THE WARMEST ROOM
IN THE HOUSE

THE WARMEST ROOM
IN THE HOUSE

*How the Kitchen Became
the Heart of the Twentieth-Century
American Home*

STEVEN GDULA

BLOOMSBURY

Published by Bloomsbury USA, New York
Distributed to the trade by Macmillan

All papers used by Bloomsbury USA are natural, recyclable products made from wood grown in well-managed forests. The manufacturing processes conform to the environmental regulations of the country of origin.

LIBRARY OF CONGRESS CATALOGING-IN-PUBLICATION DATA
Gdula, Steven.
The warmest room in the house : how the kitchen became the heart of the
twentieth-century American home / Steven Gdula.—1st U.S. ed.
p.   cm.
Includes bibliographical references and index.
ISBN-13: 978-1-58234-355-6 (alk. paper)
ISBN-10: 1-58234-355-1 (alk. paper)
1. Kitchens—United States—History.   2. Cookery—United States—History.
3. United States—Social life and customs.   I. Title.

TX653.G38 2007
643'.30973—dc22
2007009768

First U.S. Edition 2008

1 3 5 7 9 10 8 6 4 2

Typeset by Westchester Book Group
Printed in the United States of America by Quebecor World Fairfield

For my parents Helen and Peter Gdula,
for Margo, and for Lon

CONTENTS

I n the house I grew up in, both of my parents cooked. As a schoolteacher, my father ended his workday and walked through the front door almost two full hours earlier than my mother. On most days, cooking duties were assumed by my dad. By the time my mom came home, the preparation of the meal was usually complete. But that didn't stop her from lifting the lid of whatever sat on the stove, plunging in a spoon, and giving the contents a quick stir.

"How much garlic did you put in here?"

"Why?" my father would ask, somewhat defensively.

"I'm just asking, that's all," my mother would answer. Her comments were always more perfunctory than critical. They were about maintaining her connection to the kitchen rather than trying to wrangle control.

When my dad would step to the counter to correct what he perceived as his culinary error, my mom would toss her head in the direction of the kitchen clock and say, "It's fine, it's fine, we have to eat, look what time it is already!"

And with that our family of six would rush to the dining room and sit down, each of us gabbing about our day between gulps of food.

This mealtime scenario was a common one, enacted in our house on most workdays through the 1960s and '70s as my parents did their best to give us what they felt was the most important requirement of the family dinner—the time we spent together at the table. Often the food itself was secondary, though both my parents were very good cooks. Despite the push and pull of their counterside exchanges, their kitchen operations were a tag-team effort. They had to be. With financial hardships making it necessary for both of them to work outside the home, they traded roles inside the house. Mom took the helm on weekends and holidays while Dad kept us on course the rest of the time. This did not seem unusual to me. Nearly all my neighborhood friends had working parents who shared cooking responsibilities, though I admit I always thought my dad was more skilled than theirs. This was, after all, the guy who made chive dressing with fresh produce from his garden, who gutted and fried the trout he reeled in from local streams, and who stir-fried chicken in the wok he received for Father's Day.

Regardless of how I felt about the cooking prowess of the other fathers on our block, I respected other families' mealtimes. In my hometown, dinnertime was family time. Period.

Despite my view of my parents as better-than-average cooks, I never thought there was anything that made our kitchen all that different from those of my friends. Until, that is, a lesson on colonial spice trade in my fourth-grade history class made me wonder if maybe the similarities were outnumbered by the differences.

When we were asked to name some of the spices used in our kitchens I raised my hand knowingly. "Paprika," I replied, pronouncing it as I'd always heard at home. I was always eager to participate, but this time my contribution to the class made my teacher step closer, her head cocked inquisitively. I thought for one second I'd stumped her, or at least impressed her, having chosen something more exotic than salt and pepper, those obvious tabletop twins.

"Paprika," I said again, this time a little self-satisfied. My classmates giggled. Obviously we were all aware of something our teacher wasn't as she leaned in farther, her expression now more puzzled than before.

I was about to repeat myself when she finally registered recognition and, with it, a bit of relief. "Oh! Paprika, yes," she said with a nod.

The word she uttered sounded strange to me.

"*Pap-REEK-a?*" I said it as she did, drawing out the short *a* so that the first syllable rhymed with *cap*. Pap-REEK-a. I said it aloud again. The second syllable rose and fell quickly, as if the person saying it were suddenly startled, and I noticed I lifted my eyebrows for added emphasis as I said it again.

Something that was so familiar now sounded, and felt, very foreign to me.

"That's the English pronunciation," my mom explained at the dinner table that evening.

"But we speak English," I countered. "And we don't say *pap-REEK-a.*

We say *PUHP-rree-kuh*." I accented the first syllable and rolled my *r*. Said this way, the word was musical and playful, not harsh and clipped.

"That's because we pronounce it the Hungarian way," she said.

If our way of saying *paprika* was different, I wondered if the way we used the spice was also different. I knew *how* the output of our kitchen was unique, but that day's history lesson made me begin to think about *why*.

There's history in every kitchen, and my family's pronunciation of *paprika* was part of ours. My father was Slovak, my mother Hungarian, and paprika was a staple of the kitchens they were raised in, as it was now in the kitchen they shared. Cans of the powder were always within easy reach of the stove, as my parents used the spice in almost every recipe they made. My dad dusted it over pan-fried potatoes, and the spice encrusted the humble spuds in reddish brown. They were always served perfectly crispy on the outside, warm and steamy on the inside. My mom blended paprika with sour cream in her Chicken Paprikash to impart a mild, sweet richness to the dish's sauce. Served over dumplings—called *nokedli* in our house—there was no food more comforting than this.

I knew the aromas of these dishes wafted out of our kitchen and made their way through the neighborhood in the warmer months when windows and screen doors were open, just as the distinctive smell of oregano would drift across our yard from our next-door neighbor's house when Mrs. Bonfanti's pasta sauce simmered on her stove.

The kitchens in our small Pennsylvania town represented the European ancestry of the people who had moved to work in the region's coal mines in the early twentieth century. With these immigrants came their recipes. Sometimes the foods from their ancestral kitchens retained their ethnic purity, but often those recipes were adapted out of necessity, dictated by the ingredients at hand. Improvisation didn't always give way to inspiration, though—my Slovak grandmother, having seen the spaghetti sauce made by her Italian neighbors, once served my father and his siblings noodles covered with ketchup, circa 1939.

These kitchens from my town and from my family's past supported an observation that the famous gardener and gourmand and third president of the United States, Thomas Jefferson, once made. Jefferson said that if you really want to know a culture you have to look into the people's pots and eat their bread. The ingredients in use, and the manner in which they are cooked, give insight into the economic, geographic, ethnic, religious, and even political influences that come in and out of that society's kitchen doors. My parents' kitchen did, and so did Jefferson's.

Jefferson's kitchen reflected a well-traveled man who was interested in horticulture. His garden at Monticello, where he grew more than 250 varieties of indigenous and imported fruits and vegetables, supplied his dinner guests with the freshest produce, while his French-trained chefs dazzled them with lavish cuisine. My father's garden likewise provided our table with zucchini, cauliflower, onions, garlic, chives, carrots, lettuce, radishes, green beans, yellow wax beans, and kohlrabi, not just in the summer but into the fall and through the winter, as my mother canned the harvest. We didn't have French dishes, but my parents would occasionally participate in the latest cooking trends, even if only in a modest way: We had a fondue pot and the aforementioned wok. Neither was purchased on a fantastic trip to China or Switzerland; instead, both came courtesy of the local Sears.

My grandmother's makeshift spaghetti sauce was an example of the adaptation that had defined the American Kitchen for as long as immigrants had been rebuilding their lives, and their traditions, on these shores. Jefferson's countrymen in his era, for example, had slowly adapted their kitchens and their palates to the grain the Native Americans called maize. Maize, or corn, had sustained the first European colonists in America ever since their own gardens had failed. The Powhatan, the Native Americans who'd first shared their gardening tips as well as their corn supplies with the British in Jamestown, had survived for centuries on the trio of corn, squash, and beans. Lifting the lid on the Powhatan's pots would have revealed a society similar to the American culture that would develop some three hundred years later. Like the families in my hometown, the Powhatan men and women both contributed to their kitchens, through gardening and hunting, fishing and foraging. With both parents working outside the home, one-pot meals became a family staple. A clay vessel bubbling with Pausaromena, a soupy stew of corn and beans, was kept warm over the Powhatan's fires for family members or guests to eat their fill of, day or night. In our kitchen, the advent of the electric Crock-Pot in the 1970s allowed our family to have a hot meal at the end of those days when my parents were too busy to cook. On those evenings when school and work functions staggered our returns home, we were able to serve ourselves as needed. Though they might have missed the shared family time at the dinner table, my parents could take comfort in knowing that we were all well fed.

The convenience of the Crock-Pot was something my parents took advantage of when needed, as they did with frozen foods like Swanson's Turkey Pot Pie (my personal favorite), but most meals were prepared with ingredients that were pulled from the cupboards or the fridge (and when in season, the garden) in a less processed state. That more than one hundred years of thought had gone into the process that eventually created that prepackaged frozen potpie was not important to me, and probably not to my parents, either. The fact that they bought and cooked them, whether because of time constraints or simply due to a need for a break from standing over the stove, was proof enough that the mission of the domestic-science movement was a success.

When it came to a matter of recognition, Swanson, Hunt's, and even Betty Crocker were the household names in our home, rather than domestic scientists Catharine Beecher, Fannie Farmer, and even Sarah Josepha Hale. But it was the research and work of the latter, and their idea for making the nineteenth-century kitchen a cleaner, less labor-intensive room, that informed the work of food technologists in the twentieth century. And that information enabled my parents, and millions of others like them, to take the occasional TV dinner from the oven to the dinner table with little effort expended in the cooking or the cleanup.

Whether it was one of the foods from our Eastern European background such as *halupki*, or a dish that had crossed over from another culture like lasagna, or a new recipe that my mom clipped out of a magazine like Steak Diane, nothing about the preparation of a meal ever seemed like backbreaking work in our family's kitchen. The end of summer's canning season, with its sanitizing of rows of jars and the snipping and scrubbing of bushels of various vegetables, was the only time when the goings-on in my parents' kitchen echoed the drudgery so often associated with the room in centuries past.

As a working model, the kitchen that I grew up in was a time capsule of everything that had influenced its development. There was indeed history in that kitchen, one that Jefferson's formula, with some time, could decipher.

We continued our ethnic heritage through traditional foods.

We preserved the vegetables and fruits we'd grown, partly due to economic necessity, partly because the Great Depression and World War II had taught important lessons about self-sufficiency when there was a hungry family to feed.

We relied on a variety of one-pot meals, which saved time when economic demands on my parents required longer hours at work, allowing for fewer hours in the kitchen. And those recipes also stretched budgets, making the most of the ingredients on hand at a time when a strike forced my parents into the humbling position of accepting food stamps.

Even during those tentative times the kitchen was hardly dark. I remember dinners that were eaten at the kitchen table, as we carried in extra chairs from the dining room. Making the kitchenette's seating for four accommodate six meant that we were tightly crammed in that smaller setting, but I think my parents did it to pull the family closer. With such uncertainty looming beyond the kitchen door, the message my mom and dad were trying to impart was that regardless of what happened, we always had one another. Despite the threat of change, my parents were showing us how to turn the foreign into the familiar; we did so by staying together as a family in the room that helped keep our traditions, and our past, alive.

My family's kitchen was the warmest room in the house. And often it was the hottest room in the house, as the combined heat from the oven, the stovetop, and the bodies that had congregated into the space to be nearer the hearth—and heart of the action—made it nearly impossible to move, let alone cook. Our family has grown over the years. Grandchildren and now great grandchildren assemble for holidays, birthdays, and reunions. Over the years that kitchen has grown, too. Additional recipes have been added, some older recipes have been adjusted, and accommodations have been made for family members with health issues (high cholesterol), social and moral issues (vegetarians), and religious restrictions (kosher laws). And, on occasion, allowances are made for the little ones as they protest, "But I don't *like* poe-tay-toes!" These changes caused few ripples because my parents, ever the gracious hosts, knew that in the end it was the essence of the food—and its connection to familial enjoyment—that was the most important dish they could serve.

That need for the convivial is why in a matter of days, barely two weeks into a new home and with a significant portion of the kitchen's battery still boxed away, I am hosting ten guests for Chinese New Year's Eve. Unlike the sliver of a galley kitchen in which I cooked for years, friends and family seemingly unaware of the narrowness of the space as they crowded in, our new kitchen has an island and no walls. It opens directly into the living and dining rooms.

This new kitchen is waiting to write its history, and it's fitting to me that its first official celebration will be the observation of a cultural event that has nothing to do with my ethnic heritage. But it does have ties to my past. My parents' openness to culinary exploration made me less shy when setting out on my own similar travels.

Adaptation has shaped America's kitchens and the stores that supply them through the centuries, which is why thirty-plus years ago a small Sears outside of Johnstown, Pennsylvania, was selling woks in their kitchenware department. We saw it as a fun Father's Day gift for a dad who loved to cook, but it was indicative of so much more than that. It exemplified the growing American love affair with food and cooking, as well as the influences that constantly changed the American Kitchen's terrain.

Now, in the twenty-first century, I can buy nearly all the ingredients I need for my Chinese dinner thanks to my neighborhood Whole Foods in Washington, D.C. I can scroll online for the hard-to-find items and have them delivered to my front door.

I'm not sure how the recipes I'm making will turn out this coming weekend. But what I have learned from my kitchen's history is that the simple act of sharing a meal with friends is its own reward.

Because the experiences that seasoned my kitchen, and my parents' and grandparents' kitchens, occurred with the immigration of my ancestors to this country in the early twentieth century, I have set this book's focus accordingly. Of course the indigenous souls who first occupied this land, and those from other shores whom they welcomed to it, established a kitchen that in turn welcomed my family. For readers looking for more in-depth studies I recommend the books and materials listed in the annotated bibliography. While some of the titles cover eras and events not addressed directly in this book, I relied on the histories they presented to inform this finished product.

This is by no means a definitive history of the American Kitchen of the twentieth century, but rather a selection and examination of some of its influences and representations during that time.

As for the history of the room's warmth, well, that's something that is determined by each kitchen, by each cook, by each meal. We've all written our own histories, and I hope that if nothing else, this book encourages you to consider, and ultimately share, yours.

CHAPTER ONE

This Is the Modern World: 1900–1909

*Fannie Farmer lost the drudgery but kept the domestics in her scientific approach
to making the American Kitchen a well-lit, clean, workable space.
(Courtesy of Corbis.)*

The American Kitchen at the start of the twentieth century existed in a highly charged atmosphere. Electricity was in the air. While steam and gas had powered the changes of the previous century, electricity was about to light up the next hundred years. Changes were occurring so quickly in American society, science, politics, and popular culture that more advances were now made in twenty or thirty years than had been made in previous centuries combined. The first cross-country trip by motor car occurred three years into the new century. Telephone lines were suspended in the air. Radio waves broadcast voices and music through the atmosphere. And the Wright Brothers were taking to the skies as well. Moving pictures were a source of entertainment, as were the comings and goings of moneyed-up personalities like Rockefeller, Carnegie, James "Diamond Jim" Brady, and J. P. Morgan. Baseball players were about to become superstars, and movie stars would soon become icons. The human body was projected on theater screens and examined under microscopes. New research into the physiology and anatomy of humans led to discoveries about what made the body tick. Humankind was now taking giant steps toward its future. Things were changing faster than ever before, and Americans had to look no further than their kitchens to see the difference a few decades could make.

The down-hearth fireplace so prominent at the turn of the last century was replaced by freestanding cookstoves, metal boxes and barrels that held the fire that cooked the family's meals (and, in some cases, heated the rooms of the house). The switch, which writer Nathaniel Hawthorne had all but warned would lead to the unraveling of the family unit now that "fire" was imprisoned in its "iron cage," happened without incident.

Root cellars where provisions had previously been stored were moving up into the kitchen itself and getting a makeover along the way as butler's pantries, larders, cabinets, and cupboards offered plenty of shelves where tidy rows of preserved foods, either store-bought or home-canned, could all be stored within arm's reach. Sleek indoor faucets replaced clunky water pumps, and the gas lamps that cast a dim light upon the kitchen's domain were being left in the shadows as electric lights began to blaze overhead.

At the beginning of the twentieth century, Americans were nostalgic about their own past. In the first decade of the century, historical books about the country's westward expansion, *54-40 or Fight*, were popular. Dramas that portrayed women's struggle to gain social and political clout were popularized in books like *Red Pottage* and *The House of Mirth*. Despite the advancements made in the name of domestic science toward easing the drudgery that had defined kitchen work for centuries, for some Americans the hardships of just getting by on a daily basis were never far from the front door. Stories with impoverished, sympathetic characters were popular. *Mrs. Wiggs of the Cabbage Patch* told the story of the working poor in Louisville, Kentucky, whose economic means forced them to live in shanties in an area of town where cabbages had once grown.

For those Americans who could reap the rewards of the last century's progress, the first decade of the 1900s was a confusing time, especially for the lady of the house. With so many changes reorganizing and often dismantling the elements that composed the very structure of a woman's daily life, it became difficult for some women to reorient themselves to a lifestyle where the responsibilities of maintaining the kitchen did not occupy their every waking moment. An essay titled "The Home of Today and Tomorrow," which appeared in a 1907 issue of *Good Housekeeping*, addressed these concerns. "The plexus of interests constituting home-life has shrunk with the shrinking of home industries," the writer expressed. The author, Charlotte Perkins Gilman, presented her case that the advancements in technology that lightened the load of most women's housework came with some significant consequences. Comparing the "telephone . . . exquisite plumbing . . . [and] refrigerator" of the early twentieth-century home with the "smoke-house . . . loom and wheel . . . pig-killing . . . and wood fires and warming pans" of the "rural great-grandmother" and the duties that defined her nineteenth-century house, Gilman declared that "home-life" was on its way out: "It is true that there is less of that." Rather than have the woman of the house sit idle, fretting over how to redirect her energies, Gilman encouraged her readership to become involved in their communities.

Stepping outside the kitchen, American women found a world of causes to which they could devote their energy. Their predecessors had already opened the door.

And leading the way was science.

Two cookbooks making an impact in the American Kitchen in the first decade of the 1900s were Sarah Tyson Rorer's *Mrs. Rorer's Menu Book* and Fannie Farmer's *Fannie Farmer Cookbook*. Both books traded on the power of their author's names, as Rorer and Farmer had established themselves as leaders in the movement that was bringing science into the kitchen and elevating domestic duties out of the home fire's ashes.

Domestic science and home economics were disciplines that had their beginnings in the nineteenth century with writer Sarah Josepha Hale, the writer and Martha Stewart prototype Catharine Beecher, and their contemporaries. At first glance, the mid-nineteenth-century mind-set of these women might appear to have been the polar opposite of the twentieth-century movement Farmer and her colleagues championed. The distance between Beecher's intuition-based apple pie recipe and Farmer's methodically detailed instructions for baking the same pie seems like it can be measured in more than decades: Beecher's recipe makes allotments for interpretation and personal preference, not to mention taking into consideration the individuality of the kitchen—and the cook—baking the pie, while the precise measurements in Farmer's recipe aim to narrow the margin for error. In Beecher's kitchen, a woman worked through her mistakes. In Farmer's kitchen, there were no mistakes. Accidents didn't happen; every attempt was made to avoid them. Both of these women were working

toward the same end, however, and it was something more than just a perfectly baked pie.

Beecher's design for domestic harmony was the platform on which the domestic scientists (as they would come to be known) and administrators at
Farmer's Boston Cooking Schools would base their whole philosophy. All of
these women were focused on lifting household responsibilities out of the
realm of the scullery. They elevated the role women played in the home and
christened themselves domestic scientists along the way. In this role, and
with this title, domestic scientists had more control over their domain and its
subsequent product. In *Perfection Salad*, Laura Shapiro writes, "If the housekeeper could be made to think of herself as a scientist, calmly at work . . . in
her laboratory, then every meal would emerge as she planned, pristine and
invariable." Shapiro chose a telling quote from one of Helen Campbell's lec-
tures at the University of Wisconsin that perfectly encapsulates the prevalent
thinking of the movement: ". . . even the intelligent housekeeper still talks
about 'luck' with her sponge cake. Luck! There is no such word in science,
and to make sponge cake is a scientific process!"

There were several factors motivating this new approach to cooking, and
flaky piecrust and springy sponge cake were just two of them. Prior to the
advent of the domestic scientists, kitchens were as close an approximation to
hell on earth as one could find. They were hot, dirty, smelly, dangerous
places, and the work done there seemed interminable. As advancements in
technology and science started to ease the burden of other types of labor,
women looked at the backbreaking kitchen chores they faced every day and
realized that there had to be an easier way. If industrialization was making
work less demanding, and if science was making life safer and cleaner by
identifying elements that led to illness, then surely the principles behind these
disciplines could be applied to the workings of the kitchen. A group of women
across the country, including Fannie Farmer, Sarah Tyson Rorer, and Ellen
Richards, was determined to find out.

Here was the good news: The application of scientific principles to the
workings of the kitchen did take the guesswork out of cooking. Recipes that
formerly called for "a teacup full" of flour or a "walnut-sized" dollop of butter left too much room for interpretation. All teacups and walnuts were not
created equal; where was the regulation? Farmer's insistence on level, precise
measurements implied order and set a standard that could be universally followed. *Good Housekeeping* routinely advised its readers of the benefits of
properly measuring ingredients. But old habits were apparently hard to break,

and even as late as 1917, some ten years after Farmer brought her message to the masses, *Good Housekeeping*'s articles warned: "Don't guess—measure!" To further make its point the magazine resorted to tactics of inclusion, writing, "The days when any old cup at all would do for a measuring-cup have gone by, and the modern housekeeper uses cups specially designed." And given the choice, who wouldn't want to be included among the "modern" house-keepers, considering the alternative?

Another benefit of this new scientific approach to cooking was the consideration given to the nutritional quality of the food American women were serving their families. The diet reformers of the nineteenth century, all the way back to Sylvester Graham, had already brought Brillat-Savarin's "you are what you eat" message to the American Kitchen. Graham had created a stir with his strong messages against the increased interest in store-bought bread, often made with the white processed flour that was at the center of his crusade. Primarily a vegetarian, in his sanatoriums he railed against the carnal desires that foods like red meat, processed flour, and spicy condiments like mustard allegedly excited in the body. His desire to keep morning arousal to a minimum among the adolescents in his facility led to his development and serving of cold breakfast cereals. In his opinion, meat fueled animal lust in the body, so the Graham diet was predominantly a vegetarian diet.

His beliefs had two very important effects on the kitchens of America: His cold-breakfast whole-grain biscuit, the precursor to the graham cracker, would eliminate hours the cook spent "getting the stove hot enough to fry up some ham in the morning," says writer and food historian Barbara Haber; and Graham's crusading for pure flour and pure cow's milk, both of which were stretched with chalky additives by unscrupulous salesmen, helped bring awareness to a growing problem in the food industry as it attempted to feed a population that was requiring more and more food.

The domestic scientists of the twentieth century, inspired in part by Graham, wanted Americans to take a closer look at the foods they were eating, and by 1901 the United States government would establish a Bureau of Chemistry within the Department of Agriculture for that very purpose. The job of the chemists was to examine the composition of foods and make sure that there was nothing in them that didn't belong there—for example, additives and adulterations such as the chalk previously added to milk. By the last decades of the nineteenth century, the Department of Agriculture was also focusing on what *was* in the foods Americans were eating. Under the leadership of W. O. Atwater, a professor of chemistry at Wesleyan University, the federal government dispatched domestic scientists to the kitchens of America. The purpose of these reconnaissance missions was to record what the woman of the house was serving her family, how she cooked it, how much it cost, and how much each family member ate, and then, by determining the number of calories and proteins in those foods, establish the amount of food that would be needed to adequately meet the nutritional requirements of that family. Atwater's intentions were good even if his method was flawed; his assessments of caloric needs didn't take into consideration factors like individual metabolism and those things that influenced a person's own body chemistry, like pregnancy. But Atwater's study did help to acquaint Americans with the idea that they should limit their ingestion of certain types of foods while eating more of other types. The discovery of vitamins in foods in the first decade of the 1900s would further help Americans understand the effects food had on their bodies and their health.

Ellen Richards was one of the first, if not the first, woman in the American Kitchen to turn a chemist's analytical eye toward food. Richards was the first female student to enter the prestigious Massachusetts Institute of Technology in 1870. After her graduation, she opened the Women's Laboratory, where women could learn the fundamentals of chemistry. Her plan for educating women about the science that occurred in their very own kitchens was fully actualized in a course Richards designed, titled Household Chemistry. Women were taught how to spot contaminants and additives in their foods, as they were made familiar with the chemical structures of those foods. They also learned about the changes that took place in foods during cooking, as well as how foods were digested in the body. But for all of her emphasis on utilizing the benefits of technology to modernize the kitchen, Richards was also sentimental in her view of the room as a place that was uniquely feminine: While the application of the intellect would help a woman run her kitchen using precise scientific principles, it would be her love of her family that would ensure that the kitchen remained the warmest room in the house. Richards, like Beecher, believed that housework, and cooking in particular, served a higher purpose than just keeping a household up and running.

Isabel Bevier was a like-minded pioneer in the American Kitchen who followed in Richards's footsteps by bringing the essentials of domestic science into the academic realm. Bevier instituted the Household Science curriculum, and its subsequent bachelor's of science degree, at the University of Illinois at the start of the twentieth century. Bevier held the belief that for a woman to be most effective in the management of her home, she needed to be well educated in a variety of scientific, mathematic, and artistic disciplines. She went beyond merely bringing the kitchen into the classroom, however: Bevier's students were required to study sciences like botany, physiology, and math as well as "special work in household chemistry, domestic bacteriology, domestic architecture, and decoration," according to Shapiro's *Perfection Salad*.

Bevier wanted to be sure that no one would confuse the serious academics of her course work with the Cooking School movement that had come before her. Bevier may have had something of a superior attitude toward the group who had spearheaded the organized instruction of women in the ways of domestic science, but the public felt otherwise. The Boston Cooking School's Fannie Farmer had achieved a modicum of fame thanks to her connection to the school, and her popularity increased even more after the publication of *The Boston Cooking-School Cook Book*. (The book went on to be known as the *Fannie Farmer Cookbook*, confirming her appeal.)

Sarah Tyson Rorer, a guiding force behind the Philadelphia Cooking School, had also published a cookbook bearing her name. The combo of her Cooking School background and her status as a cookbook author gave her credibility among homemakers who looked at the domestic scientists as how-to gurus. Her popularity made her an ideal candidate when *Table Talk* magazine was looking for someone to respond to questions sent in by readers seeking answers to their cooking and domestic conundrums. Rorer possessed a strong authoritative voice in her writing, and after several years working for *Table Talk*, she decided to start her own magazine, which she called *Household News*. Rorer's reputation and financial success were both sealed when advertisers came to her to endorse their products. Not only did Rorer lend her name to ads for kitchen staples like Niagara Corn Starch, she also lent her cooking know-how to several other brand names when she penned cookbooks for Shredded Wheat, Tabasco, and Wesson Oil.

The good news that accompanied the increased visibility of these women and others in the domestic-science movement was that in some ways the management of the household and the running of the kitchen became somewhat easier, thanks to their efforts. The kitchen also became a healthier environment, as adulterated foods and germs were considered targets that were every bit as dangerous as poorly managed time, ill-prepared meals, and nutritionally questionable eating habits.

The bad news was that the prescriptive sameness they preached in regard to menus and recipes robbed the American Kitchen of its uniqueness—individuality was something to be sanitized and, along with the germs, food contaminants, and unhealthy lifestyles, removed from the kitchen. And there certainly wasn't room on the Cooking Schools' menus for meals born of tradition or heritage. A homogeneous kitchen was the domestic scientist's goal, and where was the sacrifice? It would seem that sentiment, and even flavor, had no place in the diet and were seen as impeding progress. If a woman followed the advice of the domestic scientists, the Cooking Schools, and the government's new guidelines for nutrition, she could be secure in knowing that her family was eating healthy.

The U.S. government played a big role in this whitewashing of the American Kitchen, and its efforts, coupled with those of the domestic scientists, would further change the way Americans ate, giving the kitchen's appearance a face-lift along the way.

The government of the United States had assumed an early role in the evolution of the domestic-science movement, when Atwater and the Department of Agriculture began studying the chemical effects and compounds of the foods in the American Kitchen. As the twentieth century began, the government became more involved with the regulation of what Americans were putting on their kitchen tables, and eventually in their bodies—and with good cause. The need for some sort of policing of food manufacturers was old news. As early as the middle of the nineteenth century, questions had been raised about the purity of foods like milk and flour. But as the studies of Louis Pasteur had shown, there were more dangers lurking in bottles and cans than such known additives as unwanted chalk dust and molasses sweeteners. Germs were no longer considered to be only airborne, and people were learning that inherent bacteria could contaminate foods.

There was also a growing awareness that some of the unwelcome and alien substances found in foods were placed there deliberately, sometimes to preserve the foods, but often to deceive the buyer. One of the tasks of the Department of Agriculture's Bureau of Chemistry was the detection of such unwanted particles. It was Atwater's responsibility to determine the chemical analysis of foods. Criteria had to be established to control the quality of packaged and preserved items. What was the percentage of product to preservative? What were acceptable amounts of additives? When should the public be warned about the dangers of a particular product? And how should the information about their foods' contents be presented?

How were Americans to know what they were eating? The solution was simple: Packaged food would carry labels truthfully detailing their contents.

The job of making this labeling a law fell into the hands of Dr. Harvey W. Wiley, the chief chemist at what became the Bureau of Chemistry in the U.S. Department of Agriculture.

Wiley began his campaign for cleaner, or purer, foods in 1883. He conducted numerous experiments, scrutinizing the chemical compounds found in various food products, and his methodology became the litmus test other chemists used when analyzing foods. By 1902 Wiley had launched an all-out crusade to get the U.S. government to act in the best interests of the American public. Wiley wanted a law mandating that food companies list the contents of their products on their packages, one that limited the types of preservatives used in foods and placed a cap on the amounts of those preservatives present.

Wiley wanted a pure food law. The problem was that the rest of America didn't appear very concerned. Besides, there wasn't much inherent drama in the idea of preservatives, especially compared to the horrors of lead poisoning in canned foods (which had killed several sailors in the nineteenth century), or the dangers of botulism. Wiley had to find a way to increase public awareness. Being a scientist, he knew all about cause and effect. He also knew human nature and how to capture and maintain an audience's interest. To that end, Wiley assembled a group of volunteers who would sacrifice their bodies to science while the American public looked on. Given the name the "poison squad" by one of the reporters covering the story, the dozen men were fed foods containing various amounts of preservatives and additives while America awaited word of the results. Newspapers started to report daily on the poison squad and the experiments being conducted on them by Wiley and his staff. The story sparked the public's curiosity. Unfortunately, from the press's point of view, the food additives Wiley fed his poison squad weren't producing immediate or visible effects, and with no hard news to report to the hungry public, members of the media started to spin their own tales. It would be four years before Wiley's tests were concluded, but support for pure food laws had grown among American citizens in the meantime. Dr. Wiley's findings showed that certain preservatives and additives currently found in food products posed a danger to the public's health. Wiley took his message to President Theodore Roosevelt, and in turn Roosevelt took his message to Congress. In a statement released on December 5, 1905, Roosevelt declared: "I recommend that a law be enacted to regulate interstate commerce in misbranded and adulterated foods, drinks, and drugs . . . Traffic in foodstuffs which have been debased or adulterated so as to injure health or to deceive purchasers should be forbidden."

The vote for the Pure Food Act took place in Congress and was passed in

June 1906. Six months later, on January 1, 1907, the law went into effect. Public sentiment ran high in favor of the law. By this time Americans were fully aware of the dangers of adulterated and contaminated food. While the public watched and waited to find out the fate of Wiley's poison squad, Upton Sinclair's book *The Jungle* told the story of the hellish practices in the U.S. meatpacking industry. Sinclair wrote about foreign substances in sausages and lard that made the chemical additives in preserved food seem harmless in comparison; his graphic but truth-based descriptions of the horrific neglect in the meat industry brought about the Meat Inspection Act in 1906, the same year that the Pure Food Act was voted into action.

Sinclair's book raised such a stink and turned so many stomachs that homemakers took to the streets, barged into local butcher shops and meat markets, and demanded sanitary conditions. But some women didn't need Sinclair's book to tell them about the ugliness that existed in the food industry. Just as *Good Housekeeping* had urged its readers to channel their energy into projects that would benefit the community, the same magazine had reported in the spring of 1905 that a group of women in Portland, Oregon, had stormed their local markets, insisting that lax attitudes toward cleanliness be addressed immediately. Lilian E. Tingle reported that "many [shops] were open to the street, so that flies, dust, and dogs did damage unchecked; and the late passer-by at night might catch glimpses of rats holding high carnival in the midst of unprotected food material of all kinds. Joints of meat, whole carcasses of sheep and hogs, hanging outside unscreened doors and windows, converted many a fastidious newcomer to vegetarianism."

Tingle concluded her article by placing the onus of a clean market in the hands of every homemaker: "The blame . . . for unsatisfactory markets lies primarily with the individual housewife." She laid the responsibility on the homemaker because she believed that the modern convenience of phoning in market orders, or the practice of allowing "Chinese servants"—a minority subject to endless suspicion and discrimination since the Chinese Exclusion Act of 1882— to do the housekeeping and shopping, helped contribute to the unhealthy conditions prevalent in Portland's shops. The woman of the house needed to keep a watchful eye focused on all matters in the running of her home, and this included affairs that occurred under her roof as well as those beyond her front door.

The events of the first decade of the 1900s shocked the American Kitchen into action. But despite growing public awareness and all the advances in science and industry, food could still be deadly. And so could the hired help.

*   *   *

In 1906 the American public didn't need any more evidence to convince them that there were potential dangers lurking in their foods. The problem was that all the highly publicized inspection, from Wiley's human guinea pigs to *The Jungle*'s testimony of horrors, focused on food *prior* to its entry into the American Kitchen; although more emphasis was being placed on the cleanliness of the cooking environment, contamination of food during the preparation process was still a very real threat. And Americans were about to learn that this contamination could come from an unsuspected source.

The American Kitchen of the new century was not as crowded as it had been in the decades that closed the previous one. There were more, better-paying jobs now available for young women and immigrants who were looking for work outside the realm of domestic service. Good help was hard to find, and the heads of households looking to hire experienced workers knew they faced serious competition from other homeowners who were willing to pay top dollar for experienced cooks and servants. The value placed upon reliable kitchen help might have been one reason why one of the most notorious personalities in the history of the American Kitchen was able to continue working, even after mounting evidence suggested that she could be exposing her employers, their families, and their guests to a deadly disease.

In the summer of 1906 Mary Mallon was just a cook working in a beach house on Long Island that had been rented by Charles Henry Warren and his family. She had not yet been branded Typhoid Mary, the name she would end up taking to her grave. In fact, no one considered her a threat; she certainly wasn't a suspected killer. She was just one of countless immigrants employed in one of the countless kitchens in her adopted homeland, like thousands of others had been before her. There was no reason to suspect she had anything to do with the illnesses, let alone the deaths, that were sometimes left in the wake of her departure. Every time someone contracted typhoid in one of the homes in which she worked, water was considered the culprit. The infection had to have come from a tainted source outside the home; certainly it wasn't something that was coming from someone or something *inside* the kitchen. Cleanliness was one of the main tenets preached by the domestic scientists in their reformation of the American Kitchen, and every effort was made to keep the kitchen as free of dirt and germs as the most sanitary laboratory, conditions that were most definitely present in the swank home Warren rented.

As Anthony Bourdain writes in *Typhoid Mary*, his sympathetic biography of Mallon, "Rich people didn't get typhoid," a disease which was "widely associated with poverty and filth," two terms one would not have associated with the Warrens or the Oyster Bay community where their rental property was located.

It was only after the sleuthing of a Dr. George Soper, a sanitary engineer from New York City, that Mallon herself became the prime suspect. Soper looked into Mallon's employment history and found that in at least three other homes in which she'd worked family members or other servants in the house had been stricken with typhoid. Mary was the one thing the otherwise disparate cases had in common.

There was no criminal intent on Mallon's part, but there was no denying that she was the source of the infectious disease (especially after her stool samples tested positive for the bacteria known as *Salmonella typhi*). Simply put, Typhoid Mary was infecting her victims because she did not always wash her hands properly after using the bathroom. It may have initially been a relief for George Thompson, the owner of the house the Warrens had rented, to learn that the disease was not lurking in the water pipes or work surfaces of his kitchen. But the discovery that Mallon was a carrier of the disease presented new anxieties in the American Kitchen at a time when the war against contaminated foods and unclean food-preparation areas was one most Americans thought they were finally starting to win.

Around the time Mary Mallon was becoming the poster girl for typhoid, "sanitation was a mania in kitchens," Bourdain writes.

The fight to eliminate the drudgery of housework had already resulted in the application of new technology in the American Kitchen. Catharine Beecher's designs from the mid-1800s for a well-built, user-friendly workspace were an offshoot of the increasing industrialization of America. The emergence of safer, cleaner-burning, more fuel-efficient gas stoves at the century's close helped women—at least the women who could afford them—sweep the dirt and dust from their old coal stoves out of their kitchens once and for all. The discovery of the causes behind diseases like cholera had ushered in a new urgency when it came to cleanliness in people's daily lives, and especially in the kitchen. Following the lead of scientists in other fields, domestic scientists began regarding the kitchen as a laboratory. They overhauled recipes as well as the appearance of the kitchen itself in their quest to regulate the room's output. They even began to create not only new dishes, but new foods as well.

In 1907, *Good Housekeeping* featured a Professor Thomas B. Stillman in an article titled "Foods Made in the Laboratory" in which the good professor declared that "it is now possible to produce artificially all food substances except meat albumen and starch, which is the same as saying, Give a chemist a laboratory with seventy elements, starch and albumen, and he can make any vegetarian dish on the menu."

Stillman's disclosures were more akin to science fiction at the time, but the laboratory discoveries of saccharin and of artificial milk made from santogen reflected what domestic scientists thought was best for America's kitchens. Nature, which supplied the food Americans ate daily, could not be controlled, whereas experiments in a lab could be closely monitored and their outcome manipulated. This type of regulation had to be brought into the kitchen and applied to cooking.

This new regard for cooking as a science went beyond mimicking the efficiency and precision of experiments of chemists and other scientists in the preparation of food, however: It also meant that the space where these meals were prepared had to be as clean and orderly as the most sanitary medical or chemical lab.

The layout of the kitchen would have to reflect this.

Laboratories had cabinets and shelves where the tools of the scientist's trade were stored, waiting until they were needed, at which point they could be quickly put into use. The kitchen would have to have shelves and cabinets and drawers where dishes, pots, pans, and utensils could be kept, protected from dirt and dust. Just as the instruments used in labs were routinely disinfected, so too would the kitchen's utensils and tools have to be sanitized. Anthony Bourdain writes that carbolic acid, a powerful disinfectant, was widely used in American kitchens during the time Typhoid Mary was employed. Ammonia was another sanitizing agent used to clean surfaces in the kitchen.

Manufacturers tapped into America's new obsession for cleanliness in their advertisements. Ivory soap suggested that kitchen utensils and baby bottles be sanitized with "a few shavings" from a bar of Ivory soap, dissolved in a quart of hot water. The dirt and germ phobia was an easy fear to target via ads. McCray Refrigerators promoted the health benefits of the easily cleaned "opal glass, tile, or white-wood-lined" interiors of its appliances, warning that its competition sold "unsanitary refrigerators."

Since most laboratories were white, paint companies focused on how their products enhanced the cleanliness of a house, especially the kitchen. One paint manufacturer included close-up photos of a wall covered in its product, comparing it to the surface of a wall painted with the competition's product. An application of the advertiser's paint resulted in a smooth, sleek, easily cleaned surface, whereas the competitor's paint dried unevenly, leaving bumps, nubs, nooks, and crannies marring the wall's surface. As the copy for the ad was quick to point out, these blemishes provided plenty of places for dirt and germs to hide as they waited to infect the house. Laboratories couldn't allow such imperfections, and neither could America's kitchens. In a 1905 article titled "A Convenient Kitchen," *House Beautiful* advised its readers that two coats of paint followed by a coat of varnish was the best way to keep a kitchen's walls from becoming germ colonies.

Laboratories also needed good lighting, and the same *House Beautiful* article stated that "the things most desired in a kitchen are plenty of light and ventilation and a convenient place for cooking utensils where they are free from dust." Dust may have been a nuisance, but dirt was a crafty enemy. It could hide in shadows and be easily overlooked. Suddenly, strong electric lights reached into every corner of the kitchen, exposing dirt and its lairs. Strategically placed windows flooded the room with sunlight and allowed for ample circulation of air that might otherwise become stale and odorous.

Germs were more cunning than inanimate mounds of dirt or tumbleweeds of dust. Because they could not be seen, they could remain undetected in a sink or go unnoticed on a countertop. They could even seep into absorbent wooden floors. Hard, nonporous surfaces that could be quickly wiped down with a disinfectant would make it more difficult for germs to survive. The American Kitchen would have to replace its wooden worktables and wooden floors with something else, something that wouldn't provide such a hospitable home for germs. Enamel sinks were already popular, and enamel-coated utensils and enamel-clad countertops and cabinets were becoming increasingly available. Formica, a protective laminate first invented in 1913 to fit snugly around electrical wires, would eventually offer homemakers a cheaper alternative to enamel, porcelain, and steel surfaces in their kitchens. At the turn of the century linoleum was giving the American Kitchen a floor that was as easy to clean as the kitchen's other hard surfaces.

Linoleum was developed by the Nairn family of Kearny, New Jersey. In the latter part of the nineteenth century the Nairns had emigrated from Scotland, where they had established a prominent business manufacturing sailcloth. In the tough fabric of the sailcloth, Michael Nairn saw a durable floor covering that could be as decorative as it was protective. By the time the Nairns had set up house, and shop, in America they had taken their painted sailcloth and morphed it into another type of floor covering—linoleum, the by-product of linseed oil that had been mixed with ground cork and then adhered to a backing of canvas or burlap. The Nairns later used their formula for topping hardy canvases with materials that would create a hard, smooth surface and developed Congoleum. (The name came from the Congolese asphalt material used in the process.) Congoleum Gold Seal Rugs were very popular in American kitchens in the 1920s. Not only were they easy to clean, they also spruced up the kitchen with some style and color; a novel idea for a room that had never really experienced much of either. Ads for Congoleum promised a "happy" and "liveable" kitchen, the color and patterns of the floor covering replacing the "workplace" appearance that used to define the room.

Kitchen design, in terms of the room's floor plan, was becoming more prevalent, especially in wealthier homes where butler's pantries and new appliances were positioned so that the transition from cooking the food to serving it was as smooth as possible.

Still, the emphasis was on waging war against dirt and germs and in making the room more efficient. *House Beautiful* readers who wrote in, asking the magazine's design experts for renovation and decorating advice, circa 1905, rarely mentioned the look of their kitchens, even though they gave detailed descriptions of the makeovers the rest of the rooms in the house were given. When the same magazine printed the plans for a small country home designed by Frank Lloyd Wright in 1906, the article emphasized that the room's design made it impossible for dirt to squeeze through the cracks in the tight-fitting seals between the enamel sink, countertops, and wall.

While all this attention to the eradication of germs threatened to leave the American Kitchen looking sterile and uninviting, the new emphasis on efficiency and precision was creating a bright spot in the form of the beloved Hoosier, which was about to give the American Kitchen the answer to its prayers.

The Hoosier hit the scene in 1903 when the Hoosier Manufacturing Company of Indiana began making the cabinet that would launch a mini-revolution in the way Americans cooked. The idea for the Hoosier—as all freestanding cabinets of its design were soon called—was simple. The makers of the cabinet took a page from Catharine Beecher's call for order in the kitchen, and to this they added the emphasis on fluidity and ease in the execution of tasks seen in entrepreneur Frederick Taylor's Efficiency Movement. Taylor's philosophy of industry that aimed to make the most of a worker's time and space was brought into the kitchen by *Ladies' Home Journal* editor Christine Frederick. Frederick, like Beecher before her, sought to bring to housework an ease of preparation along with an elevation of spirit. Finally, they considered the precise measurements and cleanliness of the domestic scientists' approach to cooking. The result was a workstation where entire recipes could be assembled without the cook having to move until the time came to actually heat the food.

The Hoosier consisted of drawers for utensils and cabinets for storing pots, pans, dishes, and bowls. Filling the role once played by pie safes, the Hoosier had bins where baked goods could be kept safely away from any vermin that might succeed in sneaking into the kitchen. While it also had room to store containers of flour, sugar, and spices, what made its design so ingenious was the inclusion of fixtures like built-in sifters. Cooks no longer had to worry about steadying a sifter over a bowl since the Hoosier had the device securely attached to its back wall. The problem of storage was eliminated, too; the cabinet featured a work surface that was initially made of wood, but eventually also offered in zinc and aluminum. Competitors of Hoosier Manufacturing who made similar models offered their customers freestanding cabinets and countertops clad in sheet steel and "porce-namel," a porcelain-based material.

As Hoosiers developed to meet the needs of the evolving aesthetics of the kitchen, options like oak and enamel finishes with names like Wedgwood, Silver Oak, Hoosier Gray, Italian, and Navajo were made available.

Hoosiers became more elaborate and presented more storage options and more accessories as butler's pantries and domestic help were phased out of American kitchens. The cabinets started to make allowances in their design for the inclusion of storage areas for electric appliances like irons, add-on shelving units to accommodate glassware and food items, and space for small desktop items like pencils and pads for jotting down grocery lists and recipes. Kitchen Maid, another Indiana company, made a Hoosier unit that "grew" through add-ons. Ironing boards, refrigerators, ranges, and even sinks could be built into and around the Kitchen Maid models.

With fewer people milling about the room, the kitchen started to become smaller, and so did American houses. The bungalow was the popular style for homes, and kitchens, which were separated and practically detached from the floor plan of the main house, were becoming integrated into the "block" of the house. The Hoosier carried the counter space, cabinetry, and shelves that had once been relegated to the servants' work areas between the kitchen and dining room and plopped them into the kitchen of these smaller homes.

The all-in-one feature of the unit made it indispensable, especially when extra space became scarce.

As Terry Uber, professor of Interior Design at Kent State, says, the beauty of the Hoosier was that the makers of the cabinets seemed to design them with the philosophy that "these are all the things everyone needs all the time, so let's put them in one compact unit."

Fitted cabinets that wrapped around the kitchen and had countertops running parallel to them underneath would eventually replace the Hoosier in the decades that were to come. The Hoosier would become less prominent after the Great Depression, but its design of cabinetry, drawers, and work surface all contained in one operation changed the way the American Kitchen looked, and worked, from its inception on.

Cabinets and shelves weren't the only parts of the kitchen that were getting a redesign in the first decades of the 1900s. Electricity was livening up the room, and the appliances in it. Only slightly more than 10 percent of American homes had electricity before World War I. The Hillman House of Schenectady, New York, was "the first house ever built representing the complete application of electricity to the uses of domestic life," touted *House Beautiful* in 1906. The Hillman residence, with its strange and exciting switches, knobs, and gadgets, was part funhouse, part laboratory, and part time-travel opportunity for the general public. Magazines devoted entire spreads to the house and its electrical curiosities. Appliances such as the Electrical Four Combination Cereal Cooker were so new to homemakers that they seemed like they belonged in H. G. Wells's futuristic novels rather than in the kitchen of the day. Likewise, the average American had never witnessed anything like the Cooking and Baking Outfit, with its "Seven Regulatory Switches," a stove with a control panel that could "reduce or raise the temperature" of a cooking pot to "desirable levels in a matter of minutes." (The temperature settings cooks could choose from included "maximum, medium, and minimum" heat.)

It was boasted that every chore in the kitchen, including "chopping the meat and vegetables, cooking them, and boiling the kettle," could all be done by electricity in the Hillman House. And while convenience was the main selling point of the new form of energy, some of the appliances were actually a nuisance, as they really didn't eliminate any steps in the cooking process. In fact, in a few cases, they created more work. For instance, the Electrical Four

Combination Cereal Cooker crowed that it boiled water for coffee, but what was not disclosed was that the hot water then had to be poured into the coffee pot and set to percolate.

This new application of electricity to centuries-old chores might have come with the best of intentions, but it wasn't always well thought-out. Like the Hillman's Four Combination Cereal Cooker, the first electric toasters, made by General Electric, had a few flaws. The toasters, which started to pop into the American Kitchen as early as 1908, had to be closely monitored, as they had no automatic mechanism to time the toasting process. The first toasters also did not have the ability to toast both sides of the bread, so users had to take the slice out and turn it over to ensure even browning. But this was still an exciting innovation, even though the public wouldn't be able to buy the pop-up, uniform-toasting machine until the mid-1920s. At least the ordeal of steadying long-armed baskets, in which the bread used to be suspended over a fire, was being replaced by a safer method. Now all the kitchen needed was to find a way to slice the bread before it came into the house.

The century's first decade was nearing its end and the kitchen as Americans had known it barely ten years earlier, had become cleaner, safer, cooler, and more efficient. Calling the room "welcoming" was still a few years off, but the American Kitchen's new charms were beginning to beguile the family. As the primary source of heating the home was moved to another part of the house, the warmth emanating from the kitchen was of a more inviting essence than the unbearable inferno that once characterized the room.

The kitchen in America, however, was about to begin serving a higher, and different, purpose than any of the domestic scientists had ever conceived, as the next decade would see the kitchen playing a role in a worldwide drama.

CHAPTER TWO

Soldiers All!: 1910–1919

Home cooks stocked an arsenal of homegrown foods in the American Kitchen,
as the country's fields fed the war effort. (Courtesy of Corbis.)

The American Kitchen has been subject to global influence ever since the first ship of settlers arrived on this continent's shores. But when the United States became involved in World War I in the second decade of the twentieth century, America's kitchens would become the first line of defense on the home front. As every American quickly learned, fighting a war required more than just guns and ammunition; it also required raw materials and natural resources. Winning a war depended on a strong military, and those strong servicemen needed provisions to keep them fit and healthy. Americans at home were encouraged to make sacrifices in their own kitchens for the sake of the war effort. THE MAN AT THE FRONT AND THE WOMAN AT HOME ARE EQUALLY IMPORTANT IN OUR GREAT AMERICAN ARMY, declared a headline accompanying an article by Helen Irene Weed called "Soldiers All!" in a wartime issue of *House Beautiful* magazine.

The pressures on the homemaker during the 1910s brought an element of lack that the kitchen had not withstood since the previous century. The war was a true test of all the advances that had been made in the name of industrialization and domestic science during the last hundred years. Aside from the demands the war placed on all the room's resources, the American Kitchen was on the verge of becoming the loneliest room in the house. Loved ones were leaving home, being sent overseas. And the domestic help that had formerly created a type of sisterly bond among women working side by side in the kitchen was also disappearing. The use of hired domestic help had been on the decline since the Industrial Revolution had created more jobs outside the house, and in particular outside the kitchen. Kitchens in cities and towns across the country had provided a de facto intern program, courtesy of the large number of immigrants relocating to this country and in need of work. The American Kitchen provided a cultural training ground for new arrivals into the ways of this country, continuing the long tradition of domestic apprenticeship. But by the 1900s, this practice was going the way of dirt floors and communal water wells. Immigrants continued to relocate to America, but now another tradition was set to welcome them: the occupational training centers run by women who'd immigrated earlier, who often shared the same religious background if not nationality.

The domestic scientists had also helped create a working environment that wasn't as arduous for women of the day compared to the kitchen of their mothers and grandmothers. But just as Americans were becoming accustomed to a different way of thinking about cooking and food preparation, the war began placing limitations on their kitchens. Thomas Jefferson had enjoined Americans in his day to "make the most of our labour, land being abundant," and a hundred years later his words were again a creed the kitchen could take stock in. While the circumstances were different, the sentiment remained the same. With all that was at their disposal, Americans were expected to succeed. Much had changed since the last major war effort in the United States, and the country had certainly never before seen the horrors of this type of global conflict. Now, the same automation that had given farmers reapers and thrashers that could do the work of five men in one day could also be harnessed to unleash a barrage of bullets, or produce an assembly line of bombs.

As news and images from the war overseas made the crossing back to the States, a new level of anxiety began to build in homes across the nation. The kitchen felt lonely, even cold, with so many young Americans being called to duty. Their homecoming would be cause to celebrate and, just as it had done its part to guarantee their safe return, the kitchen stood ready to welcome them back.

Every calorie mattered when it came to the feeding of American troops, and no morsel of food was too small to save if it could be used to keep a hungry soldier fighting. Helen Irene Weed reminded readers that "the value of grains and crumbs cannot be misunderstood, for a mouthful saved here means a mouthful over there, and in the terms of sugar a lolly-pop or a piece of frosted cake here means a sugar bun to those tortured souls across the sea."

Americans back in the States were encouraged to substitute foods whenever possible. Weed instructed her readers to abstain from "heavy cuts of beef, pork, and mutton" so that those portions could be used to feed the army. She made allowances for the occasional indulgence but warned that eating these foods "more than once a week [was] not in the line of patriotism when it is so easy to substitute fish, eggs, fowl, cheese, peas, beans and nuts."

U.S. Food Administrator Herbert Hoover asked Americans to impose voluntary restrictions on their diets in the summer of 1918. The schedule he proposed suggested that Americans forgo wheat and wheat products on Mondays and Wednesdays, eschew meat on Tuesdays, and refrain from eating pork on Thursdays and Saturdays. "Victory bread," a dark loaf made from coarse mill, was encouraged as a filling alternative.

Cooking magazines and other household guidebooks took up Hoover's cause and offered readers all sorts of alternatives to what had been their typical diet. With forced good cheer, writers suggested that homemakers try using boiled mashed potatoes instead of eggs when making omelets.

One recipe for a dish called Potato a la Hoover instructed:

Take mashed potato and mound it in a mountain shaped loaf. Scoop out the center leaving the walls an inch or more thick. Fill the center with left-over gravied meat, creamed fish or vegetables. Cover the top with liberty bread crumbs, and corrugate the sides with the back of a fork. Brush over with a little milk or left-over egg. Place in the oven to brown. Serve garnished with a bit of green.

The things that could be done with a scooped-out mound of mashed, boiled potatoes were seemingly endless. Anything and everything could be used to fill the depression left by the hollowing out of the mound. Potato mounds and vegetable loaves were common as homemakers were urged to put their patriotism ahead of their palates. Loaf of Green Peas was another wartime concoction, in which cooked peas, "war bread crumbs," a beaten egg, and chopped onion were mixed together and patted into a loaf and then baked in the oven.

The homemaker's role in the war effort was emphasized at every turn, from the names given to ingredients like "war bread crumbs" and "liberty bread crumbs," to the names of the dishes they were making, such as the Potato a la Hoover and Corn Meal War Pie Crust, to the sources the foods came from, as in "war gardens."

A woman was expected to treat the kitchen as her base of command, and every domestic duty was to be done with a single aim—the winning of the war. Even measuring cups and spoons were enlisted in the effort. "Don't guess!" *Good Housekeeping* warned its readership, acknowledging in its scolding tone that not every cook was using the still relatively new kitchen implements. The adherence to the use of precise measurements, as insisted on by the domestic scientists and in particular Fannie Farmer and the Boston Cooking School in the last century, could make the difference between success and defeat if cooks were careless and wasteful in their kitchens.

Similarly, the canning and preserving of foods was still common in many American kitchens, but the need became greater when food-packaging companies were called upon to send their goods overseas. War gardens were encouraged, and advertisers were quick to find ways to position their products as serving the noble war effort. Trowels, mats to kneel on while gardening, and lawn ornaments were all sold as a means to an end, and of course that end was winning the war. "A garden set is an acceptable present for the industrious and patriotic woman who will care for her war garden this summer," read one ad for matching gardening tools. "The gardens of 1918 will be sanctuaries in which, for a moment, we can find peace," consoled another. And by the end of that year, the war was over. But there was still a lot of work to be done before any celebrations could begin.

For one thing, all the fruits and vegetables from those war gardens had to be harvested, cleaned, and canned. Women were practically shamed into stashing their homegrown produce away for the winter or times when market prices put such foods out of the average homemaker's price range. In anticipation of such conditions, Weed wrote, "we then have our stores of dried and canned vegetables which we had foresight and patriotism enough to put away in the summer."

The canning and drying of foods was hardly a lost art form in the kitchen of the 1910s, as plenty of people still relied on their own preserved food supplies, yet most magazines that dealt with domestic responsibilities ran how-to articles during the war years to offer a refresher course in those tasks. Since every morsel of food was to be put to good use, marmalades were suddenly en vogue. The fruit spread used every bit of the orange, grapefruit, apricot, or prune in the recipe, and since people were familiar with its tart, often bitter taste, an excess amount of sugar was not required to brighten the pot. Cooks were further encouraged to substitute corn syrup for sugar when possible.

If appealing to Americans' patriotism wasn't enough of a motivation, some magazines resorted to stirring up the competitive spirit of the American homemaker. *House Beautiful* rallied its readers in a story about home-canning by announcing that "Germany is fifteen years ahead of us in this work, but our American Women will prove themselves to be equal to the emergency." The article delivered the news that the Germans had perfected a way to outfit their army with a supply of dried food that could sustain a stranded soldier for up to one month; the provisions were all neatly tucked into the confines of a box eight inches long by six inches wide. The writer bearing this news was Caroline G. Peeler, who attempted to galvanize readers into canning by declaring that "we should heed this loudest of all calls this year." A one-month supply of food in the enemies' hands would not only be enough to keep them alive as they starved out the Americans and their allies, it could also be a sufficient amount to carry them across the Atlantic. The American homemaker was to beat back this imminent threat by preserving and conserving as much of the harvest as possible today so there would be plenty of provisions in the cupboards come tomorrow.

The ability to preserve food in such a manner that it could be stored long enough to travel had been one of the most challenging issues facing the human race ever since the first tribe ran out of supplies during a migration. A depleted supply of staples was one of the reasons why the *Mayflower* came ashore when it did, and Napoleon would have conquered more land, sooner, had it not been the for the lack of rations that kept turning his troops around and making them hightail it back home to restock and refuel.

Those preserving foods in the American Kitchen had always relied on centuries-old methods. Pickling and potting (the latter being the practice of first cooking large amounts of meat, then sealing the pieces in a large jar lined and topped with lard) were popular, but the sheer size of the vessels that housed foods preserved in this manner made mobility and storage difficult. Meanwhile, salted and dried foods could sustain a family, but after a while the meats and flesh of fish became too pithy even to swim in pots of soup or stew.

On their own boats, the Acadians of the eighteenth century had relied on a one-pot staple, heating potatoes, onions, and dried cod in a cast-iron vessel until the ingredients transformed into something edible and worthy of being called chowder, the dish that became one of the staples of New England and Louisiana. But while this all-in-one meal was just what the experts ordered for American homemakers during World War I, it wasn't the kind of meal that could keep armies, or that armies could keep.

Throughout American history, troops had been hindered by food-related battle tactics, including the British blocking of salt supplies to Washington's army during the Revolution and the North's commandeering of the South's salt reserves during the Civil War. Without salt, meats could last only so long, as the sodium was needed to rid the flesh of moisture. Potting meat was one alternative, but large vessels were cumbersome and difficult to haul.

It was Napoleon Bonaparte's quest for a food that traveled and stored well during his military campaigns that eventually led to a safe means of food preservation. By offering a cash reward to the individual who could successfully preserve foods in a manner that kept freshness in and bacteria out, the French ruler became the benefactor of the modern-day canning industry. Nicholas Appert, the Frenchmen who won Napoleon's challenge to find a way to preserve food to sustain marauding armies, patented his vacuum-packing technique in 1809. Appert immersed his food-filled jars in vats of boiling water and then covered them with a piece of cork and sealed them with a smear of tar. This was revolutionary stuff at the time; old means of preserving food relied on larger vessels and heavy globs of lard. Appert's methods made it possible for food to be kept longer in more manageable, easily transported containers.

Appert's method eventually crossed the Atlantic and, soon after, new industrialized plants for packing foods in metal cans were creating a new market. John Landis Mason took Appert's original idea off the battlefield and into the home with his revolutionary Mason Jars in 1858. The arrival of the glass canning jar and the grooved lid, which, with a good twist, tightly sealed the contents safely inside, allowed homemakers to preserve their crops in smaller, more convenient containers. As James Trager wrote in his *Food Chronology*, Mason's jars enabled farm families to survive the winter without "having to rely on pickle barrels, root cellars, and smokehouses."

Even though the war effort of the 1910s occupied top-of-mind awareness in the country's kitchens, not all the means of food preservation in the modern American home had been motivated by war. While Napoleon's conquering ways were eventually responsible for the appearance of Mason Jars in America's kitchen cupboards and pantries, one means of food preservation widely in use across America by the start of World War I actually owed its beginnings to one man's humanitarian efforts.

Gail Borden was a successful agent of land lots in Galveston, Texas, in 1848 when news reports began carrying word of the tragic end met by some members of a group of pioneers from Illinois who'd tried to take a shortcut through Utah en route to California in the winter of 1846/47. The Donner party, as the ill-fated group became known, had taken a different road rather than the Oregon–California Trail traversed by most westbound settlers, but veering off the beaten path proved deadly for the party as the rough terrain slowed them down. An early snowstorm in the Sierra Nevada Mountains caused them to become stranded. Several members of the group ventured out in search of help, but provisions were running low for those remaining at base camp. When the search parties finally returned to rescue the pioneers, only forty-seven of the original eighty-seven men, women, and children were still alive. It didn't take long before the horrifying truth emerged—the remaining members of the Donner party had survived the winter by eating the corpses of those who'd died from starvation and malnourishment.

The news startled the world. Rumors of cannibalism were one thing; that was nothing new. But the fate of the Donner party was not gossip or conjecture. The evidence was there for the rescuing parties to see. While severe weather had definitely hampered the group's progress, the biggest threat they'd faced was their dwindling food supply. Unfortunately, the party's members who remained alive had to confront the difficult question of what if?

If Gail Borden could do anything to prevent it, such quandaries would never have to confront travelers or pioneers again. Borden's efforts to formulate a foodstuff that could travel were motivated by concern for friends who were about to make their own westward journey. Fearing that they might meet the same unspeakable fate as the Donner party, Borden began conducting experiments to create a food that was a source of energy and nutrition, and that would also keep well over long periods of time. By dehydrating meat, mixing it with flour, and then baking it in the oven, Borden created a cracker-like item that travelers could store away and munch on when hungry.

As any cook knows, creating a new recipe can require a lot of trial and error. Borden's efforts to create his "meat biscuit" spanned six years and cost him more than sixty thousand dollars. And while it didn't become one of the lasting items in the American Kitchen, its creation did lead Borden to achieve another breakthrough in food preservation.

In 1851 Borden had taken his dehydrated meat biscuit to the Great Exhibition world's fair held in London's Crystal Palace, where it was awarded the Great Council Gold Medal. The meat biscuit had been used by explorers to Arctic regions as well as by those on naval expeditions. In promoting its benefits, Borden emphasized that families could survive on it during hard times. The meat biscuit was a hit.

In returning from England, however, Borden was again confronted by tragedy. On the ship carrying him back to the United States a young immigrant's infant died because the cows onboard, which had been providing the baby's milk, were too overcome with seasickness to be milked. And at that time, there was no means of treating milk to safeguard it for long periods of time, so the child went without and starved.

This loss of life inspired Borden to find a way to put milk in a can. He eventually succeeded when he found a means to heat milk to a degree that killed off any microorganisms that might have been living in it. He then added sugar to thwart any further bacterial growth. By 1853 he developed a patent-worthy technique, and by 1857 he was selling his canned condensed milk in New York. By 1861 Borden had established an empire, and his numerous factories were capable of supplying the Union Army with countless cans of milk for its rations during the Civil War. (Unlike Appert's, Borden's initial efforts were not motivated by war.)

The saving of fuel during wartime was just as important as the saving of food, and both noble efforts were combined in casserole cooking. There were few ways to cook that were more economical than tossing vegetables and meats into a pot with some broth and allowing them to stew for hours over low heat. In fact the casserole was really nothing more than an update of that old standby, the one-pot meal, which had been present in the American Kitchen for centuries. In a 1917 article in which readers were encouraged to use casseroles, *Good Housekeeping* even paid tribute to the kitchen's ancestors, stating, "The primitive woman herself was the inventor of casserole cooking, and in her pottery dishes she boiled and stewed meats, vegetables, and fruits, everything which she did not cook in the ashes or on a hardwood stick over the fire."

There were a number of casserole and one-pot meals that had become traditions in America's kitchens that cooks could rely on during the war years. The aforementioned chowder was a one-pot regional favorite whose popularity had spread, as was the oft-made dish known simply as baked beans, or sometimes Boston Baked Beans. Both dishes made the most of ingredients that could be slow-cooked, and the baked-bean casserole served double-duty, as it allowed the Sabbath-observing Puritans to have a meal ready on the day of the week when their religion required that they abstain from work.

The fireless cooker was another fuel-saving weapon in the arsenal of the American Kitchen. The forerunner to the Crock-Pot, the fireless cooker was an apparatus in which pots containing foods were submerged into an insulated structure *after* they'd already been brought to a boil over a fire. The construction of the fireless cooker contained protective layers of materials that wrapped around the pot and kept the temperature inside constant. The type of insulation varied depending on the manufacturer; materials used for this purpose included asbestos, excelsior (curled wood shavings), cotton cloth, and even old newspapers. Some guides suggested that homemakers build their own fireless cookers. Since the pot was sealed inside these cookers, the insulation helped retain the heat as well as the flavor of the food being cooked. With less domestic help in the American Kitchen and with more activities taking place outside the home, the fireless cooker freed up valuable time that could be used on other activities. The typical cooking time in the cooker was three to four hours, but when compared to the fuel saved and the other work that could be done in that time, the wait was worth it. "Saving in fuel is now every woman's duty," ran the ad for the Rapid Fireless Cooker, a popular model of the day that claimed it helped households "save two thirds fuel costs" each year.

Food, fuel, and energy costs could be saved in the kitchen in other ways, too, and advertisers slyly worked this message into their sales pitches. McCray Refrigerators featured an Uncle Sam–like character in its ads that cautioned homeowners to Prevent Waste of Perishable Food in their kitchens. McCray's ad quoted from the wartime bulletins issued by the U.S. Food Administration: "If we can reduce the waste and unnecessary consumption of food, by a matter of only six cents a day, we shall have saved two billion dollars a year." Western Electric's ads showed "the man of the house" presiding over his wife as she used the company's appliances to wash clothes, iron, vacuum, sew, and, of course, cook his meals. HELP YOUR WIFE KEEP DOWN EXPENSES, the headline read. "Economizing to meet war-time conditions is a man's size job," the ad continued. The message was that the use of Western Electric's products was every bit as patriotic a gesture as canning and preserving since their electric range "save[d] fuel, labor and food."

Women on the home front also contributed to the war effort outside the kitchen. In Bedford, New York, a group of young women took to the fields to work the farms because the community's men were off at war. They were featured in several magazines and praised for their strength, endurance, and commitment. For women who didn't have fields to plow or backyards to plant, their patriotism manifested elsewhere. HOW ARE YOU USING YOUR PARKS? *House Beautiful* asked its readers in September 1918. The question was the lead-in for an article about public park space in Boston that had been enlisted as a garden plot. "The Women's City Club of Boston received permission to turn a portion of The Commons into gardens," the story reported. Several photos of the women's handiwork documented the fruits of their labor.

World War I ended with the declaration of Armistice Day on November 11, 1918. The rationing of sugar, which the government had imposed in the summer months of the year, was lifted by December, as were other voluntary restrictions on foods. The American Kitchen had contributed to the survival of its soldiers and the winning of the war, and now it was ready to welcome its heroes back home.

When World War I ended and soldiers started to reunite with their families, Americans again began to enjoy things that they might have taken for granted before the war. The hard times imposed on the kitchen by the scrimping and saving of every crumb of food had created a great deal of strain in the household. Now, with peace and prosperity seemingly on the horizon, homemakers could loosen their grips on their budgets and their menus and come out from the pall of austerity under which they'd been living for the past few years. "This is about to be a new world!" cheered Helen Irene Weed, the *House Beautiful* columnist who had championed the role of the homemaker during the war. "Let us make our homes fit into the new order of things! And where better can we begin than in the heart of those homes—the kitchen?"

One new development waiting to help create the new kitchen for this "new order of things" was Pyrex cookware, though the initial reception the glassware received from American homemakers was hardly warm.

Like waxed paper and other breakthroughs that eventually led to advances in home cooking, the arrival of Pyrex in America's kitchens was somewhat accidental. The Corning Glass Works Company had been tinkering for years with borosilicate, a form of glass that withstands the effects of extreme temperature changes. Corning initially perfected their heat-resistant glass, which they called NoneX, in the lenses and lanterns it produced for the railroad industry. NoneX proved to be so strong that the company's orders started to drop significantly—the glass wasn't breaking, and the product simply didn't need to be replaced. Corning needed to resume their cash flow, so the company's scientists took their NoneX know-how and went back to the drawing board. If NoneX could withstand the rigors of industrial use, then certainly it could stand up to the demands of domestic use.

After four years of experimentation, in 1915 Corning was ready to introduce Pyrex bakeware into the American Kitchen. The company expected Pyrex to be an immediate hit. The new glass dishes were much lighter than the heavy metal wares cooks had been hoisting in and out of ovens and to and from stovetops, and the cleanliness of glass cookware fit in with the domestic scientists' emphasis on sanitation—dirt, grease, and stains had nowhere to hide in the transparent Pyrex vessels. Corning even relied on "celebrity" endorsements. In one ad, a Professor L. B. Allyn of the Westfield Pure Food Laboratory proclaimed, "Not only does food cook more readily in Pyrex, but all danger of chipping, so prevalent in some types of oven-ware, is eliminated. We regard Pyrex as a valuable asset to any kitchen." Unfortunately the majority of American homemakers ignored Allyn's message, and despite Pyrex's winning combination of being strong and lightweight, its acceptance into the nation's kitchens was a slow one. Why? The problem was one of timing: Pyrex debuted right as the world was erupting into war. By the time the fighting had ended, the global mind was set on new beginnings. Corning had positioned Pyrex as another manifestation of the domestic scientists' call for cleanliness and order; after witnessing the death and destruction caused by the war, Americans wanted to move forward with as few reminders of the past as possible.

Many leaders of the domestic movement saw the end of the war as a time to make a new start in all aspects of living. In her essay "Reconstruction! Are

We Ready?" Helen Irene Weed continued the domestic scientists' mantra "Simplify!" but now there was a different tone to that old chant. If the enemy before the war was the drudgery of housework, the enemy after the war was the loss of quality time. The early domestic scientists and home economists were determined to lift housework up out of the ashes of wood and coal stoves. The new attitude that seemed to emerge in America's kitchens after the war was a more relaxed one than had ever accompanied the days of arduous labor from the last century. Home magazines were suggesting that women pull up a stool and sit down while baking or washing dishes. Americans were even encouraged to consider adding a breakfast nook to their kitchen, complete with benches and table, so that they could enjoy their food as soon as it came off the stove.

Before long, Americans were feeling the need to kick up their heels. The war was over and the country felt the need to live it up. And in this new era, with this new attitude, the efficiency preached by the prewar domestic scientists seemed too rigid. Years of sacrifice and personal denial for the greater patriotic good had taken their toll, and Americans were looking to celebrate. Cleanliness was still in, but sterility was definitely out. Americans wanted to embrace life after so many years of death, and the kitchen was a good place to start.

CHAPTER THREE

The Greatest Thing
Since . . . : 1920–1929

Style came into the American Kitchen in the 1920s, and so did a more relaxed
attitude. Homemakers were urged to pull up a chair and enjoy their time in
the room. (Courtesy of Corbis.)

The decade following World War I earned a reputation as being the one that roared, but its beginnings could hardly have been called raucous. At a time when families and friends should've been celebrating peace and looking toward an era of prosperity, somber news continued to come in from around the world. The United States had emerged from the war as a leading global power, and its involvement had helped prevent a prolonged conflict. Yet that victory was not without consequences. For starters, the devastation caused by the war demanded attention. Reconstruction required funds to rebuild the parts of Europe that had been blown apart. But while the war had not been waged on American soil, and there was no need for reparation monies in the States, the country had financial issues of its own. Falling farm prices created economic instability early in the twenties. Industrialization and automation developed since the last century had helped increase crop production, but maybe they had done their jobs a little too well; an overabundance of wheat contributed to the plummeting economy when farmers had nowhere to sell their harvest domestically. Other advances in food production were also contributing to bumper crops. A chemical pesticide that would become known worldwide as DDT was now sprayed in fields, helping farmers combat an enemy against which they'd formerly had no defenses.

Contributing to the increasing surplus on American farms was the abundance of grains that would have otherwise been made into alcohol. New laws were clamping down on the manufacturing, distribution, and consumption of alcoholic beverages, killing the buzz in more ways than one. The Prohibition laws, as the new restrictions on alcohol were called, threatened to stop the party in the 1920s before it could even get started.

But while Americans couldn't wind down with their favorite cocktail, there were plenty of items at the ready to wind them up. Americans were getting a rush from all the prepackaged foods now available at newsstands, drugstores, and grocery stores. Candy was dandy in the 1920s, as manufacturers and advertisers raced to position their confection as the It snack of choice with postwar America's In Crowd.

A great deal of emphasis was being put on appearance, inside and outside of America's kitchens. The suave and svelte demeanor of F. Scott Fitzgerald's Gatsby, even if only idealized, replaced the fat-cat style of "Diamond Jim" Brady. And another idealized image, one in sharp contrast to the stern expressions and starched white uniforms of the domestic scientists, was that of a smiling homemaker by the name of Betty Crocker, the fictional spokesperson for Gold Medal Flour.

Things were definitely changing. It didn't take long for the prevailing attitude in the country to go from somber to almost superficial in the 1920s. The troops were home, the economy was starting to gain momentum, and Americans tried to convince themselves that they'd never face the adversities of war and lack again. Surely the world had grown wise from seeing the devastation science and technology could now bring to warfare, and no civilized country would ever allow such a thing to happen again. That kind of thinking, however, was too depressing. In the new decade, Americans wanted to Charleston their cares away.

On the morning of January 1, 1920, the American Kitchen must have nursed some of the worst hangovers in its history. Before the first month of the new year would end, an amendment to the U.S. Constitution would take effect, making alcoholic beverages—their manufacturing, distribution, selling, and consumption—illegal. If New Year's Eve celebrants wanted to party like it was 1999, who could blame them? The decade of the Great War was over. It was time to move forward, but the Prohibition Amendment was putting a gigantic cork in any future plans, party or otherwise, that involved alcohol.

Alcohol had been part of the American Kitchen since the first immigrants to North America had struggled to grow the hops, barley, and fermenting agents needed for their beer. Drinking water was not always safe, so home-brewed beer was often consumed from sunup 'til sundown. Even the Puritans, who are most remembered for their austere and "puritanical" ways, were so fond of their beer that their funerals could easily turn into drunken blowouts, according to Daniel Sack, author of *Whitebread Protestants*.

Beer was considered perfectly acceptable in America's kitchens until the Revolutionary War, when, for a period of time, the British and European roots of beer made it politically incorrect for colonists to partake of it regularly. "Cider, now that was an American drink," says Frank Clark, historian and director of Foodways at Colonial Williamsburg in Virginia. One of the more colorful characters in America's folklore, Johnny Appleseed, helped foster cider's popularity in America. The seeds that John Chapman (his real name) was spreading on his way westward would help guarantee settlers a grove of apple trees—necessary for their home stock of cider.

Unfortunately, alcohol also darkened many pages of American history, with the role that rum and molasses played in the slave trade during colonial times. Benjamin Franklin, writing as Poor Richard, opined in his alter ego's famous *Almanack* that too much beer made a man lose himself, but too much rum made him "lose his soul." The connection to the slave trade was one of the reasons abolitionists and reformists in the nineteenth century strongly opposed rum, along with other hard liquors.

Meanwhile, the proliferation of readily available liquor was another sign of the excess that the age of industrialization and modernity was bringing into the kitchen. With comparatively less work needing to be done to keep a household running, Americans had more leisure time. The ruin that awaited anyone with proverbial idle hands had long been preached, and it was thought that it would be only a matter of time before one of those hands reached for the bottle. If alcohol had the potential to destroy a man's soul, as believed by the temperance movement, backers of the twentieth century's Prohibition laws, it could in time destroy an entire nation.

The restrictions against alcohol consumption had several long-lasting effects on the American Kitchen. Breweries went out of business, wheat farmers had a surplus crop, and wineries were prohibited from fermenting the drink for any purpose other than as needed for religious observances. The lack of quality wines in the United States for several years following the repeal of Prohibition in 1933 was attributed to the disappearance of wine-growers from America. With no one to buy or enjoy their craft, many wine-growers relocated outside the country.

But while one industry suffered due to the ban on alcohol, another boomed. Soft drinks such as Coca-Cola and Pepsi-Cola were already putting a spring in the step of those who favored them, but soon other carbonated beverages were bottled for consumers looking for a new kind of, legal, kick. Nehi began bottling Royal Crown Cola as an alternative to the two major cola drinks, and lemon-lime-flavored 7-Up was introduced as the alternative to the alternative. Kool-Aid fruit-flavored drink mix also found its way into America's kitchens. Finally, coffee and tea, which had been part of the American diet since the days of the Revolution, were increasingly turned to as an end-of-the-day pick-me-up or an after-dinner drink.

One thing the bottled soft drinks all had in common, besides profiting from Prohibition, was their reliance on sugar to sweeten their formula. While the "Sweet Twenties" doesn't have quite the same ring to it as the "Roaring Twenties," the decade could easily have been tagged as such. Whether it was due to the search for a new vice in the age of alcohol prohibition or because the lack in the kitchen during the previous decade's war years made some Americans throw caution, and moderation, to the wind, the country developed a sweet tooth that demanded increasing amounts of sugar to keep it satisfied. Fortunately—or unfortunately, depending on your cravings—there were plenty of the white granules to go around: The price of sugar on the world market had dropped nearly 75 percent in 1920. That drop sent consumption of sugar in the American Kitchen up to a hefty 106 pounds per capita. Food manufacturers were making it easier than ever for Americans to get their sugar fix. The Good Humor bar, Baby Ruth, Oh Henry!, Butterfinger, Mounds, Reese's Peanut Butter Cup, and Milky Way were just a few of the treats for sale in the first half of the decade. It seemed food companies were looking for any and every opportunity to sell their products. Oh Henry! bars came with serving suggestions, including a recipe for Tomato-Stuffed Salads. The stuffing in the tomato was, of course, a chopped-up Oh Henry! bar. The popular dance of the decade had a candy bar named in its honor, the Charleston Chew, as did the first transatlantic pilot, Charles Lindbergh—Lindy Bars and the Flying Lindy.

If the events of the 1920s couldn't be honored or celebrated legally with a bit of the bubbly, then candy bars were guaranteeing Americans at least one source of a giddy rush.

The American Kitchen had been the scene of contrasts in the past, and the 1920s were no different. The sugar fixation was offset by a trend toward salads, and "dainty" foods became all the rage.

Despite the clamoring for sweets, many Americans were eating what they thought were "quality" meals, as scientists had discovered vitamins in the first part of the twentieth century. An emphasis was placed on the ease of digestion of foods, in addition to the concern of their nutritional content. Quaker Oats and Puffed Rice were some of the first foods to pick up on this trend in their advertisements. Quaker maintained that their products "agree[d] perfectly with even the weakest stomachs," and offered a "dainty crispness." Minute Tapioca likewise promised to help cooks make "Dainty Desserts," while Sunkist growers assured consumers that their oranges would perk up a "sluggish" liver and deliver "better digestion."

What did the digestibility of certain foods and vitamin contents have to do with whether or not something was dainty? A lot, actually. The domestic scientists and their preoccupation with dainty cuisine had unwittingly played a hand in launching the American obsession with being thin. Ever since the last century the domestic-science movement had preached a message of purity and control in the American Kitchen. It was only a matter of time before that same message started to pertain to the American appetite. With the introduction of calorie-counting, it was determined that women did not need as much food as men (regardless of how physically demanding their workday was). Smaller portions became stylish, and soon so did smaller figures. The domestic scientists were already fond of salads by the time Florenz Ziegfeld featured fifty thin dancers in his production *The Follies of 1907*. The ideal woman prior to this was buxom to say the least, but Ziegfeld's model began a revolution. The following year the "sheath" dress emerged, leaving little to the imagination and causing many a man's eye (and other body parts) to wander when it debuted in American cities. Terribly fashionable in Paris at the time, the sheath dress was so named because of its glove-like fit over the body. Women couldn't wear petticoats underneath, as they'd disrupt the garment's smooth lines. Thus, by 1923, the emphasis on a woman's figure was becoming a weighty issue. Magazines for women were starting to pick up on the "thin is in" trend. In an issue of *Women's Home Companion* an essay addressed how food and fashion could work to a woman's advantage or inadvertently create a less-than-desirable image. "Weight," the author wrote, could now be "a liability, both physical and esthetic." Women were being told to count their calories if they wanted to slim down, and salads were thought to assist them to that end. In addition to being served in smaller portions, these dishes were also less messy since they were often "imprisoned in gelatin to be fit food for civilized people," as Sylvia Lovegren writes in *Fashionable Food*. While the amount of cream cheese that existed in some of these "salad" recipes made for anything but light meals, the petite servings guaranteed that the women eating them were getting fewer calories.

There was something amusing about the continued emphasis on lighter foods and smaller portions that carried into the 1920s, considering that the country had just come out of a decade when Americans were urged to restrain their appetites; all of this at a time when the American Kitchen had more access to, and availability of, a variety of foods than it had ever had before. Grocery stores, like Alpha Beta Foods and A&P's Economy or "cash and carry" store, were offering canned foods such as Dole pineapple, peas and corn from the Minnesota Valley Canning Company (which was soon to become Green Giant), and Sunshine Biscuits. Tea was now available in small, sealed bags, perfect for single servings of the beverage—another example of how food manufacturers raced to fill the void, and the empty drinking vessels, left by Prohibition in the American Kitchen.

Wheaties, Pep, and Rice Krispies cereal were in cupboards and on breakfast tables, their presence in the American Kitchen of the twenties a tandem success for both the reformists and the domestic scientists of the nineteenth century.

The Kellogg Company, maker of breakfast cereals, grew out of the research done by John Harvey Kellogg on behalf of Ellen White and her religious sect, the Seventh-Day Adventists. In the latter part of the nineteenth century, Kellogg had experimented with a number of corn- and wheat-flake cereals for the group at their enclave in Battle Creek, Michigan. The Adventists' vegetarianism made them abstain from the popular breakfast foods of the time, which often included bacon, ham, or some other type of animal flesh. Kellogg was already working from Sylvester Graham's idea of a breakfast that was as good for the body as it was for the soul when he developed the Adventists' meal. Before the century would end, Kellogg would have a competitor in C. W. Post. Post's Grape-Nuts would go on to become a favorite with a different kind of social reformist in the 1960s and '70s, but in the 1920s the popularity of his cereal was more attributable to its quickness and ease of preparation. Like the other boxed cereals entering the American Kitchen in the first quarter of the twentieth century, one of the biggest selling points for Grape-Nuts, Wheaties, and Pep was that nothing more was required to enjoy them than a spoon, a bowl, and milk. No fire, no domestic help, and virtually no mess. The sterile kitchen environment favored by the food technologists and domestic scientists was left intact.

For Americans who could afford it, boxed cold cereal was the greatest thing to hit the American Kitchen's breakfast table until sliced bread. Pre-sliced, commercially packaged bread wasn't widely available until Wonder Bread hit store shelves, wrapped in plastic, in 1928. To understand how exciting and important an innovation this was for homemakers, one has to look no further than a helpful hint in an early *Better Homes and Gardens* "For Better Housekeeping" column. Discussing how to make kitchen work less stressful, the magazine suggested: "A combination of bread knife that really cuts, and conveniently small cutting board, kept near the bread box will save you several steps and possible loss of temper three times a day."

More Americans were purchasing commercially baked bread in the twenties than ever. Less than half the population still baked their own. The switch was one of necessity for some, convenience for others. While sliced bread met with some resistance—critics admonished that it did not stay fresh as long as a whole loaf, regardless of what it was wrapped in—the way it helped transform the breakfast table quickly won over its detractors. Uniform slices of bread were less likely to burn in the new electric toasters. Plus, they had another appeal: They were like blank canvases, just waiting to be covered with jellies, preserves, butter, or the new jarred peanut butter that was now available in stores. Sales of these spreadables increased significantly with the arrival of sliced bread. A piece of toast, slathered with jam or jelly, might not have been a complete breakfast, but it was a portable one!

As the introduction of sliced bread and the electric toaster demonstrated, the American Kitchen was continuing to get the makeover that had been under way prior to the start of the war of the last decade. New conveniences and new designs were proving that science and aesthetics did not have to be mutually exclusive, and one invention that would make a colorful impact in the kitchen was Bakelite by Leo Baekeland. Baekeland was a chemist who was working to create a type of plastic when he created a resinlike material from formaldehyde and phenol, a substance that would later be used in everything from the manufacturing of nylon to cough medicines. Bakelite, as the substance would come to be labeled, was an immediate success when it hit the market: It allowed cooks to grip pot handles without burning themselves. The properties of Bakelite prevented it from absorbing heat, so it could be safely used on pots, pans, lids, and even cooking appliances.

From an aesthetic angle, Baekeland's invention brought a little bit of wow into America's kitchens, as it became a favorite among designers during the Art Deco craze. Coffeepots and utensils were adorned with Bakelite handles that had a jewellike tone to them, which in turn echoed the opulence of the Deco movement. Consumers liked it because it made glamour accessible by lending a little bit of elegance to objects that would ordinarily be considered utilitarian.

In a country made up of and founded by immigrants, international influence was unavoidable. Yet America's taste buds were still somewhat provincial in the 1920s in the sense that the menu of the English, who settled the country in the largest numbers, was for the most part still the dominant cuisine in the new nation. Regional foods also had an effect on what Americans ate and cooked, but the American Kitchen was opening its doors wider after the war, even if with a bit of initial hesitation.

Americans were introduced to international flavors in food and design in the expos and world's fairs that began as far back as the initial fair in London in 1851. Expos in America in the last quarter of the nineteenth century sparked an interest in Asian design in the United States, and Victorian homes started to see Oriental flourishes in the design of their banisters and furniture spindles. Bamboo became a popular material used in homes of the time, too. (Interestingly enough, while their aesthetics were permitted in American homes, the Chinese and Japanese themselves were unwelcome in the country and their immigration was blocked.) The Chicago World's Fair in 1893 and the St. Louis World's Fair in 1904 further exposed Americans to authentic cuisines from around the world. Eating foods in a pavilion at the fair apparently was deemed safer than eating in an ethnic restaurant, as Americans still remained somewhat suspicious of foreign cuisines. That the fairs could influence American eating habits had already been proven by the popularity of peanut butter, ice cream cones, and hamburgers—all foods that were first enjoyed at world's fairs—in the American Kitchen.

After World War I, the nation began to experience a shift in attitude toward other cultures. A number of things contributed to this change of heart. Art Deco and jazz were the movements driving the culture at the time. Art Deco drew upon a variety of global influences for its designs. Mesoamerican temples, Egyptian hieroglyphics, African tribal art, and Asian architectural elements all came together in the new and exciting high style. The look of Deco was not overtly foreign, but just exotic enough to first tease, and then appeal to, America's tastes. Jazz had a similar allure. The music was striking and unconventional, and the fact that it was made predominantly by black musicians sharpened its edge. With the visual and musical aspects of different groups being embraced, it was only a matter of time before more daring Americans began to step up to the plate and enjoy the cuisines other countries had to offer.

Chinese food had intrigued Americans for years because the Chinese diet seemed to give Chinese railroad workers more stamina than their American counterparts enjoyed in the 1800s. But Americans were slow to adopt Chinese cooking in their own kitchens, preferring to have bastardized dishes like chop suey (a meal about as Chinese as pizza) instead of more authentic items like chow mein.

The American love affair with foods that would cause them to exclaim "That's Italian" years later also began in the early twentieth century. It was the prohibition of alcohol, however, that would really give Italian cooking a chance to impress Americans as many Italian restaurants continued serving alcohol. The only problem was that while the Italian hangouts offered their share of booze, the foods they were cooking weren't appealing to the average American's taste buds. In fact, the biggest complaint among Americans who patronized the Italian restaurants was that the sauces lacked one crucial ingredient: beef. Since long before the ranchers in Texas drove their cattle north, Americans had had a love affair with red meat. The solution, fortunately, was an easy one. Meatballs were added to the tomato sauce that was spooned over the pasta, and suddenly an "authentic" Italian dish became a favorite in America's kitchens.

Foods with a Mexican or Spanish influence also started to spice up the nation's kitchens in the 1920s. The American infatuation with spicy peppers was evident in the way Tabasco Sauce had become such a hit in the nineteenth century. As more cultural mingling continued in the southwestern United States, the offspring of these merging cuisines began to pop up in kitchens and restaurants around the country. Chili parlors became popular at the turn of the century in major American cities, and chili con carne—a one-pot budget stretcher if ever there was one—became fashionable in the years that followed.

All three "international" cuisines—Chinese, Italian, and Mexican—had companies canning foods to promote their cause by the beginning of the third decade of the twentieth century. La Choy (which would later sing that they made "Chinese Food that swings American") got its start when an American entrepreneur teamed up with a Korean businessman to can bean sprouts. Progresso Foods also began to line stores' shelves, and Old El Paso brand foods got their start on a farm in New Mexico when a family with the last name of Powell began canning vegetables from their fields.

After an initially slow start, as the nation's confidence grew, Americans were dancing and eating their way through the 1920s. There were lots of reasons to celebrate, even if Americans had to do it without alcohol. The Great War was over, the country was hard at work, and the increasingly inviting American Kitchen had plenty of food and new appliances to keep meals on the table. Things weren't just looking up; they were also looking different.

Unfortunately, not even a full decade had passed before new worries entered the American Kitchen. The 1920s may have roared, but they were about to come to a screeching halt. The party was definitely over.

CHAPTER FOUR

Heroes: 1930–1939

Shared caring meant that friends, neighbors, and even strangers made the most of a little during the Depression era. (Johnstown Soup Kitchen by James Du Pont. Courtesy of Johnstown Area Heritage Association.)

W hen the stock market crashed in October 1929, most Americans had to have been wondering when the partylike atmosphere that characterized the decade that roared would come to an end. In the ten years leading up to the twenties, Americans saw war divide the world and poverty widen the gap between the classes at home. While progress in industry and science continued to offer ways to improve American quality of life, the century had so far proven that the only thing that was certain was uncertainty.

In the period following the crash, the faith and fortitude of Americans would be tested by economic ruin, natural disasters, and the devastation of another world war. This was not the future they had planned; threats like these were supposed to be things of the past. The breakthroughs in medicine, science, and technology had been moving America forward. In a society where procuring food was no longer a full-time job for all, the American population had the time, money, and resources to engage in leisure activities and to follow artistic, educational, and spiritual pursuits. Being able to properly can, or "put up," jars of preserved foods was no longer the issue of life or death that it had once been. Americans could now buy their sustenance at their local Piggly Wiggly.

The new century had promised access and abundance for all. Democracy and capitalism were purported to be equal-opportunity employers. Anyone who wanted to get ahead could do so as long as they had ambition, motivation, and dedication. Regardless of his or her current lot, the chance to live the good life was one every American was supposed to share. It was only a matter of time before everyone was living on Easy Street, with a car in the garage and a chicken in the pot: This image of a prosperous America was such a sure bet that Herbert Hoover ran his 1928 presidential campaign, and won, on the promise.

But in the aftermath of the crash of '29 the one thing most Americans had in common was anxiety. As they stepped apprehensively into the unknown they began looking for comfort and solace in old customs, just as they looked for hope and salvation in new innovations: Family and friends began gathering for home-cooked meals, all the while hoping that technology and science would eventually find a way to eliminate the hardships they were facing.

The balance of such dichotomies would be typical in the American Kitchen during this new era. *Gourmet* magazine would premiere just as more "fake" foods were being engineered. Breadlines wrapped around soup kitchens while streamlining was applied in manufacturing. And Prohibition was finally repealed, even though there weren't many reasons to toast. But Americans would survive the Great Depression and World War II, and as a result their kitchens would be stronger and more productive than ever.

"We ate better in this country when we were poor," Anthony Bourdain says, looking back over the evolution of American cuisine. "We ate more heroically, more fearlessly when we didn't have so much money and ease." And if ever there was a time when life in the American Kitchen was exemplified by a lack of money and comfort, it was the period following the stock market crash of 1929—the Great Depression. With millions of people out of work, the indulgences of the 1920s were a thing of the past. Keeping one's family fed was the first priority, and one that was often difficult. Americans met this challenge with a stiff upper lip and steely resolve. "The food sections of popular magazines never mentioned the terrible plight of many of their readers and only occasionally ran a feature on economical meals," writes Sylvia Lovegren in *Fashionable Food*. And even now, when reading accounts of people who lived through the Depression, the impression left by the testimonials isn't one of a brooding, dour population but rather a selfless, charitable, and industrious nation that pulled together during a tough time, determined to make it through.

"Perhaps it takes the worst of times to bring out the best in people, but with all of the shortages it was a time that drew many people closer," writes Bill Jones, a retired senior writer for the Johnstown *Tribune Democrat*. In an essay titled "A Time of Sharing," Jones describes the way people in the various neighborhoods of Johnstown, Pennsylvania, looked out for one another. "Neighbors shared what little they had, often exchanging items from their small gardens—a cabbage for green beans, some carrots for tomatoes."

This spirit of sharing and swapping pervaded the American Kitchen during the 1930s. Generosity wasn't limited to those who had something to give in exchange, though. Families joined together to come to the aid of a neighbor who was facing particularly hard times. People gave food to homeless men, or hoboes as they were called then, who usually road the railways from town to town, sometimes offering to perform odd jobs in exchange for something to eat, sometimes not. The presence of a drifter at the back door was a common sight during the Depression. For their part, these men often lived in makeshift camps called "hobo jungles" where they cooked for themselves, assembling a stew from vegetables begged from townspeople, along with scraps of meat from local butcher shops. Men weren't the only drifters, however, as recounted by Nancy Pyle Johnston, a former Johnstown resident. In a special edition of the Johnstown *Tribune Democrat* commemorating the 1930s, Pyle Johnston writes: "I remember the day a desperate, poverty-stricken woman appeared at our back door, begging for food." Pyle Johnston's mother was facing her own hard times and had only a can of bacon fat, which she'd saved by draining the frying pan after each use. "The woman was so grateful for this meager offering that, despite my mother's protests, she scrubbed our kitchen floor."

The poor economic conditions leveled the social playing field, as most people were living in similarly dire straits. Families bought what they could afford from local grocers. Company stores, grocery and department stores owned and operated by the coal mines that employed people in different regions of the country, extended "credit" to their customers, only to take the money out of the shopper's next paycheck. Other establishments were more straightforward with their generosity, allowing customers to pay when they could, if they could. According to Bill Jones's article, at the start of the

Depression about three hundred independent grocery stores existed in Johnstown. By 1941 nearly 20 percent of those had folded.

Prices at the time weren't overly inflated, but few customers had the means to pay for foodstuffs. In 1931, bananas sold for 19 cents a dozen, a bushel of peaches was 89 cents, and coffee averaged 19 cents a pound. In the middle of the decade a quarter bought a dozen oranges, and 90 cents would get you 24 pounds of flour. By the end of the 1930s, prices would show the economy had improved, if only slightly; coffee was selling at 17 cents a pound, and sugar had dropped from $1.23 for twenty-five pounds in 1931 to $1.13 in 1939.

When Americans couldn't afford to shop for their foods, they foraged or resorted to growing their own. Elderberries were a favorite of the American Kitchen in rural areas. The wild berries were picked and canned, baked into pies, or made into jellies that were preserved right alongside the vegetables from the family gardens. In addition to picking wild fruits and nuts, most rural families never stopped planting vegetables. But now gardens also sprouted in the cramped backyards that ran behind urban row homes. The harvest from these gardens was essential to the nightly meal for many families, often the only variable in an otherwise routine diet. Historian Frank Alcamo, who chronicled his Pennsylvania hometown's growth in *The South Fork Story: The First 100 Years*, writes, "Food was scarce. In our Italian family our meals were predominantly pasta dishes—one day with spinach, another with kale, then beans, endive or anything that was grown in the back garden. Meat was a rarity."

Mr. Alcamo's experience was typical. Dr. Shirley Wajda asked her father about his ordeal growing up on a farm in Ohio during the Depression; his response was, "We ate macaroni every night for dinner and I wore your Aunt Francis's shoes to school." Dr. Wajda's parents raised chickens and cows, but the eggs and milk were always sent to market. The family couldn't afford to eat the output from their own industry.

For those families who had sufficient space on their property, fruit trees provided a rich source of vitamins and flavor. Pear, peach, apple, and cherry trees were popular during the Depression. Centuries of cultivation in North America had produced hybrids that grew well in most regions and in most soil types. Fruits were canned or dried at home and stored away. As Mr. Alcamo writes, "Who could afford canned goods?"

The American Kitchen relied heavily on the budget-stretching, one-pot meal during the Depression, and it took on different forms in different regions of the country. Cabbage and potato soups and stews were prevalent.

"Popular" probably doesn't best describe the reason for their presence; they were cheap, filling alternatives for feeding a hungry family. Homemade noodles and pastas were also in wide use. For Helen Kalwasinski, a native of Portage, Pennsylvania, lima beans were the recurring item on her family's dinner table. "We mostly had lima bean soup," she writes. "To this we always added browned flour gravy in which tomatoes were smothered. If a person had potatoes," she adds, "these were cooked for soup. If we were short tomatoes and lima beans, we cooked macaroni."

Just as one often hears about meals based on macaroni, potatoes, and cabbage during the Depression, stories surface about neighbors banding together to help one another regardless of their religion or nationality: "Neighbors cared and shared with each other despite their ethnic background," writes Johnstown native Helen Gehosky in the *Tribune Democrat*'s 1930s' coverage. And Bill Jones recalls that "the Depression years . . . helped to draw people of various ethnic backgrounds closer."

In these testimonials a missing link in the evolution of the American Kitchen can be found. Taste buds in America have grown increasingly adventurous since the earliest days of the American Kitchen. The characteristic pickiness exhibited by the British at Jamestown, Virginia, was abandoned when survival was at stake (though not always soon enough). Former national boundaries were erased when immigrants arrived in America. As it had during the earliest days of the colonies, the common enemy of hunger made people turn to one another for survival. Suddenly the ethnicity of a food mattered less than its ability to nourish. This was certainly the case in the decade of the 1930s.

It's been said that America's great culinary expedition began after World War II, when soldiers returned home with a taste for the international foods they'd eaten while abroad. More than likely, though, the willingness of Americans to embrace the cuisines of other countries was born of necessity during the Depression—not out of the pages of a magazine or around the tables of the numerous women's dinner clubs—as neighbors shared what foods they had with the family next door. Fresh vegetables and fruits and loaves of bread were shared, but so were cooked dishes. Potato pancakes, baked pastas, noodle kugels, and other foods served as culinary ambassadors as they made their way into kitchens that had never experienced such dishes.

During the 1930s there was a strong need for shared caring. There were more Americans facing starvation than ever before within the nation's borders. As early as 1931, eight million Americans were out of work. With so many of its citizens facing hard times and empty cupboards, the U.S. government, under the leadership of President Herbert Hoover, decided that feeding the hungry was a role better suited to charitable organizations like the American Red Cross. The following year, funds that had provided assistance and relief checks in various urban cities were depleted. Congress released forty million bushels of wheat that had been previously purchased by the Federal Farm Bureau to feed hungry Americans. (The original purchase was part of a checks-and-balances system that was supposed to protect consumers from lofty prices driven up by unscrupulous farmers and salespersons.) Long lines poured out of soup kitchens, and breadlines fed the unemployed and the underemployed. By the end of 1932, more than fifteen million Americans would be out of work. The average income for those fortunate enough to have a job was approximately sixteen dollars a week.

Desperately in need of a government that cared about their plight, Americans voted Hoover out of office, and in 1933 Franklin D. Roosevelt took control. Rather than making promises about how prosperous the country would be with him at the helm, Roosevelt inspired Americans to face the challenges of the era. Instead of guaranteeing Americans "a chicken in every pot," Roosevelt stirred the country with the message "The only thing we have to fear is fear itself."

Roosevelt got down to business quickly by turning his attention toward the American farm. Both the Emergency Farm Bill and the Farm Mortgage Act were created to help keep farmers and their lands producing the staples needed by the rest of the country. A Crop Loan Act was later passed to keep farmers in the black until their autumn payday.

In addition to creating jobs, like the building of the American highways through the Works Progress Administration (WPA), the Roosevelt administration proposed a New Deal for America. Working Americans were hungry Americans, so the government began issuing surplus cheese, butter, bread, potatoes, and even occasional cans of meat. Stenciled on the side of the products' packaging were the words NOT TO BE SOLD. Edward Semich of Elton, Pennsylvania, shares somber memories of that packaging in the *Tribune Democrat*: "One day my brother and I walked to get a free bag of potatoes. NOT TO BE SOLD was conspicuously printed on one side of the bag," Mr. Semich writes. "We twisted and turned that bag every which way on our four and a half mile walk back home so passersby wouldn't notice. Our pride was on the line."

In listening to stories told by Americans who lived through the Depression, what can be heard is a sense of pride for having survived the toughest of times. The spirit of sharing and caring for one's neighbors turned strangers into heroes, and heroes into friends. A reversal of fortune was never far away: Those who had an extra head of cabbage or loaf of bread to share knew that in the uncertainty of the era they could soon enough find themselves in the position of need.

Backyard gardens and the kindness of strangers weren't the only noncommercial sources of food the American Kitchen relied on during the 1930s. Homemade chicken coops and henhouses were just as common as cabbage patches or carrot beds in American backyards. Raising chickens provided a constant source of protein from the eggs collected each morning. Slaughtering the chickens, however, was done only when the birds grew too old to produce a steady supply of eggs.

Poultry meat had always been expensive in America, especially compared to the price of beef. In the 1880s, chicken cost approximately ten dollars per pound. By the 1930s, that price had dropped to twenty-two cents per pound, but that was still out of the reach of most family budgets. A pound of beefsteak could be had for a few pennies more. And with so many Americans raising chickens of their own, if money was going to be spent on meat, beef was what was for dinner.

The prohibitive cost of eating chicken was why Hoover's 1928 campaign promise of putting one in every pot was so effective. An America where chicken was eaten regularly was a prosperous country, indeed. Part of the reason for the bird's high cost was the fact that chicken was not yet farmed commercially as extensively as cattle or pigs. Chickens were also susceptible to a host of different diseases that could spread quickly through a henhouse, decimating their numbers. Investing a lot of money in a chicken farm was a gamble, but in 1920 the Perdue family had just ventured into the chicken farming business in Salisbury, Maryland. The Perdue farm, started by Arthur Perdue, was originally founded with fifty leghorn chickens with the intention of relying on their eggs for income.

The cost of keeping chickens, even for a commercial affair like Perdue's chicken farm, was evidenced in the decline of "layers on hand" between 1925 and 1945. According to statistics collected by the USDA's Economic Research Service, the years leading up to the stock market crash of 1929 were boom years for chicken farmers, with 1927 being particularly productive: American poultry farms averaged 329,576 layers on hand. That number dropped by tens of thousands during the Depression years, as the cost of feed—not to mention the lack of a market—affected the poultry industry. There were 275,919 egg-producing birds in 1938. In the next decade, the war effort's demand for eggs would bring the numbers up and over the pre-Depression count, with an industry high of almost 400,000 layers in 1944. In that year, chickens in America were doing their patriotic duty by producing an average of 148 eggs per year, per hen.

For the backyard chicken enterprise, a family of six would house about fifty chickens to meet their needs, as each hen averaged almost a dozen eggs per month. Some of the eggs were eaten, while others were allowed to hatch. And protecting those hatchlings was crucial, especially in the colder months.

"Be prepared!" advised the makers of Cel-O-Glass, a heat-reflective covering used for chicken coops. "A small investment in Cel-O-Glass now will earn big profits in more eggs and healthy chicks all winter long." Even the government was offering assistance to the novice poultry farmer with its brochure "How to Raise Poultry for Profit."

One of the more unorthodox tools of the chicken-rearing trade was the Harwood Plastic Spectron. It was believed that the presence of red light increased egg productivity in otherwise aggressive hens; somehow the hens became more approachable or more receptive to the advances of roosters when the color red was introduced into their environments. So Harwood manufactured a type of lens to be fitted over the chicken's beak so that they would quite literally see red, turning backyards all across America into red-light poultry districts. The plastic contraption looked more like half-spectacles with opaque "lenses" replacing the glass. How the poor chicken was supposed to see anything *other* than the red blind in front of it is anybody's guess.

Publications like the *American Poultry Journal* and the *Poultry Tribune* targeted the backyard chicken farmer, and magazines told compelling stories about fortunes that were waiting to be made. In one article in *Better Homes and Gardens* readers encountered the story of a "Mrs. Cotcher," who had undertaken a "small poultry venture" by keeping chickens in her garage. (The whereabouts of her car was unknown.) Within one month of beginning her chicken-raising enterprise, Mrs. Cotcher had sold 150 eggs. At the price of about 30 cents per dozen, Mrs. Cotcher was contributing $3.75 to her household income during a time when every penny mattered.

Having chickens roaming in the backyard was so common during the Depression that the tools of the poultry trade were even incorporated into the kitchen in unique ways: Sylvia Lovegren writes in *Fashionable Food* that the *American Home* magazine suggested that homemakers use "galvanized iron chicken feeders with their neat little rows of oval holes" to serve olives and hors d'oeuvres at their dinner parties. In the homes of those who could afford to entertain guests, this whimsical serving suggestion was one way to alleviate some of the stress of the Depression.

But chickens weren't the only birds being raised to feed hungry families. Pigeons and squabs were also reared in backyards, though the pigeons were eaten more readily than chickens. And of course, regardless of what kind of bird was being served, there was that pesky problem of killing and cleaning it—which, when considering the amount of work involved, might have been reason enough to rarely eat them. Once the bird was killed, the carcass had to be drained of its blood, gutted, and plucked. This latter task—which required that scalding hot water be poured over the dead bird as a means of loosening its feathers from the skin—is generally considered the most difficult and least appealing part of the job.

Despite the thriving backyard chicken industry, however, Hoover's promise turned out to be a sham. By the middle of the 1930s Americans could not have been blamed for not believing everything they heard, whether it came from Washington or Madison Avenue. There was a growing sense of mistrust, not only because of the dire economy but because the dust storms blanketing the Midwest with dirt were partly the fault of the government. The opening of land, years earlier, to increase wheat cultivation had depleted thousands of acres. The overfarming had allowed the topsoil to quickly erode when severe droughts plagued the nation's farmlands in the middle of the decade.

Americans were also being exploited by the bogus claims of advertisers who routinely swindled customers. The government had tried to crack down on dishonest "snake-oil salesmen," but consumers were still being bilked. In an attempt to court integrity, companies would seek endorsements from the likes of the domestic-science movement's "celebrity cooks." The Good Housekeeping Seal of Approval was another sought-after imprimatur. Advertising agencies even had test kitchens. Earning the trust of the public was crucial to a product's survival; everyone was vying for what little spare money Americans had to spend during the Depression. Who was the public going to believe?

The American public, and the American Kitchen, found powerful advocates in the authors of *100,000,000 Guinea Pigs*, Frederick Schlink and Arthur Kallet. A best seller in 1933, Kallet and Schlink's book was a whistle-blowing exposé about the products that many Americans ate or used every day. The first chapter of the book, "The Great American Guinea Pig," told consumers in rather blunt language that they were being duped, and that their health was at risk as a result:

> In the magazines, in the newspapers, over the radio, a terrific verbal barrage has been laid down on one hundred million Americans, first, to set in motion a host of fears about their health, their stomachs, their bowels, their teeth, their throats, their looks; second to persuade them that only by eating, drinking, gargling, brushing, or smearing with Smith's Whole Vitamin Breakfast Food, Jones' Yeast Cubes, Blue Giant Apples, Prussian Salts, Listroboris Mouthwash, Grandpa's Wonder Toothpaste, a thousand and one other foods, drinks, gargles and pastes, can they either postpone the onset of disease, of social ostracism, of business failure, or recover from ailments, physical or social, already contracted.

With an opening salvo like that, it was clear that Kallet and Schlink were sticking up for American workers and how their hard-earned dollars were being spent.

Schlink was no stranger to consumer advocacy. As early as 1926 he was already advising consumers about faulty versus favorable products through a mimeographed list he distributed in White Plains, New York. The next year he and economist Stuart Chase took on the advertising world with *Your Money's Worth*, a publication that was leery of product sales based on "the fanfare and triumphs of higher salesmanship." A best seller, the book spawned the Consumers' Research organization and the Consumers' Research Bulletin. The bulletin tested products that were currently on the market and reported the research group's findings in its pages. Consumers' Research made a point of refusing advertising dollars to assure its readership it was not being swayed in any way.

With *100,000,000 Guinea Pigs*, Kallet and Schlink ratcheted up the intensity of their message by speaking directly, and urgently, to the consumer: "That All Bran you eat every morning—do you know that it may cause serious and perhaps irreparable intestinal trouble? That big juicy apple you have at lunch—do you know that indifferent Government officials let it come to your table coated with arsenic, one of the deadliest of poisons?" Since street sales of apples were a common way for down-and-out businessmen to make a buck during the Depression, it's a wonder that this sort of rhetoric didn't cause hysteria. But the tempo and directness of Kallet and Schlink's message was what made it so successful. Their opinion of the Pure Food and Drug Act (which they referred to in lowercase letters) was that it offered "feeble and ineffective" guidelines.

Guinea Pigs relied on testimonials from accredited doctors, like one Dr. Edwin Oakes Jordan of the Department of Hygiene and Bacteriology at the University of Chicago. Schlink and Kallet got Oakes to go on the record against the potential dangers lurking in the foods of the American Kitchen: "For aught we know to the contrary, the relatively high death-rates from degenerative changes in the kidneys, blood vessels, stomach, and other organs may be in part caused by the use of irritating chemical substances in food." They also got the inside scoop from eyewitnesses, like George W. Wickersham of the National Civil Service Reform League. After investigating the habits of food inspectors, *Guinea Pigs* reported that Wickersham and his crew observed that "the trusting confidence of the American public in the efficiency of laws was never more clearly shown nor more grossly betrayed than in the matter of food inspection."

These were harsh words and frightening accusations. Americans had less money to spend than ever before, and the thought that rules and guidelines implemented by their own government couldn't protect them from being cheated, or even poisoned, was disheartening to say the least. On a state level, the laws in Pennsylvania, which required food-production facilities to be routinely inspected in order for their foods to be sold in the state, appeared to be effective. The products that met the standards required by the law were issued a REG. PENNA. DEPT. AGR. stamp on their packaging. For its part, the U.S. government eventually signed a new Food, Drug and Cosmetic Act into law in 1938. The new law replaced the outdated Pure Food and Drug Act, but still it was not very stringent.

100,000,000 Guinea Pigs made heroes out of Kallet and Schlink. In 1936 the Consumers' Research group the duo had founded almost ten years earlier expanded its bulletin and turned the missive into a full-fledged magazine titled *Consumer Union Reports*. The first issue rated goods like milk and breakfast cereals with grades of Best Buy, Also Acceptable, and Not Acceptable. "Scientific testing" promised to be the determining factor in judging the products, and within ten years' time *Consumer Reports*, as its name was short-ened to, would have a circulation of one hundred thousand.

Americans now had a test kitchen whose results readers felt they could trust.

Despite the best efforts of Kallet and Schlink, and their scientific approach to consumerism and bettering Americans' lives, cynicism remained. In fact, the title of the 1933–34 World's Fair, "A Century of Progress," must have seemed like a cruel joke when the exposition got under way in Chicago. The country was sinking deeper into the Depression, and there weren't many signs of improvement the public could feel excited about, at least not in their immediate daily lives. But the message that this fair intended to deliver was one of hope. Americans needed to be shown that the institutions they'd come to place their trust in—democracy and capitalism in particular—would not only survive, but would prevail. This prosperous future would be brought to them through the marvels of science. In fact, one of the themes of the fair was "Science Finds, Industry Applies, Man Conforms." Science and indus-try would save the day by creating more jobs, safer work environments, cleaner homes, and bountiful food supplies. Democracy would allow sci-ence's most brilliant minds the freedom to pursue their wildest dreams, and capitalism would provide the finances so that industry could make those dreams come true. And humankind would reap the rewards.

One of the ways science proposed to make life better in the America of the future was by extending the cold, metallic helping hand of Robby the Robot. As envisioned for the 1933 World's Fair, Robby made everyday life easier by eliminating hardships in the home for American women. With can openers built into his arms, the robot could make dinner. He could vacuum the floor with the intake vents in his feet, and he could light candles to help set the mood for the evening thanks to the butane lighters in his fingers. But Robby's helping hands would need to do only so much. The American Kitchen of the future was a state-of-the-art, stylized center with conveyor belts on counter-tops and inside cabinets. The refrigerator had revolving shelves, much like a vending machine's, and every chore—putting away plates, selecting dinner items, and washing the dishes—was just a push of the button away. An even more advanced model of the American Kitchen of the future featured an atomic-powered family food center. Underneath the center's plastic shell was a series of workstations and appliances, all conveniently hidden away under a roll-top dome. With the flick of a switch, the center sprang into life as its shell rolled back and its stations came into view like cars on a Ferris wheel. In addition to being able to "atomically irradiate food," the family food center could clean the dinner dishes with its "supersonic dishwasher" and, afterward, put the plates away in its convenient storage station.

Most kitchens in America in the early 1930s didn't even have electric refrigerators yet: There were approximately one million fridges in use in America as of 1931. As of 1935, a full year after the World's Fair's fantasy kitchen had been unveiled, President Roosevelt was still trying to get electricity into rural America, as only 10 percent of those households had electric power. The idea of an electric pancake maker, which not only mixed the ingredients into batter but also tilted the mixing bowl to pour that batter onto the hot griddle, was stupefying to most Americans. The "Century of Progress" and all the high-tech wonders the fair had touted probably seemed more like "A Century Away" to Depression-addled Americans. But surely if science and industry could produce atomic-powered kitchens and house-cleaning robots, they had to be able to eliminate droughts, famine, poverty, sickness, and war—or at least their ill effects.

One example of science working hand in hand with nature was exhibited by the folks at Ford Motor. Fairgoers learned that the kitchen of the future would have strange new foods sitting on its conveyor-belt shelves and cooling in its revolving-rack refrigerators. The "chefs" at Ford had seen the future, and in it Americans were eating soybeans. The protein-rich legume had been introduced into the gardens of America with little fanfare and even less initial acceptance in the early nineteenth century. During World War I, the U.S. government had tried to convince its citizens that a good alternative to foods like ground beef and wheat flour—which were rationed because of the war—could be found in the overlooked and underappreciated soybean. Even though a pamphlet was distributed by the Department of Agriculture containing recipes that relied on the beans, few Americans knew what to do with them. The Ford exhibit at the World's Fair set out to change that. Soy candy, soy milk, green soybeans with butter, cake made with soy flour, piecrusts made with soy, and soybean cheddar cheese were only a few of the new ways in which the versatile food could be eaten. It seemed the food engineers backed by Ford had found as many uses for the soybean as George Washington Carver had discovered for the peanut at the turn of the century.

The Chicago World's Fair closed without the salvation it proposed bringing about any immediate changes. The country sank deeper into its economic depression as drought and dust storms ruined crops and any chance for a quick recovery.

When the next world's fair opened in Flushing Meadows, New York, at the end of the 1930s, science was still the driving force behind new marvels like the electric cow-milking machine displayed at Borden's electrified farm, and the new dishwasher built by Westinghouse. In contrast to the sci-fi food-ways presented at the Chicago World's Fair six years earlier, the New York World's Fair of 1939 introduced a new generation of Americans to haute cuisine courtesy of the French Pavilion. While patrons of the fair might not have been ready for foie gras, the introduction of the pressure cooker was an idea most Americans could appreciate and use. The cooker, a large pot whose lid locked in place and had a valve gauge, sterilized foods for canning in record time, allowing homemakers to preserve more food than ever before.

The 1939 fair started to lose its international participants, as war overseas had cast a pall over the festive atmosphere. The theme of the short-lived fair was "The World of Tomorrow"—a phrase that had an unintentionally ominous ring to it, as the Nazis were already terrorizing Europe.

Science and technology did brighten the American Kitchen during the 1930s, albeit on a smaller and less dramatic scale than having a can-opening robot of one's own. Toasters were becoming more popular and more readily available. Chafing dishes, those old standbys from the turn of the century, now had an electric successor. Electric griddles and waffle irons were hot items and were often the center attraction at dinner parties among the haves in America. Just as Americans in poorer communities shared their vegetables for stews and soups and gathered together to share the pot, so the more financially secure Americans would invite friends and family over for toned-down dinner parties. Dinners where guests were encouraged to make their own grilled cheese sandwiches at the table were considered "fun"—or at least that's what cooking magazines at the time tried to convince their readership. This DIY method had a no-fuss sensibility to it during an era when garish displays would have seemed unsympathetic. It also broke down the wall, figuratively, between the kitchen and the dining room. If cooking could now be done in front of the guests, there was less of a barrier between the room where the food was cooked and the one in which it was eaten.

Despite the gloomy economic outlook of the 1930s, or maybe even because of it, manufacturers like General Electric continued working on new ideas for the kitchen with an optimistic eye to the future. Prosperous days had to lie ahead, and when those days finally arrived there would be a mechanical staff of new appliances waiting to serve Americans and their kitchens. In addition to Westinghouse's dishwasher, better-off homemakers could now have the convenience of a garbage disposal in their sinks. General Electric unveiled what was affectionately called the "kitchen pig" in 1935. Like most proto-types, the first in-sink disposal was too loud, too large, and too costly, but GE's device was welcomed as yet another drudge-defeating ally. Another convenience that appeared in the 1930s was the Waring Blender. Named after the popular bandleader of the time, the nuts and bolts of the first blender were actually the brainchild of Stephen Poplawski of Racine, Wisconsin. Back in 1922, nearly fifteen years before he and Waring went into business together, Poplawski had perfected a blender to support his malted habit. Waring en-countered Poplawski's design in 1936, and after having a "with my name and your invention" conversation, Waring got his name on the blender and the American Kitchen got a new toy on its counter.

Technological breakthroughs in the 1930s didn't always manifest in gadg-ets with motors and switches, though. One such innovation was the gable-topped milk carton. This seemingly humble invention debuted in 1932 and revolutionized the milk industry. The first milk cartons actually appeared in 1915 when a man by the name of John Van Wormser created a cylindrical con-tainer for milk. The gable-topped carton solved one of the problems that had plagued Van Wormser's original design, which was how to make use of a re-sealable container without a lid. The inventor's perseverance paid off eventu-ally when, with the help of some like-minded technicians, Van Wormser finally came up with a design for a machine that would manufacture milk car-tons with the now familiar pitched-roof top. The closeable spout would not appear widely on milk containers until the 1940s, but the waxed cartons elim-inated the need for sterilizing customers' returned bottles, and they were lighter and less cumbersome than their glass counterparts. This innovation led the bottling companies to have a cow. Their grudge became a legal grievance when the Milk Control Board tried to force dairies using the new cartons to charge one cent more per quart of milk than the dairies that used bottles. The New York State Supreme Court eventually decided in favor of the milk car-tons. (With this sort of tension in the air, not to mention the anxieties of deal-ing with daily life during the Depression, the arrival of the technology that could easily produce beer cans was probably real cause for celebration.)

Not all developments that related to the American Kitchen in the 1930s caused as much drama as did the introduction of the milk carton, and not all of them even found their way into the kitchen proper. Sylvan Goldman of Oklahoma got grocery store sales rolling when he invented the wheeled shopping cart in 1937. Bigger, more easily maneuvered grocery baskets would allow customers to load up on more items, bringing about an increase in sales in the Piggly Wigglys, A&Ps, and other stores that were beginning to dot urban landscapes. Goldman's invention was a runaway success.

The shopping cart came at a time when Americans were finding more and more foods in the aisles of their grocery, even if they couldn't always afford them.

Interestingly enough, with fewer resources available, a portion of American cooking started to turn toward shortcuts that used ingredients that were acceptable if only for the fact that they were new. Campbell's soups had been in the American Kitchen for several decades by the time the Depression hit, but their use as a budget-stretcher for cream sauces and dips was suddenly hitting an all-time high. And there was probably no other soup used more widely than Campbell's Cream of Mushroom. Making its debut in 1933, Cream of Mushroom soup, reconstituted or as-is and out of the can, became a kitchen staple almost immediately. Its versatility was the biggest component of its popularity. It could be used in casseroles, soups, dips, and sauces. By adding a can of the soup to egg noodles and peas (or carrots or celery or whatever was on hand) a homemaker could put a meal on the table that was filling and relatively inexpensive. More adventurous cooks used the soup as a starting point for a white sauce to pour over fish or meat loaf. Furthermore, Campbell's Cream of Mushroom soup was similar enough to—yet different enough from—another Depression-era stalwart, macaroni and cheese. Cooked pasta baked with cheese was a favorite of penny-pinching cooks in the 1930s. Blocks of cheese were one of the foods given out at government-sponsored relief stations to help families make ends meet, and it found its way into many a casserole dish, mixed with boiled elbow macaroni. Topping those dishes of macaroni and cheese with crunchy bread crumbs not only gave the dish another textural dimension to balance the softness of the macaroni, it also gave it a little bit of pizzazz, if only on a modest level. (Broccoli, which had become more visible in the American Kitchen during the previous decade thanks to Italian immigrants, was served beneath bread crumbs or even crackers that had been sautéed in butter or margarine. Cauliflower was similarly dressed up for the dinner table.)

Homemakers would get another break, if only in their investment of time, when Kraft packaged all the fixings for macaroni and cheese in one box. Kraft Macaroni and Cheese became available in grocery stores in 1937, and while it may have lacked the warm touch of the homemade original, it soon supplanted the old-fashioned version and enjoyed equal status as a comfort food. Another Kraft product that had been introduced a few years earlier and became equally popular was Miracle Whip. Miracle Whip dressing, which appeared in jars in 1935, became *the* ingredient of choice in salads and dressings. Like Campbell's Cream of Mushroom soup, Miracle Whip gave many Americans a version of white sauce for their meals that actually had some flavor, at least when compared to the often-tasteless paste the domestic-science movement had promoted for years.

SPAM was one of the oddest creations to enter America's kitchens in the 1930s—or any decade, for that matter. Canned meats were old news by the time the Depression rolled around, thanks in part to the efforts of Hormel, the company that would eventually bring SPAM to the world. The George A. Hormel Company was started in the 1890s when its namesake converted an old Minnesota creamery into a meat-processing plant. According to James Trager's *Food Chronology*, Hormel "personally split 100,000 carcasses before letting anyone else do the job" of butchering the hogs that were the lifeblood of his business. At first Hormel concentrated primarily on fresh pork products, but at the turn of the century he began putting his hams in cans, becoming the first meat packager in the United States to do so. Business was booming; the only problem was that with canned hams being such a big seller, there was a lot of spare pork sitting around the Hormel plants. Jay Hormel, the son of George, had an idea for using the surplus pork shoulder the company had in abundance. Hormel mixed the shoulder meat with ham, salt, sugar, spices, and sodium nitrite (to make it nice and pink!), put the jiggling slab in a can, and then tried to think of an appropriate yet catchy name for his new product. "Spiced pork shoulder and ham" wasn't particularly memorable or appealing. So, as the legend goes, Hormel turned the naming of the company's latest foodstuff into a contest. On New Year's Eve that year, as the now-legal champagne flowed and 1936 gave way to 1937, the name "SPAM" was pronounced by one Kenneth Daigneau, who walked away with the hundred-dollar prize.

SPAM would go on to become the top-selling canned meat in the world, serve its country in the form of military rations over the next decade, inspire a series of haiku, and of course share its name with unwanted junk e-mails.

Meanwhile, Clarence Birdseye's contributions to the American Kitchen might not have been as kitschy as Hormel's SPAM, but they were every bit as revolutionary. Like the naming of Hormel's most famous product, the story of how Birdseye's name became synonymous with packaged foods is practically a legend in the world of food engineering. As the story goes, Clarence Birdseye was on assignment in the Arctic for the U.S. government as a "field naturalist" when he noticed that the catch of local fishermen became frozen solid, almost in an instant, after the fish were pulled from the water and laid on the frozen terrain. The icy wind only added to the effect—just as cod fishermen had strung up their fish on the decks of their ships to "freeze-dry" the creatures centuries earlier.

Birdseye inspected the ice-zapped fish and discovered that this quick-freeze process somehow protected their cellular structure. But the real surprise came when the fish were thawed and eaten: They tasted nearly as fresh as if they'd just been caught. Clarence Birdseye set to work on re-creating this phenomenon in the controlled conditions of a food-production plant. He found that by placing the food item to be frozen between two pressurized refrigerating plates he could replicate the deep freeze he'd witnessed in the Arctic. By the 1930s Birdseye had a line of frozen foods in grocery stores. The only problem was that Birdseye's product had to be stored in a freezer at a time when most American kitchens were still relying on iceboxes.

Science had found a way to get the fish from the Arctic's depths into the nation's stores in Birdseye's freezing methods. Now, a new efficient network was taking those fish, and other foodstuffs, from the stores and into American homes.

When Route 66 connected Chicago to Los Angeles in 1938 the highway did more than just provide a litany of mileposts for the song that would bear its name. It opened up the country in a way railroads never could by shortening the distance between urban and rural America. America's kitchens had already benefited from the train deliveries that brought everything from California produce to Texas beef through their front doors. But now, with the completion of Route 66, shipping could become more localized and ultimately cheaper. Two developments from the industrialized world were adding to that lower cost, and lessening the load as well. The first was the invention of the tilting forklift truck that made the stacking and packing of delivery vehicles faster and easier work. The second was the creation of cardboard boxes. Food had previously been shipped in wooden crates that were prohibitively heavy; only so many could be placed on a truck before the machine's shocks and axels were stressed. With the lighter cardboard boxes, more items could be sent out in one shipment, thus reducing the number of trips and ultimately the price the consumer had to pay for the items.

Now, with another route taking their goods to market and to their customers, food industries in the Midwest flourished.

New foods and new appliances weren't the only changes in America's kitchens in the thirties. The line of dishes known as Fiestaware, created by the Homer Laughlin China company along the banks of the Ohio River, and the aptly titled cookbook *Joy of Cooking*, by Irma Rombauer of Missouri, were finding themselves right at home as well.

Fiestaware embodied the spirit of streamlining, an industrial design trend that could be seen everywhere in the 1930s. The silhouettes of trains, planes, and automobiles were all given the sophisticated sleek lines that characterized the style, and it was only a matter of time before streamlining reshaped household items like radios and refrigerators. The Burlington *Zephyr* was unveiled at the 1934 World's Fair, and its design threatened to outshine the spotlight directed on the vehicle. Manufacturers who were concerned that such an edgy design might seem too decadent in an age fraught with low wages and even lower morale were encouraged by the reception the *Zephyr* received. Soon design stars across America were rethinking everyday objects and reshaping them in the motif of the sexy new style. Tiffany, that perennial arbiter of good taste, released their "Century" flatware series. The lofty name accompanied the forks and knives whose handles bore the emblematic insignias that usually graced the facades of Deco-inspired buildings of the era. As for the average American, who might be charmed by the design but chafed by the price, Homer Laughlin China gave them what they were looking for in Fiestaware: a household item they could use every day that had a look that was both functional and fashionable. According to the Smithsonian Institute, a 109-piece set of Fiestaware sold for $13.95, with department stores often offering a one-dollar-down layaway plan.

Fiestaware also reflected the popularity of the Art Deco movement that was the epitome of high style at the time. Its festive colors—orange-red, blue, egg yellow, ivory, and cucumber—and the artisan references in its contours were reminiscent of Mesoamerican pottery, one of the influences on Deco design. The dishes were sturdy, attractive, and affordable at a time when those words were seldom used.

Families who could afford the new dishes might have used them for meals they prepared from Rombauer's *Joy of Cooking*. The book, which has gone on to become an institution in the American Kitchen, was well received immediately upon publication. But not everyone was turning to the book for recipes, despite its popularity: As Barbara Haber points out, what's interesting about *Joy of Cooking* is that it demonstrates the "regional differences" that exist in the American Kitchen from one part of the country to another. Having grown up in Milwaukee, Wisconsin, Haber explains, "I never heard of Rombauer's *Joy of Cooking* until I was grown and on my own. Go into most homes in [Wisconsin] and you will find [Lizzie Black Kander's] *Settlement Cookbook*."

The idea that Americans were choosing one kitchen bible over another addresses the issue of ethnic preferences that remained strong in the American Kitchen. Kander's book was based on recipes that were intended to help assimilate Eastern European homemakers into their new kitchens (and homeland). Haber sees a similarity in some Americans eschewing *Joy of Cooking* in favor of their *Settlement* recipes, just as Kander's audience was disinterested in the then popular *Boston Cooking-School* cooking guidelines.

"While Fannie Farmer's British-style recipes were not appealing to this population, the ethnic recipes found in the *Settlement* [cookbook] were," Haber observes. The popularity of *The Settlement Cookbook* showed that despite the domestic scientists' insistence upon a prescribed sameness in the American Kitchen, many Americans were still devoted to the recipes that originated in their ancestral homelands.

An implied link between the mentality of domestic scientists like Farmer and Rombauer's views on cooking can be seen in *Joy*'s cover art: an illustration of a woman in silhouette, holding her ground as she fends off a dragon (with what appears to be a broom raised above her head) as it threatens to constrict and consume her. Is the dragon a metaphor for kitchen drudgery? The original book's graphic is playful, but the message it imparts seems hard to mistake. At a time when conveniences had arrived to lighten the homemaker's load, she was now burdened with other hardships like the cost of feeding her family during the Depression. The book's tone was sympathetic without being condescending, conversational without being chirpy. It also gave its audience "recipes in the most minute detail, telling the cook exactly what to look for," writes Trager in his *Food Chronology*.

Like *The Settlement Cookbook*, Rombauer's *Joy of Cooking* would become a lasting addition to the American Kitchen's library. Other cookbooks that joined these in homes across the country were the *Better Homes and Gardens* cookbook and *Le Petit Cordon Bleu*. Though the latter was initially published in London, it would grab the attention of American cooks who had more adventurous leanings, making the international cooking school a success when it made its American debut a few years later.

Accentuating the positive was the key to surviving life during the Depression. Americans garnered their strength from their families, their faith, their communities, and their leaders. Households would gather around the radio, a source of entertainment and information, to listen to Betty Crocker, who had been giving cooking advice since 1924 with her show, *The Betty Crocker Cooking School of the Air*. In 1936 fans of the show could finally get a peak at the General Mills spokesperson thanks to a portrait that appeared in ads for Gold Medal Flour. On the other hand, the identity of the host of *The Mystery Chef*, another popular cooking show on the radio in the 1930s, would remain a mystery. According to legend, he did not want his mother to be embarrassed by his chosen profession. The home kitchen was still considered the domain of women, so a certain amount of shame was mixed in with that title's intended intrigue.

Radio was an important ally of the American Kitchen, and of its advertisers, in the thirties. In addition to General Mills, scores of other food manufacturers promoted their goods on the air. Spammy the Pig, the spokes-mascot for Hormel's SPAM product, used to plug his wares on George Burns and Gracie Allen's radio program. Thanks to the audio-only aspect of radio programming, Spammy's identity could remain as secret as that of the Mystery Chef.

As the 1930s ended, however, a few lucky Americans got a preview of something that would change their worlds forever when President Roosevelt delivered an address live from the 1939 New York World's Fair. Roosevelt's message was received by approximately 150 television sets—the total number in existence at the time.

The age of television was about to dawn in the American Kitchen. The revolution would, indeed, be televised. The images television presented, however, were not depicting a future any more secure than the era this new age of technology was supposed to succeed.

CHAPTER FIVE

Duty Now for the Future: 1940–1949

After years of lack, Russel and Mary Wright proposed a new attitude, and new dinnerware, for the American table post–World War II. (Russel Wright. Pieces from the White Clover service. Philadelphia Museum of Art: Gift of Matthew Singer in memory of Hyman B. and Naomi T. Schwartz, 1993.)

Survival took on a whole new meaning in the American Kitchen in the 1940s. A country that had just suffered through the lack that characterized the years of the Great Depression now had to endure further deprivation as rationing brought the fight of World War II into the home of every American. With the bombing of Pearl Harbor in December 1941, the United States found itself in the middle of war as fighting raged on both sides of its bordering oceans. Americans had to keep their spirits up and their bodies strong. Budding green thumbs whose hands were still dirty from growing their own vegetables during the Depression now tended their "victory gardens" with patriotic dedication. Food production stepped into overdrive across the country. Just as Napoleon's empiric aspirations had sparked Nicholas Appert to discover new ways to preserve food for the French armies, so the United States' involvement in World War II led to breakthroughs in the preservation, processing, and packaging of food. Food was just as responsible for winning the war as were the armed services and ammunitions. In fact, leftover grease from America's kitchens found its way into the manufacturing of bombs. The slogan "Food Fights for Freedom" was used in schools, on posters, and even in pamphlets distributed by food manufacturers like Pillsbury.

These decades of trial, and especially the call to arms of the early forties, brought the American family closer as President Roosevelt delivered fireside chats to an anxious nation. Gathered around the radio, Americans listened with their families, friends, and neighbors as news reports of the war's progress and serialized shows came over the airwaves. The atrocities committed by the Nazi Party were dramatized in one such radio program, *You Can't Do Business with Hitler*. The show, presented by Douglas Miller, the former American attaché to Berlin, included Miller's reports from European capitals as well as short skits depicting Germany's evil actions. Meanwhile, the Mystery Chef aired instructions on how to make the most of rationed sugar while canning fruits. By the war's end, the Mystery Chef would be celebrating VE Day with a show on preparing Armenian Artichokes.

Meanwhile, the kitchen's appearance was beginning to resemble the space that we identify with today, as more cabinets and cupboards were being built in and freestanding workstations were being taken out. Fiestaware now had to compete with the cool green tones of Fire-King's affordable Jadite dinnerware when it came to giving the kitchen a splash of color. Wallpaper was being used to brighten the room, but the white bead-board style popular since the turn of the century was still widely in use. This sterile, monochromatic color scheme was about to get what Washington, D.C., interior designer Walter Gagliano calls "an explosion of color" once the 1940s ended and the 1950s burst on the scene. But the American Kitchen first had to live through several years of darkness before sighing with relief over this eventual dawn.

Scarcity was nothing new in the American Kitchen when the government instated mandatory rationing of foods in May 1942. For the generation of Americans who were born on the eve of the Depression of the 1930s, making do was a way of life. Older Americans, who had lived through World War I, remembered the food substitutes and meal-stretchers that had been encouraged during that time. The system of rationing that was put in place to help guarantee food resources for the armed forces during World War II, however, was unlike anything younger Americans had ever seen. Their European allies, like the British, as well as the Axis power enemies, had already been limiting the amounts of foods their citizens could consume for several years. Britain began issuing rationing coupons in 1940. Japan had reduced the amount of rice its people were permitted to eat. And while Germany starved Russians, Finns, Norwegians, Poles, French, and Greeks into submission, it saw to it that its own soldiers were well fed, often slaughtering thousands of head of livestock in countries it invaded.

The first food item to be rationed in the United States during the war was sugar. Candy delivered a good dose of quick energy to the service personnel, and with the Japanese taking control of the Philippines, an important source of America's sugar, the sweet granules were considered a highly valuable commodity in the war effort. Americans at home were initially asked to keep their sugar consumption to eight ounces per person, per week. (That's one full cup in dry measurements. To put it into a context of use, most cookie recipes call for at least three quarters of a cup of sugar for a batch of dough that will turn out about two dozen cookies.) That quotient was later raised to twelve ounces. Part of the reason for the initially scant amount allotted per household was that many homemakers, no doubt having heard about Britain's rationing program, had begun stockpiling sugar. Preliminary assessments of the U.S. sugar supply foretold a shortage in the near future if restrictions weren't put into place.

Sugar pills were sent overseas and included in each soldier's daily food, or K ration. Chocolate and candy bars were also given to the military. With the U.S. Army purchasing candy by the tons they were endorsing its dietary benefits by default. As James Trager writes in *Food Chronology*, "In emphasizing the food value of candy, the Army [was] not only the best customer for candy but also its most effective publicist."

The next food item in the American Kitchen to be rationed was coffee. In November 1942 the government began limiting Americans to one pound of coffee every five weeks. While that might sound like a dreadfully meager amount, it should be noted that the average American coffee drinker now requires about ten pounds per year to supply their daily habit, which averages slightly over three cups a day, the war's rationing fell just slightly short of meeting the needs of today's caffeinated society.

Gas rationing was enforced two months prior to the restrictions placed on coffee. The effect this had on the American Kitchen was that it disrupted the delivery systems that brought foods to market and, in some cases, to the consumer's front door. Milk delivery services, for instance, had their schedules reduced or altered, causing a few determined dairies to deliver their goods the old-fashioned way—by hitching horses to carts.

Meat, cheese, and butter were all rationed in 1943. Each household was allotted twenty-eight ounces of meat per week, per person. How much meat did that actually mean was going on the dinner table? Well, a one-pot budget-stretcher like chili will generally call for one pound, or sixteen ounces, of ground beef. With a meal like meat loaf, a recipe might require approximately a pound and a half of meat, which would use up almost all of a family's meat rations for the week, unless other food items were added to stretch the ingredients. The goal of the rationing was to ensure food for the armed forces overseas, while guaranteeing that at least one meal per day in the American Kitchen featured meat.

Cheese was rationed at four pounds a week, and butter was limited to four ounces under the wartime system. Canned goods were rationed similarly to meat and dairy products.

Since meat, butter, and cheese coupons were all red in color, they could be used interchangeably. This presented a problem for families, though, when they made their weekly budgets and grocery lists. While cheese could be used as a protein alternative and as an effective meat substitute, using red coupons for the dairy product meant that fewer coupon points could be put toward meat purchases. At least with butter, margarine—which was not rationed—could be substituted, but it was somewhat cost prohibitive. First Lady Eleanor Roosevelt lobbied for tax breaks on the price of margarine. She was such a champion of the vegetable oil product that years later, in the late 1950s, she would appear in a television commercial for Good Luck Margarine. In her pitch she recalled the initial aversion to using margarine in the American Kitchen, saying, "Years ago most people never dreamed of eating margarine."

The biggest stigma facing margarine, or oleo, wasn't its taste but its pasty white color. Packets of yellow dye were still available to mix into the food so it could masquerade as butter, and in its colorless state it was less expensive. Mrs. Roosevelt's campaign was directed toward providing a break for consumers who bought their margarine already dyed.

But choosing between margarine (colored or not) and butter was the least of the American homemaker's worries during the war. The rationing system was difficult to understand at best and frustratingly ill-conceived at worst. When the rationing system was first implemented, households were issued coupons according to the size of their families, as well as according to their on-hand supplies. Just as inventories were taken of sugar supplies, home-makers were required to take stock of the canned goods in their pantries and cupboards. Unfortunately, having too much of a surplus resulted in a family being penalized for each can of food they had in their larder.

Adding to the confusion involved in using the coupons was a series of letters, numbers, iconic images, and colors that could have given a military code-cracker pause. The letters went from A to Z, and the numerical values assigned to the rationing coupons were 8, 5, 2, and 1. Shoppers were re-quired to use the appropriate stamps to "pay" for the ability to purchase the food item. (The coupons had no monetary value of their own.) For in-stance, if a can of corn was assigned a value of 12 rationing points, a store-keeper could accept either one 8 and two 2 coupons, or two 5 and one 2 coupons, as long as the total equaled 12. And the customer would pay the cost of the can. Problems arose near the end of the month when the versatile lower-number coupons had already been used. If a homeowner wanted to purchase the same can of corn, but had only coupons valued at 8 left in her month's rations, she would have to sacrifice the 4 surplus points; there was no system in place for making change. The 4 points were lost and could not be recovered.

If the complicated system of colors and images (which could be anything from tanks to airplanes, guns to cornucopias) wasn't maddening enough, and if the inability to get change for one's purchases didn't leave Americans feeling somehow cheated, a new book of rationing coupons was issued each month, making the previous month's stamps null and void, worthless. To paraphrase a line from *The Skin of Our Teeth*, the popular Thornton Wilder play from 1942, Americans had to "eat their ice cream while it was on their plate" or risk losing their coupons' values entirely. There were no extra points awarded to anyone who frugally managed her way through one month in the hope of living a little more comfortably in the next month via some ingen-ious budgeting.

There was also no guarantee that the number of coupons required to pur-chase an item one week would be the same the next. Inventories and crop yields were affected by a number of variables, such as transportation prob-lems and poor growing seasons. A can of green beans could jump in "price" as many as ten ration points or higher from one shopping trip to the next. It wasn't until the fourth book of rationing stamps was issued that a more user-friendly system was put in place. Tokens worth one point could now be given in either blue or red, and as if to buoy the morale of the Americans who used them even higher, the coupons in book number four were inscribed with patriotic quotes and passages.

Despite the hardships and confusion, most Americans didn't seem to mind. Besides, there were ways to get around the system. Grocers and butchers would allow patrons to slide if they were short a rationing point or two. Favoritism and popularity also came with privileges, as storeowners saved choice cuts of meat for their better customers.

One sure way to make the most of rationing coupons was to augment the family's food supply with items that had been grown in one's own backyard. Victory gardens sprung up across the country and planting, canning, and preserving were considered every homemaker's patriotic duty. As for eggs and milk, many Americans still raised their own chickens, and some even raised cows. The sale of livestock from larger ranches, however, was closely monitored, as a thriving black market existed.

The government did its part to make sure that all Americans were eating well—not just the soldiers overseas, but the people at home, too. Storeowners were given posters to display that outlined how to use the rationing coupons. Customers could consult the posters as they waited in line to be served.

Newspapers also did their share to help Americans make the most of the food in their kitchens. Following the guidelines provided by the National Livestock and Meat Board, newspapers would carry articles that detailed ways in which cooks could stretch their meat rations into multiple meals. The copy that accompanied the article marched along with patriotic overtones and a "we're all in this together" air of camaraderie. A spread from the *Ipswich News and Chronicle* from March 1943 titled "Hints for Housewives in Solving Wartime Meat Problems" provided "tricks" so that families could "maintain the American tradition of at least one daily meal with meat." Farther down the page was the suggestion that Americans "get better acquainted with variety meats such as heart, kidney, [and] liver." Recipe examples were given to illustrate how one meat ration could serve triple duty. For instance, the leftovers from the first meal's pork roast could be dressed up as a pork salad for the second meal. The remains from that meal, which couldn't have been much, could then be recycled yet again and served for the third meal as scrapple. There were also suggestions to help cooks get "better acquainted" with those "variety meats," complete with a three-part plan. If a shopper was using rations for organ meats, some butchers might throw in extras. With this in mind, the Ipswich paper proposed a three-meal plan that began with liver, moved on to sweetbreads (the pancreas and thymus, and sometimes brain, usually of veal but sometimes of beef), and ended with tongue. (Eating tongue and other offal meats wasn't uncommon practice even prior to the war, as nothing went to waste in the American Kitchen.)

Other support material came from the United States Department of Agriculture, which issued a how-to guide for canning fruits and vegetables at home. Kerr, the manufacturer of lids and jars used in canning, also printed booklets that instructed cooks in how to can the harvest from their victory gardens. Numerous food manufacturers published similar cost-cutting, meal-stretching recipe pamphlets during World War II.

There were similar publications available for aspiring gardeners. Even the Standard Oil Company printed a manual for would-be green thumbs. Victory gardens were inspired by the war gardens of World War I and the vegetable beds maintained by the British. "Dig for Victory" was England's equivalent of "Food Fights for Freedom." And in America, the victory gardens delivered a significant punch in that fight, as nearly 50 percent of all of the vegetables eaten in the United States during World War II came from backyard garden beds.

Of course, having the know-how to "put up" one's own vegetables was something that was taught in public schools once home economics became part of the curriculum after the turn of the century. But during World War II there was a greater sense of urgency to the material taught in home ec classes, as instruction manuals stressed the importance of knowing how to run a kitchen with maximum efficiency and minimum waste. The message, "Food Fights for Freedom," reminded students that every action in the American Kitchen, no matter how small, played a role in winning the war.

Canning and preserving were urged in home economics classes and in America's kitchens as ways to augment the foods available in stores. With rationing limiting the amount Americans could buy, it was wise to have provisions at home to fall back on. Rationing was intended to ensure a fair distribution of the available foods. Unfortunately, it did mean that a family would have to go without certain food items if they ran out of coupons, or if certain foods were temporarily marked up in price. For this reason, canning once again made good sense in the American home.

Most homeowners during the war were raised on pantry items they'd preserved themselves. But for anyone who had been privileged enough to rely solely on store-bought foods, home canning probably seemed so nineteenth century. Fortunately, the makers of canning products, like Kerr and Mason, distributed comprehensive, easy-to-follow instruction booklets to walk first-timers through the process.

Homemakers were advised to first make a canning budget. The "budgeting" in this case referred to how far one quart or pint of a canned food would go in the home. Extensive charts listed the various vegetables, fruits, meats, juices, and jellies commonly eaten in the American Kitchen at the time, along with suggested servings per week. For instance, beets, cauliflower, lima beans, and soup mixture were categorized together. In their guide "10 Short Lessons in Home Canning," Kerr suggested that the home canner should figure on serving one of these foods between three to five times each week, with the amount per individual varying. For example, tomatoes, which Kerr encouraged homemakers to eat five to seven servings of each week, were to be canned in quantities of twenty-five to thirty quarts per person per year. A family of four would require 100 to 120 quarts of tomatoes by Kerr's account.

Over half a year's worth of menu items would have to be canned in similar multiples. Basements, cellars, and pantries had to be lined with sturdy shelving to handle food stores of this capacity. In order to get this amount of food canned, an orchard's worth of apples (two and a half pounds per quart jar), numerous rows of corn (with seven pounds of corn ears necessary to yield one quart jar of corn kernels), and a small vineyard (with two and a half pounds of grapes needed per quart) were required merely to meet the suggested servings allotted for one individual of three of the foods from the fruits and vegetables groups. The two-hour rule—which referred to the time that lapsed from when the foods were picked until they were placed in the canning jars—implied that Kerr assumed these fruits and vegetables were coming from the canners' own property. And in many cases, they did.

Canning this much food required a lot of work, but for those who could afford it, the pressure cooker, introduced at the previous decade's World's Fair, eliminated the canning time: Jars of broccoli, which needed 155 minutes to be safely preserved using the boiling-water method, could now be sealed, sterilized, and canned in a speedy twenty-five minutes. And like something out of the *Flash Gordon* movies of the time, tomatoes immersed in a pressure cooker were safely preserved in ten minutes flat.

If one was tempted to cheat a little on the canning budget and forgo a dozen or so jars of one vegetable or another, no one could blame him. Canning isn't easy work. But with the new eating guidelines coming out of Washington, it would seem foolhardy to do so. After all, the amounts and types of foods the canning-jar guides were encouraging homemakers to preserve weren't just randomly selected. Manufacturers like Kerr and Mason were relying on government evidence that supported the companies' prescription that a family of four would require each and every single one of those 120 quarts of tomatoes to meet their nutritional needs. These suggestions reflected the Basic Seven—the new daily dietary allowances, which the government had recently begun recommending that Americans follow. The unveiling of the Basic Seven chart, and the corresponding wheel, in which foods were represented by one of seven slices of the chart's "pie," announced a home-front campaign as important to the war effort as rationing. One poster for the Basic Seven had the tag line A NUTRITION TARGET FOR ALL AMERICA TO SHOOT AT! emblazoned across the bottom. Improving the diet of every American was the government's aim.

The health of every American became a grave matter of concern for the government during World War II. As men and women from every region of the country received physical examinations prior to entrance into the military, the U.S. government was seeing, perhaps for the first time, that a large number of its citizens were suffering from conditions attributable to the same cause: poor nutrition. Americans did not know how to eat properly. This discovery led President Roosevelt to establish the National Nutrition Conference for Defense in 1941. By the time of the conference's inception, the government had been concerning itself with what Americans were eating for more than fifty years. From the early days of the Department of Agriculture to the Pure Food Act to the Poison Squad, Washington had monitored the foods eaten in the American Kitchen. The emphasis, however, had been placed on increased production and the safe packaging and preparation of foods. As for the composition of the foods, worries arose over what might be added to foods. The caloric content of individual items had been addressed in the previous century, but addressing the inherent value of the foods—in terms of vitamins and minerals—was a relatively new phenomenon. Linking these vitamins and minerals to diseases was newer still.

The idea of an "eating cure" for ailments had a significant history by World War II, going back further than James Lind's mid-eighteenth-century discovery that citrus fruits were not only a preventative against scurvy but an agent of change, as they reversed the condition in sailors who were afflicted. But even in Lind's case, while the sailors might have come from different backgrounds, their travels and limited provisions were the common denominators.

The soldiers called up by the wartime draft in mid-twentieth-century America were from dozens of backgrounds and lifestyles; each represented a different microcosm and each microcosm had its own unique set of variables. Vitamin- and nutrient-deficient diets were responsible for so many diseases, birth defects (due to poor nutrition in the womb), and chronic ailments that Washington realized it had another war to fight at home. While *malnourishment* was an all-encompassing term to describe the conditions present, the ailments and their causes were so varied that there was no way a single antidote could address all the conditions. Knowing the enemy is half the battle, and the government had to survey the ills they were facing in order to form a strategy to combat the problem.

The diseases the draft board was seeing in the military's would-be soldiers included chronic gastrointestinal illnesses, metabolic disorders, skin ailments, impairments in brain function, and a host of developmental problems. Advancements in twentieth-century medical science as well as an emphasis on nutritional benefits had allowed doctors to identify and treat several diseases since the 1900s. As early as 1905 it was seen that when iodine was added to salt it became an effective preventative against goiters and other thyroid- related ills. In 1923 rickets had been successfully cured, and subsequently curbed, when studies at the University of Wisconsin and Columbia University showed that food that had been irradiated with ultraviolet light became a good source of vitamin D. Vitamin D and calcium helped the liver function better, and helped strengthen bones. Food manufacturers Borden and Pet began introducing vitamin D "fortified" milk products in the early 1930s to help prevent rickets and other diseases. In 1936 another common ailment, pellagra, was successfully treated when it was discovered—again at the University of Wisconsin—that niacin (or vitamin B_6) acted upon the skin disorders, diarrhea, and dementia symptoms that characterized the disease. The causes of other diseases were also becoming known; for instance, it was learned that beriberi was brought on by a thiamin deficiency.

The government set out to remedy the problem of poor nutrition through education. The Basic Seven chart was devised by the National Food and Nutrition Board with the hope that a better-informed America would lead to better-fed Americans. With the words "Eat This Way Every Day" encircling a family of four at the center of the wheel, and the food groups wedged around them, the diagram seemed easy enough to follow. The seven groups were broken down into food categories like "Leafy, Green, and Yellow Vegetables" (group number one); "Citrus Fruit, Tomatoes, and Raw Cabbage," (group number two); and "Milk, Cheese, and Ice cream" (group number four). Butter was not included with its dairy brethren, but was listed in a separate group (number seven) by itself with "Fortified Margarine."

Along with illustrations of the foods in each group, the recommended daily servings from each were also given: "two or more servings of potatoes and other vegetables and fruits," and "some daily" for the butter/margarine group. (Butter was considered its own category of food because it delivered what researchers called "vitamin F," or unsaturated fatty acids.) The group containing breads, grains, and cereals came without any recommendations or restrictions. With flour products not being rationed, perhaps the National Food and Nutrition Board figured Americans should be allowed to eat their fill.

"Basic 7 foods give energy and protect health," was the encouraging message from the U.S. Bureau of Human Nutrition and Home Economics. The government tried to consider the limited access the public might have to some foods because of rationing, so a reassuring tag line was added to the section of the chart that described what types of meats, poultry, beans, nuts, and eggs should be eaten: "Fresh, canned, or cured. One serving daily if possible."

In an impressive campaign to spread the word on the importance of a proper diet, the Basic Seven wheel rolled into classrooms, grocery stores, and newspapers. The posters became as ubiquitous as other wartime propaganda posters. Even though homemakers might encounter food shortages due to the enormous effort required to feed soldiers overseas, there was no longer the shortage of food that had existed during the Depression. Had the government suggested the Basic Seven a decade earlier it would have seemed like a ludicrous, if not potentially cruel, expectation to put upon the American people. But with the entire nation's industries contributing to the cause of winning the war, more Americans were employed than in previous years. There was more money circulating through the economy, and Americans were eating better than they had during the 1930s. Sylvia Lovegren notes in *Fashionable Food*, "although meat and butter almost disappeared from the shelves for a few months in the spring of 1942, Americans ate more food during the war, in total and per capita, than they ever had before."

The Basic Seven was just one way in which the government hoped to increase the population's health through diet. Enriching the foods Americans were eating was another way to guarantee a healthy home front, and what better place to start than with one of the foods of which a surplus was guaranteed: flour. In 1943 it was estimated that Americans ate about twelve billion loaves of bread. That's almost a hundred loaves per individual, and with more than 70 percent of all bread consumed during the 1940s coming from commercial bakeries or stores, the U.S. government had found a good delivery system for their health plan. And with public schools explaining the benefits of vitamin-enriched grains, the government's message was sure to be heard.

The specific nutrients being put into flour beginning in the 1940s were thiamin, niacin, riboflavin, and iron. Calcium and vitamin D were also added to flour as "optional ingredients." These were chemical versions of the naturally occurring elements found in the whole wheat berry.

In a 1942 study that identified approximately 150 diseases brought on by poor diet, Royal Lee and Jerome S. Stolzoff presented their findings concerning dietary health and the consequences of poor nutrition. In Lee and Stolzoff, the government couldn't have found better endorsers for their nutrient-adding program. Concentrating specifically on the effects of diets lacking in vitamins A, B, D, E, and F (fatty acids), Lee and Stolzoff sang the praises of two foods—whole wheat bread, and butter. With segment headings like "The Superiority of Whole Wheat Bread," "The Unique and Indispensable Place of Butter in the Diet," and "The Superiority of Butter over Substitutes," the pair urged that Americans shun bleached white breads, and especially oleo and margarine. Unfortunately, with butter being a rationed item, their suggestions could not be followed as closely as they'd have liked. But their study helped to reinforce the government's findings and suggestions, which in turn helped to continue to raise awareness that a good diet equaled good health.

The government waged this home-front battle heroically. Families were kept well informed, and every effort was made to ensure that they were well fed. The health of the men and women working in factories and plants where military goods were manufactured was just as great a concern in Washington as was the health of the Americans fighting overseas. The American Kitchen had been faced with the hardships of war before, and each time it came through stronger and smarter and better prepared for any future challenges.

The first meal of the day had been changing in the decades leading up to World War II, ever since Graham, Kellogg, and Post had revolutionized breakfast with their cold-cereal prescriptions. Shoppers in the 1940s now had several options when it came to choosing which box of flakes, squares, or crunchy nuggets they wanted to pour into their bowls each morning.

Kellogg's Corn Flakes, Post's Grape-Nuts, and Quaker's Puffed Rice had been suitable alternatives to meat-dominated breakfasts for most of the twentieth century, and their ready-to-eat nature increased their popularity during a time when domestic help had become less prominent in the American Kitchen. It was the circumstances that prevailed following the eruption of war in the forties, however, that would make a bowl of cereal—and, of course, the box it came in—such a prominent figure in the breakfast table's tableau.

Rationing changed the breakfast menu in America just as it changed the rest of a family's meals. The old favorites weren't always available during the war. The limited amount of meat Americans could buy meant that bacon was not as easily obtained as it had been in the past. If a family raised its own chickens, there would certainly be a steady supply of eggs. And there were no restrictions on flour or grains, but with rationed supplies of butter and sugar, foods like pancakes and waffles were harder to make. And unless a homemaker canned her own jellies and preserves, toast was a potentially dry and unappetizing way to start the day; store-bought jams and butter were both subjected to rationing. All of these foods required that enough time be allotted to prepare them, but with more men and women employed by wartime industries, the American Kitchen was becoming deserted earlier in the day. Busier schedules required speedier breakfast alternatives, and luckily there were boxes of cereals just waiting to be poured into bowls. This was another advantage that cold cereals had over their hot-served counterparts like Cream of Wheat, for example: Nothing had to be cooked, boiled, steamed, or baked.

The discovery of vitamins and minerals and the health benefits they carried also made prepackaged cereals more appealing. Just as flour was being "enriched" and milk was being "fortified," so the cereals on the market had their nutritional value enhanced by the addition of vitamins and minerals. With the information that was being learned about the ins and outs of each nutrient, cereal manufacturers had a marketing campaign ready and waiting for them. "Whole-grain" cereals gained the most from this strategy since the benefits of the "whole berry" had received a lot of attention. But the nutrient that got the most wordplay in the 1940s was thiamin. Described as the "good disposition" vitamin, B_1, or thiamin, was considered the cure-all for symptoms that were described in the parlance of the times as a "lack of pep." Thiamin was marketed as a must-have breakfast item, and what better way to make sure you were full of energy at the start of your day than to have a decent breakfast? The idea of thiamin as a personality enhancer was particularly played up in pamphlets and ads geared toward high school students. Want to get a date? Make the team? Get good grades? Well, the secret to a happy high school experience, according to advertisers, was to be found inside a box of Post cereal.

Cereal companies also cashed in on the protein content of their product and promoted it accordingly. Meat rationing had already cut into one good source of protein in the American diet, and cereal manufacturers wasted no time in spreading the word about the amount of protein in their products.

The versatility of breakfast cereals was also stressed. At a time when rationing limited the types of foods that could line the shelves and cupboards in the American Kitchen, that box of cereal in the pantry was an adaptable ally that could work overtime, easily moving from breakfast to lunch to dinner. Looking for something to stretch a casserole? Why not add corn flakes, or a toasted-wheat cereal? Cereals could also be used to make cookies and coffee cake recipes.

When President Truman suggested in 1947 that Americans continue to observe some days as meatless and eggless, cereal's place in the kitchens of America was guaranteed.

Another stalwart of the American breakfast table that likewise got a boost in popularity during the 1940s was orange juice. Like other things that now seem so institutionally American, the orange was introduced to the continent first by European explorers, most probably Columbus. The fruit's long voyage to the American table actually began in China centuries ago, and its arrival on both coasts of America would eventually produce two very different types of orange.

Oranges were prohibitively expensive for most middle-class Americans until the twentieth century, when irrigation helped to increase the crops from California's groves and transportation brought the fruits to market faster. Florida oranges would go on to outproduce their western kin because of the State's abundant rainfall. However, packagers of the fruit on both coasts would benefit from science and technology. In 1936, for instance, ethylene was put to use to help ripen oranges, which in turn resulted in a better product. In 1937 the first frozen orange juice concentrates were made, but with the Depression still keeping most Americans impoverished, this was a luxury out of the reach of most household budgets.

The army's search for a nonperishable form of orange juice was partly responsible for bringing the drink from the front line into the home. Just as Napoleon had offered the cash award that eventually led to Appert's preserving revolution, so the U.S. government promised three quarters of a million dollars to the individual or company who could produce orange juice in powder form.

The problem with creating a sellable and palatable juice was the inconsistencies in the batches of juice that were made, as well as in the juices themselves. The army's technicians had found a way to make powdered orange juice that had a reliable taste by first freezing, then drying, the beverage. The American Kitchen benefited because this method provided the basis for the process that would eventually churn out the thick, syrupy substance that would become reconstituted ("by mixing with 3 cans of cold water") and enjoyed over breakfast. In 1946, three Florida scientists—Louis Gardner MacDowell, C. D. Atkins, and E. L. Moore—were responsible for getting the balance right in the concentrate, producing a more even flavor from one can to the next. By the end of the 1940s, more than twelve million cans of frozen orange juice concentrate had been sold in the country. Minute Maid established itself as a leader in the industry, and actor/singer Bing Crosby plugged their product over the radio.

Another beverage that established its territory in the American Kitchen during the war years of the 1940s was black tea. Coffee had been growing in popularity since its introduction into American culture, and by the 1930s, 70 percent of the world's coffee exports were being brewed and percolated in the pots of America. But tea was still a favorite for some, and the war changed their beverage from green to black. Most of the tea coming onto American shores prior to World War II was of the green variety, but the bombing of Pearl Harbor cut off trade routes for ships coming from China and Japan. Americans turned their trade toward India and Ceylon, who continued to produce tea—albeit the black-leaf variety—during the war years. By the war's end, most Americans were sipping black tea with their breakfast.

Mobilizing an army as large as the American military in World War II required that entire industries be devoted solely to the task of food production. *Food Engineering* magazine noted, "The need to feed the troops and 'round-the-clock shifts in defense plants created the first real mass-feeding markets, stimulating new convenience foods (including C-rations) and institutional food packaging."

The U.S. government's contracts provided the necessary cash for expanding food packaging and preservation technology. Huge rotary drums capable of dehydrating meat were devised to help dry beef for C rations. Production plants across the country were filled with freeze-drying plates, robotic arms, and gigantic rollers. Foods were frozen, dehydrated, flattened, and wrapped, and then shipped where they were needed.

Some of the technological advancements, like the meat-dehydrating drums, were part of the behind-the-scenes innovations that American citizens benefited from indirectly. But there were other breakthroughs that were initially part of other wartime operations, and two accidental by-products of these experiments, the microwave oven and Teflon coating, eventually became as essential to the operation of the American Kitchen as the sink and the stove.

The idea for the microwave oven came about as a result of a melted candy bar. It seems that when Dr. Percy Spencer, an engineer at the Raytheon Corporation, was working closely with an instrument called the magnetron, the chocolate bar he was keeping in his lab coat pocket was reduced to a soft mess. (The magnetron was developed by the British as a radar warning system to alert the military to incoming enemy planes.) Spencer knew that the magnetron emitted microwaves and, figuring that these waves were responsible for melting the chocolate, decided to try another experiment by placing a few kernels of popping corn next to the magnetron tube. As he suspected, the kernels danced and eventually exploded into little white puffs. Next he placed an egg beside the radar device and, sure enough, the yolk and egg white burst out of the shell. (Safety clearly took a backseat to the thrill of watching stuff nearly combust.)

Spencer's experiments took place in 1942, but it wasn't until after the war, in 1947, that the power of radar waves, as witnessed in his experiments, was harnessed and placed inside a microwave oven. Like most applications of new technology, the resulting construction was large and cumbersome. The original ovens were as large as refrigerators and tended to get dangerously hot. Water was pumped into the microwave to cool it, and this meant that every microwave oven had to be placed in a part of the kitchen near plumbing. And at a cost of about three thousand dollars, domestic use of the Radarange, as the Raytheon-manufactured unit was named, was hindered by more than just its size.

Teflon was another item from the American Kitchen's roster spawned by wartime experiments. Beginning in the late 1930s, chemists at Du Pont were conducting research into reactions of various types of gases. Dr. Roy J. Plunkett had been working with a gas similar to Freon, the cooling agent in refrigerators and air conditioners, when he noticed that the substance known as tetrafluoroethylene became slick and impervious to chemicals when frozen. Plunkett and his fellow scientists realized that this new material was not only slick, but also seemed to be able to withstand all sorts of abuse. Initially this discovery, called polytetrafluoroethylene, was used for electrical wiring, and it even found its way into aircraft technology. In 1945 Du Pont christened the material Teflon, and in 1946 they began making it available commercially. Silicone-glazed baking pans would soon follow in 1949, but Teflon-coated pans and utensils wouldn't take up residence in kitchen cupboards and drawers until the fifties. According to a *Bon Appétit* article by Dorie Greenspan, celebrating the twentieth century's "Cook's Essentials," when it comes to giving credit where it's due, for "the idea of applying [Teflon] to cookware . . . we have a wife to thank." Greenspan writes, "a Parisian named Marc Gregoire was applying Teflon to his fishing line when his observant—and imaginative—wife wondered why this slippery stuff couldn't be used in frying pans."

Aluminum foil, another modern kitchen staple was in use prior to World War II, but the roll of foil that is used today came about through circumstances related to the war. And as with Teflon's journey from the lab to the kitchen, the vision of one housewife changed the way others would benefit from, and cook with, aluminum foil for years to come.

The Reynolds Company had been involved in the production of thin sheets of metal in the 1920s. Tin wrap was originally used on soda-bottle labels and in cigarette packs. But things changed for Reynolds after they purchased the company that made Eskimo Pie ice cream treats. The frozen confection came tightly wrapped in foil, which meant that Reynolds now had another product that required metal packaging. With an abundance of cheap aluminum available in the 1920s, Reynolds used the Eskimo Pie purchase as a springboard to concentrate on finding other uses for the affordable metal. In the late 1930s, when it appeared that America's involvement in the war in Europe was inevitable, Reynolds started digging in bauxite-rich mines in Alabama and Arkansas. When the government required tools, weapons, and machines, Reynolds was capable of filling their order thanks to the company's quarry. These mines produced such an abundance of aluminum ore that the company was able to continue experimenting with new ways to use the material. One result of the Reynolds Company's technology was the manufacturing of sturdy aluminum trays in which food could be transported, heated, and eaten; another was the ability to create very thin, but highly durable, sheets of aluminum foil that could be used to wrap foods, store them, and even bake them. In fact, the countless dinners that would eventually be cooked in aluminum foil were inspired by one Thanksgiving turkey. Again, Greenspan writes that "the wife of a Reynolds' Metals executive in Richmond, Virginia, sent her husband out to buy a roasting pan," on the morning of the holiday. "Knowing that [his] chances of finding what she wanted . . . were slim, he gave her a roll of aluminum foil earmarked for a presentation to be given at a commercial kitchen." Several hours later, the silver-wrapped bird came out of the oven, and the holiday had produced yet another tradition.

It should be noted that the dehydrated or freeze-dried advances in preserving and packaging foods weren't the only benefits to emerge from the wartime technology explosion. While they don't come with same type of lore associated with their inedible kitchen counterparts of Teflon and aluminum foil, Kraft Singles cheese slices and packages of vacuum-packed bacon, both of which debuted after the war's end, were made possible by the expanded production skills of American food manufacturers.

Convenient ways of cooking, as well as new convenience foods like Kraft cheese slices, were ready to take the cook and the drudgery out of the kitchen as American soldiers returned home from the war.

The promise of science as the century's savior seemed on its way to being fulfilled.

Some of the changes that had taken place in the kitchen during the forties were obvious. An army of appliances could be found for sale in department stores now that the military no longer required that every scrap of metal be used for defense purposes. The War Production Board had slapped a cease-and-desist order on the manufacturing of eighty appliances in 1942, and production of refrigerators, stoves, and blenders, to name but a few, had come to a screeching halt. With the ban now lifted, people who might have not been able to afford items like the new pop-up toasters when they debuted snatched up such must-have items for the postwar kitchen.

Ready-in-a-snap foods, like instant mashed potatoes, could now be made by simply boiling a pot of water. The science and technology that answered the government's call for dehydrated potatoes to feed the troops took the dried spuds from K rations to the home kitchen.

Similarly, mass production meant that other food mixes could now be sold in a box with a guarantee of in-kind quality from one package to the next. Cake mixes were now available in boxes, courtesy of Pillsbury and General Mills. Continuous cake-mix systems in large production plants flawlessly measured the right amount of ingredients into each box. Being able to bake a perfect cake was the hallmark of a perfect hostess, but for those who wanted to eliminate any room for error and even avoid the cake mixes, commercial bakeries allowed them to stake their entertaining reputations on names like Sara Lee and Pepperidge Farm, which were now supplying stores with ready-made cakes and other baked goods.

But despite the changes automation continued to bring into the kitchen during the 1940s, the publishers of *Gourmet* magazine believed that there were still plenty of homemakers who enjoyed cooking. When *Gourmet* debuted in the early 1940s, no one could be blamed for thinking it unlikely to survive—especially since the publication arrived at a time when food was viewed essentially as fuel. Certainly food was not an indulgence, and treating it as such would have seemed decadent, if not perverse. But *Gourmet* was prophetic in its ability to foresee the way the postwar American attitudes toward food would elevate cooking and cuisine to an art form; furthermore, *Gourmet* foresaw a time when American food would be able to fuse its disparate elements together and stand on its own as a unique and valid cuisine. The magazine had a strong voice, with writers like M. F. K. Fisher, who had already charmed readers with her wartime favorite, *How to Cook a Wolf*, and Ogden Nash, whose poems about his dislike of cod or love of mustard amused and beguiled those who read them. With text that put food into the context of everyday life—as opposed to trying to contain and subdue it within the confines of a kitchen laboratory—*Gourmet* managed to celebrate the accidental as well as the established, showing readers that they could find reward in the cooking as well as in the eating.

The American Kitchen as it stood prior to World War II was a much different place after the war ended and as the decade came to a close. Denial and lack had defined the kitchen for almost two decades, and an entire generation had grown up getting by on merely the essentials, and sometimes not even that much. But early in the 1940s, things had already started to change. The war had jump-started the stalled economy. American industries had been infused with government cash. There were plenty of jobs and, by the end of the war, plenty of soldiers coming back home found that the technology that had helped secure their victory by changing the way they ate on the battlefield had also changed the way they ate in their homes.

CHAPTER SIX

Cool Down: 1950–1959

*The General Electric fridge was from the forties, but the chrome-wrapped table
and monochromatic cabinet and countertop scheme was signature fifties
(and lasted well into the next two decades, longer than my dad's skinny tie).
(Courtesy of the author.)*

W hat a difference a year makes. As the 1940s came to an end, the
American Kitchen was about to close the door on what had been
nearly two decades of mettle-testing struggle. The future looked as bright
and shiny as the chrome that was starting to wrap its way around kitchen appliances, tables, and chairs. But just as Americans were about to settle into a
much longed-for (and hard-earned) era of peace and prosperity, democracy
discovered a new enemy: communism.

The advancements in science and technology over the past five decades
had presented the American home with a new blueprint for its kitchen. Doors
continued to come off hinges as barriers between the kitchen and the rest of
the home. Pass-throughs were becoming more popular, serving as an indoor
window between the kitchen and dining room. Lifestyle gurus Russel and
Mary Wright offered their *Guide to Easier Living*, in which dinner guests

were invited into the kitchen not only to serve themselves but also to lend a hand in the preparation of the meal.

In the kitchen, wraparound, wall-hugging cabinets and cupboards and lengthy countertops became the room's new signature look. There were plenty of new boxed mixes and canned entrées being put up on grocery store shelves across the country, and now there were sleek new storage cabinets to hold those foods at home, along with ample working space on which to prepare them. Appliances like refrigerators and stoves were available in matching colors. Tailor-made cupboards rested snugly around these new marvels, as well as over and under them. Kitchenette sets in dazzling yellows, soothing blues, and glitter-speckled reds were the appropriately cheerful places to enjoy the new American breakfast.

Technology was proving to be an interesting, if sometimes dangerous, ally. Scientists harnessed previously unknown powers and showed the world that an egg could be cooked from the inside out in a minute—or a city could be leveled to the ground in seconds. Science also gave the world television, and television brought the world into the American home. American life was reflected in the medium's early shows; *The Adventures of Ozzie and Harriet* and *Leave it to Beaver* portrayed what became known as the "all-American family." Dad went to work in a suit, and Mom tended the house—and the kitchen, reigning over her appliances in pearls and a dress.

As it had from its beginning, the American Kitchen integrated the cuisines of its new immigrants, as Americans slowly began warming up to new dishes. Political diplomacy might be enacted at arm's length, but culinary diplomacy? Well, that was something Americans were ready to embrace. For instance, despite the enduring Cold War and the possible Soviet threat, there was a cultural thaw in the kitchen as Americans began eating and cooking up the Russian-tinged Beef Stroganoff.

American cooks were also finding a bit of exotica closer to home in the 1950s. Hawaii and Alaska were now stars on the American flag, and their namesakes, Chicken Salad Hawaii and Baked Alaska, made their way into the kitchen. All things Polynesian captured the American imagination, and luaus were perfect for the new backyard barbecue fad. Many Patio Daddy-Os stoked the fires of the outdoor grill, while pots, pans, stoves, and recipes were still the trappings of a woman's world. But even in the early 1950s, the acknowledgment that a woman's sphere and interests went beyond the kitchen was what helped make *Sexual Behavior in the Human Female* by Alfred C. Kinsey a best seller.

Family meals were eaten in front of the television, thanks to the convenient and collapsible TV trays department stores were selling. Americans weren't yet couch potatoes, but they sure went crazy over french fries. People in the fifties might have gone out to McDonald's to escape the kitchen, but the American Kitchen went underground to escape the bomb as Americans stocked their shelves and watched the skies.

The American Kitchen of the 1950s had a sleek surface, but under that Formica veneer, a subculture was beginning to rumble.

The ongoing battle to make the kitchen less of a scullery had been waged since the days of Catharine Beecher, and by the 1950s it was a fight that was well on its way to being won. Preserved foods were de rigueur. Store-bought packaged foods were becoming equally as common. *Function* became the kitchen's watchword. Whether considering the appliances used for cooking or the foods themselves, there was an ease to operation as well as preparation. Despite the advancements that had transformed the kitchen from a smoky, dirty sweatbox to a gleaming model of efficiency, the engineers in the food industry responsible for these breakthroughs weren't going to be resting anytime soon. In the words of FDA Commissioner George P. Larrick, "Our industry will not have done its job until housewives buy most of their meals as packaged, ready-to-serve items." In other words, as long as potatoes were still peeled or batters mixed, there was work to be done in food labs across the nation.

Making the work of the housewife less of a burden was an idea that was over a hundred years old by the time Larrick made his remark in 1956. Now, a century into that mission, every meal of the day could be made with the slightest bit of effort.

For breakfast, how about waffles that come out of the new refrigerator-freezer *already* made? Just a quick pop into the toaster was all it took to have a hot breakfast now. No batter, no clouds of flour pluming out of the bag, no messy egg whites smeared on the counter. Even the toaster was being improved upon: In the second part of the decade the toaster oven was ready to nudge the pop-up toaster off the kitchen counter and out of the way. For beverages, orange and grapefruit juices could be bought premade, or in frozen concentrate. By 1959, Tropicana juice seemed quaint compared to Tang, that new orange juice that came in a jar, in powder form. Instant coffee had been introduced at the end of the war, and a simple pot and mug was all it took to enjoy the new brew. Those old-fashioned percolators with their baskets and spouts were too clumsy. But now there was an even newer breakthrough for coffee lovers who preferred the taste of coffee but not the fuel-injection that came with it: Food engineers had found a way to take the caffeine out of the beverage without altering the taste (though diehard coffee purists would claim otherwise).

Lunch was almost as easily prepared as breakfast. Grilled cheese sandwiches could be made with those convenient, individually packaged Kraft Singles. Store-bought sliced bread was old news by the 1950s. The Imperial brand of margarine was new, however, and it turned the bread a golden brown as evenly as butter; as an added bonus, the new margarine was more flavorful than its colorless progenitor. A mother could make these comfort-food favorites with confidence knowing that the new nonstick coatings in her skillet formed a burn-free barrier between the food and the pan. And of course the new electric stove heated quickly with the simple push of a button. If a soup-and-sandwich combo was on the menu, Campbell's canned soups were ready and waiting on the pantry shelves. For something a little different, an envelope of Lipton's Onion Soup Mix could be emptied into a pot of boiling water. After a few minutes of stirring and simmering, lunch was ready! Later in the day, should Mom run out of menu ideas, that same soup mix could give a little zing to her meat loaf recipe, or it could be whipped with sour cream for a zesty vegetable dip.

At dinnertime, the modern homemaker could serve the pièce de résistance of food engineering's achievements: the TV dinner. It was Swanson's name on the box, but the credit for the first fully prepared main-course meal belongs to a Swanson employee by the name of Gerry Thomas. As with any famous discovery, the origin of Swanson's frozen turkey dinner is not without its lore. The story is that in 1954 Swanson & Sons, already makers of frozen turkey potpies, had purchased a surplus of turkeys. It was the suggestion of Swanson employee Thomas that the turkeys be cooked complete with the bird's traditional Thanksgiving cohorts of gravy and mashed potatoes, placed in the disposable aluminum trays airlines were using, and flash-frozen. Thomas coined the term "TV dinner" as a way of marketing the meals to busy homemakers. The going price of ninety-eight cents bought diners turkey with gravy and cornbread stuffing, sweet potatoes, and peas. While Thomas got the credit for naming the meal, it was Swanson's in-house "food technologist," Betty Cronin, who did all the work. Or at least most of it. Cronin was responsible for formulating the process that would allow the foods to come out of the home oven "fresh" once they'd been frozen. Her initial inclusion of sweet potatoes sent her back to the test kitchen, however, according to Trager's *Food Chronology*, as they "turn[ed] watery . . . and

[were] quickly replaced by regular potatoes." Swanson packaged the dinner in a box that looked like a television screen, for added novel effect.

The TV dinner embodied the mass production that food-packing plants had relied on during the war. Birdseye's "flash-freeze" process was behind the technology that enabled Swanson to preserve the already-cooked foods. Reynolds Metals had perfected the sturdy, disposable serving tray that carried the meals a decade earlier. And of course tying the product in with the new television phenomenon added to the gee-whiz factor of it all. Sitting in front of a TV with a dinner that Mom's hands barely had to touch? Well, that was progress—and a victory for food technologists!

Of course, there wouldn't have been any point in frozen dinners had there not been advancements in home refrigeration units. World War II had put the manufacturing of such appliances on hold—every spare metal, nut, bolt, and wire was needed to make tanks, guns, ships, and planes. But now, with the economy in bloom and the country at peace, refrigerators, stoves, and—in some homes—dishwashers were being dollied into the American Kitchen.

The refrigerator had been in the kitchen for decades, but the addition of electricity to the unit, and the elimination of its pipes and pumps, was a more recent development. For the first part of the century iceboxes were still in use. In some houses, storage cabinets were built with vents that allowed the cold air from outside to circulate around the contents inside.

Even after electrical wires were laced through the walls of the family home, many Americans still relied on the block of ice, delivered once a week, that sat in the insulated food safe. Home-design and lifestyle magazines even advised homeowners to have outside access to the refrigerator via a trap door on the side of the house. This way, the iceman could make his delivery without ever stepping into the kitchen: He could simply open the trap door and slide the block of ice through the chute that connected to the refrigerator inside.

The refrigerator of the 1950s could trace its ancestry back to the middle of the 1910s, when a man by the name of Alfred Mellowes in Fort Wayne, Indiana, invented an electric refrigerator for home use. Mellowes's refrigerator was the model around which the Frigidaire would later be built; General Electric bought the rights to Mellowes's appliance, and the name Frigidaire was the winning choice in a name-the-product contest the company sponsored.

General Electric's developments led to the use of the terms *mechanical refrigerator* and *electric refrigerator* to distinguish the new appliances from their old, static counterparts. Before GE took over the manufacturing of these new marvels, an electric refrigerator cost as much as a car. But the price of a refrigeration unit wasn't only cost-prohibitive in the home. When Birdseye was first ready to market his line of frozen foods, there were few grocery outlets in the country equipped with freezers to carry the items.

General Electric did a lot to change the home refrigeration units of the late teens and early 1920s by eventually designing what would become known as the "monitor top." The monitor was a drum-shaped, self-contained motor and cooling system that sat on top of the appliance. Prior to its invention, mechanical refrigerators used water and ammonia to generate the chilling effect. This system often required elaborate outer workings. An advertisement for General Electric's Icing Unit in *Good Housekeeping* from 1929 announced the company's revolutionary new monitor-top design: "The entire mechanism of the Icing Unit is housed on top of the cabinet in one hermetically sealed casing. That is *all* the mechanism—none below the box. None in the basement. There are no pipes, no drains, no attachments." The ad further crowed that the new GE appliance was "as easy to operate as an electric fan—and almost as portable." Considering the mammoth proportions of most early home appliances, this moveable refrigerator, not bound to a wall for ice access or connected to pipes for drainage, was a real revolution, as was the disappearance of the belt-driven motor that kept the compressor running in the older models (which often had to be housed in another room adjacent to the kitchen, if not in the basement).

The refrigerator not only kept foods from perishing, it also saved cooks from toiling in hellishly hot temperatures in the middle of summer. The mercury could quickly climb to 140 degrees in the American Kitchen in earlier times. The advent of coal, wood, and gas stoves helped to contain that heat, but without a place to keep meats and other perishable foods sufficiently cool, meals had to be prepared shortly before they were eaten to reduce the chance of spoilage. YOU CAN COOK IN THE COOL OF THE MORNING (IF YOU HAVE A GOOD REFRIGERATOR) rang the headline of an article in *Good Housekeeping* in the late 1920s. Homemakers were instructed to prepare menus with items that could keep throughout the day, like Jellied Shrimp Salad, Chocolate Cornstarch Pudding, Fruit Gelatine, Sliced Cold Meat, or Shredded Cabbage with French Dressing. By following these suggestions, lunch and dinnertime didn't have to mean turning a portion of the house into an inferno in order to cook the family's meals. Frigidaire seduced buyers by using this as a selling point: "You can prepare many new and tempting dishes in the Frigidaire freezing compartment." The implication was that perhaps the stove's fire didn't need to be lit at all!

Refrigerators also liberated the woman of the house from being at the mercy of the ice delivery. Frigidaire addressed this nuisance in their ads as well, suggesting that their appliance helped homemakers to "know a new freedom. Freedom from outside ice supply—more time away from the kitchen—more leisure hours." In summer, iceboxes had to be replenished often to ensure that their contents were kept safely cool, and opening and closing the doors of an icebox reduced the effectiveness of the unit's insulation. Early refrigerators weren't much better. Cooking magazines cautioned homemakers to keep a list of their refrigerator's contents handy; that way, they could open the door and go right to the item they were seeking, rather than allowing the doors to remain open as warm air seeped into the unit while they rummaged.

Before the stock market crashed at the end of the twenties, a refrigerator cost almost three hundred dollars, less than two thirds of what they'd sold for fifteen years earlier. The introduction of Du Pont's Freon gas into the refrigerator's cooling system made the appliances even more affordable (and less dangerous, since they no longer had to rely on ammonia). Despite the tough economic times of the early Depression, one million homes in America were equipped with electric refrigerators. Through the thirties, technological breakthroughs and increased mass-production capabilities brought the price of a refrigerator down to about $170 in 1939. The military's need for metal during World War II meant that Americans who did not have an electric refrigerator would have to wait even longer before getting one. By the war's end, however, homeowners had several manufacturers' appliances to choose from when outfitting their kitchens. Amana had gotten its start back in 1934 when an inventor named George Forstner had designed the refrigerator-freezer combo. Forstner's invention was first sold to grocery stores, and later its technology was adapted for use in the home. Westinghouse, the company that had wowed attendees of the 1939 World's Fair with its dishwasher, was manufacturing other household appliances.

But the real sign of the times in the 1950s was the color-coordinated refrigerators and stoves that General Electric was offering. GE's Frigidaire brand had become the first manufacturer to add the blush of matching color to their appliances. After the drab years of the thirties and forties, the American Kitchen welcomed the cheery transformation.

Just as they had in previous decades, the advancements in procuring, preserving, and preparing food meant that in 1950s America there was now more time to pursue a lifestyle outside the realm of domestic duties. Americans were participating in more leisure activities than ever before. *How to Play Your Best Golf All the Time*, by Tommy Armour, was the go-to guide for men who were looking to relax, while women's clubs, with luncheon dates, bridge parties, and museum outings, were en vogue. And of course the family could always unwind in front of the TV with *I Love Lucy*, *Your Show of Shows*, or *Our Miss Brooks*. With all these new influences, Americans were exercising their opportunity to express their individuality both inside and outside the home.

The kitchen was suddenly a much more pleasant domain for the woman of the house, and it began reflecting her tastes. The doors that had once closed off parlors and dining rooms in the Victorian era and early twentieth century were swung wide open, if not removed entirely. American houses were growing larger because American families were getting bigger: All those nights that reunited couples spent getting reacquainted after the absences imposed by World War II and the Korean War resulted in a population explosion.

The jobs that allowed the heads of households to keep the family fed were located outside of cities now, and urban neighborhoods emptied while suburban neighborhoods swelled. Americans were seduced by the sense of order and control suburbia offered. "You can *really live*!" promised an advertisement for Princess Jeanne, a development of homes near Albuquerque, New Mexico. In Princess Jeanne every kitchen came equipped with an electric range, a garbage disposal, and all the latest conveniences that science and technology could provide. This was definitely a new way of living!

This new type of neighborhood needed a new kind of home, and the flat, single-story ranch house became a popular design. It was the introduction of this style that changed how the American Kitchen would be used and designed in future decades, starting with the rooms adjacent to it. As Professor Terry Uber, Kent State's expert on interior design, says, "The disintegration of the walls between living and dining room [began] . . . in the fifties, starting with the ranch house, and the kitchen became more a center of activity and started to open up a little bit more."

Opening up the kitchen began with the bar pass-through that had been initiated earlier in the century. Pass-throughs were cut-outs between the shared kitchen and dining room wall. Generally surrounded by a china cabinet on one side and a Hoosier on the other, they allowed the hostess to keep the workings of the kitchen private. At the same time, she could avert disaster when it came time to serve her guests by sliding dishes through the pass-through space instead of navigating her way through the door that separated the two rooms.

In the 1950s, this pass-through space began to grow wider, and as it did, it provided a picture window into the workings of the kitchen. With this kind of visibility, maintaining appearances became very important. Appliances had already received a makeover, as had the kitchenette set. Wooden chairs were out. Instead, chrome chairs with new vinyl cushions were pulled up to the table in colors that matched the tabletop. Backsplashes now filled in the wall between the countertops and cabinets, and they often carried atomic or futuristic designs. Starbursts exploded from the center of tiles, while brightly colored dots orbited around them. A George Nelson sunburst clock or asterisk clock hanging on the wall of a kitchen meant the keeper of that house really knew what time it was. The American Kitchen was not only becoming more efficient, it was also becoming hip.

Cool was everywhere in the 1950s. Jazz was cool. Rock and roll was cool. James Dean was cool. And even the kitchen was cool, thanks to the new vision of designers like Nelson; Ray and Charles Eames; and Eva Zeisel. Leading this new mod squad was the husband and wife team of Russel and Mary Wright.

If ever there was a couple who could be described by the term *quintessentially American*, Russel and Mary Wright were that pair. Russel's ancestors on his mother's side of the family included two signers of the Declaration of Independence, while his father's family shared the same Quaker faith and roots as the founding colonists of Pennsylvania. Mary Einstein Wright was related to *that* Einstein, and though her grandfather's cousin Albert might not have been American-born, his acquired U.S. citizenship was as good as a birthright when he renounced Germany in 1933, came to America, and switched teams.

Russel and Mary Wright were born to change and improve the American way of life. He had a proclivity for art that eventually led to his interest in design; she was an artist who possessed a keen eye and a good marketing sense. Together, they collaborated on lines of dinnerware, cookware, silverware, linens, and even furniture with the intention of helping Americans create "a style of living that was practical, elegant, and free from drudgery."

By the time the 1950s came around, the Wrights had already established themselves through the American Modern dinnerware they'd created near the end of the Depression, as well as through their Iroquois Casual China, which they unveiled in 1946. The designs for both lines were beautifully simple. Russel Wright's love of natural elements was embodied in the warm, earthy hues, and the round, organic shapes of the pieces. The severe angles and speeding curves that characterized the Deco-influenced, streamlined designs of the thirties were softened by Wright's vision. Rather than appearing as though they were going to zoom off the table, the dishes and plates in the American Modern and Iroquois Casual sets were more relaxed. They even felt different—more welcome—in the user's hand. The indentations in the sides of the squat salt and pepper shakers felt pebble-smooth. The coffee cups bowed out generously in the middle and begged to be cradled in both hands. The Wrights' consideration of the utility of their designs was best illustrated, however, in the Highlight/Pinch stainless-steel flatware they designed in 1950: The knives had a fingertip rest that gently sloped out of the handle, allowing users more control as they cut into their food. But while the items that carried the Russel Wright signature were carefully designed, they were merely the tools for the lifestyle the Wrights envisioned and promoted.

Guide to Easier Living was the couple's manifesto on modern living. The Wrights' plan for achieving this easier life was based on their philosophies about entertaining, dining, and decorating. "We are making a new etiquette, with a new set of manners for both hosts and guests," they wrote in *Easier Living*. This new etiquette was "not counterfeit of a vanished aristocracy but an honest product of our times," one that "demand[ed], more than anything else . . . a new and more relaxed attitude on the part of all concerned." Guests and hosts alike were encouraged to drop the formalities of the past. The tableside meal preparation suggested by cooking magazines during the Depression was just the sort of thing the Wrights favored.

Anything that made for a less stressful evening was acceptable—even having guests serve themselves. "A stack of trays and tableware is laid out on the counter, and food is taken directly from the stove by the guests," they instructed. There was no room for social pretense, which was one of the threats to the Wrights' philosophy. "Certainly more than a few of today's many frustrations and guilt complexes, as well as family failures, have their roots in the struggle to fit our twentieth-century selves into an eighteenth-century corset," they wrote.

Americans had been slowly allowing guests into their kitchens ever since the servants had marched out. For the Wrights, this was perfectly natural. From their perspective, entertaining was all about spontaneity and interaction. They even suggested that inviting guests into the kitchen to share the cooking duties was "a fun leisure activity." Equality was an important part of their vision, as both men and women were responsible for making this easier living a reality.

With their "from the table outward" approach to design, Russel and Mary Wright saw the shared meal as the hub from which the rest of the day's activities, as well as the house's aesthetic, radiated. Their products allowed everyone access to well-designed, well-made tools for living. As the middle class grew, status symbols were now within the reach of a generation that had never defined itself by possessions. The Wrights hoped that by providing affordable and aesthetically pleasing household items, they would allow Americans to relax and enjoy the leisure time this new age was affording them. A functional versatility, a result of utilizing the technology of the day, allowed the Wrights' dishware to go straight from the oven to the table. This combination of technology and design—a dish that was strong enough to cook in and beautiful enough to serve with—was yet another way the Wrights tried to lessen the burdens of the kitchen.

For the Wrights and their contemporaries, science had done its job to improve the daily life of Americans. Now it was up to the culture to do the rest.

The Wrights had a kindred spirit in Eva Zeisel. Zeisel was a Hungarian-born potter who was known for her inventive ceramic designs long before she turned her attention toward the American Kitchen. Like the dinnerware created by Russel Wright, Zeisel's tableware embodied the zeitgeist. Museums around the world had been showing the works of artists whose interpretations were less representational than those of their predecessors, and Zeisel's Town and Country line of dishes echoed this abstract form of expression. Her salt and pepper shakers tweaked the idea of what these vessels were supposed to look like with their animated, whimsical forms. Like the Wrights', Zeisel's dishware came in colors that threw out the notion of matched sets: Colors were to be mixed and matched. While Eva Zeisel's approach might have seemed like it was abandoning tradition completely, the manufacturer of her Town and Country line was none other than Minnesota-based Red Wing Pottery, a company whose clay works had been in the American Kitchen since the last quarter of the nineteenth century. Zeisel wasn't the first of Red Wing's designers to court a higher aesthetic, though; the Minnesota company had begun manufacturing "art pottery" in the late 1920s.

Zeisel also designed for Nambe, another housewares manufacturer whose serving bowls, trays, and platters were carrying nuts, dips, and crudités from the kitchen to the cocktail table in the American home of the fifties. Founded in New Mexico in 1951, Nambe brought a little bit of Native American culture back into the American Kitchen of the twentieth century. The generous curves and sprawling latitude of its bowls and trays channeled the pottery and landscape of the American Southwest. The influence of the natural world on the Nambe designs was something the company shared with Zeisel and the Wrights. The inspiration of nature was seen in the forms these designers chose, and also in the simpler way of living they and many of their midcentury contemporaries espoused. There was no waste in the workings of the natural world. Nature was a model of efficiency.

With nature providing the model, science was ready to help with its mass replication. Like the Wrights, the husband-and-wife team Ray and Charles Eames was inspired by the way technology and design could create a more efficient way of life within the American home. The Eameses utilized the mass-production capabilities and mass-marketing savvy that had risen first as a result of wartime production, then as a result of postwar wealth. The couple had been experimenting with compressed plywood, trying to fashion splints and crutches for the military that were both sturdy and lightweight. The technology that had supported the limbs of injured soldiers was the same technology that would help Ray and Charles Eames create furniture that would become iconic of the American midcentury modern aesthetic. Though they were more concerned with tables and chairs, sofas and shelving units, the Eames mission statement was very similar to that of Russel and Mary Wright. Both couples were trying to offer American homemakers the tools they needed to make the most of their free time.

The advancements in science that helped to make life more livable in the American Kitchen also contributed to making it more colorful. *Plastics* might have been the word of the future in the 1967 film *The Graduate*, but poly-prefixed blends were already giving the kitchen of the fifties vivid accents. Pink bread boxes, yellow flour and sugar canisters, blue napkin rings, green bowls, and orange cups helped brighten countertops, tables, and shelves thanks to the discovery of a life-changing substance called polyethylene.

Polyethylene was the plastic compound used by former Du Pont chemist Earl Tupper to create an item that would conquer storage needs in the American Kitchen in the 1950s and beyond. By fashioning a flexible version of the plastic, Tupper was able to create the revolutionary form-fitting seals that became the selling point for the line of containers that bore his name: Tupperware!

Preserving foods wasn't the problem in the fifties that it had been in previous centuries or even decades, but storing leftovers or unused portions of canned goods was tricky. Refrigerators were no longer the cost-prohibitive luxury they once were, but even affordable items like aluminum foil and plastic wraps were relatively new on the market. Prior to their arrival, foods could be stored in the glass jars used for canning or stored in crocks and casserole dishes with tight-fitting lids. Companies like Red Wing would line the inside of their stoneware pieces with an interior glaze to prevent the contents from seeping into the vessel itself. Sometimes corks were added to ensure a better seal. But stoneware was heavy, and easily chipped or cracked, so replacing pieces could be costly. Tupperware, by comparison, was indestructible. As a result, it became practically indispensable.

Tupperware's appeal was limitless. It looked good. It came in a variety of shapes, colors, and sizes. It kept the refrigerator neat and cupboards orderly. It could be stacked to fit onto shelves. It could be dropped without breaking. It was resistant to moderate heat. It could be turned upside down, knocked on its side, or bumped off the counter, and as long as its lid had been burped into place its contents remained safe inside.

The patented Tupperware lid may have been the brainchild of Earl Tupper, but the marketing that turned it into a marvel was the work of a Detroit woman named Brownie Wise. A sharp and stylish entrepreneur, Wise convinced Tupper to yank his product out of stores. She assured him that an in-home sales routine, in which the containers were demonstrated before a captive audience of women, would turn Tupperware into a household name. She was right. Tupperware parties became an overnight sensation *and* the only way a woman could buy the nifty plastic tubs. Wise provided women of the fifties a chance to make a substantial amount of money by investing as much, or as little, of their free time in peddling Tupperware as they wished. Housewives were soon financing their children's educations, family vacations, or second cars.

Unfortunately, Wise and Tupper were at odds, and the inventor fired the person responsible for turning his name into a legend—but not before Wise graced the front of *Business Week* in 1954, becoming the first woman to appear on the magazine's cover.

The entry of other plastics into the kitchens of post–World War II America wasn't as dramatic as polyethylene's, but that didn't keep these materials from becoming any less prevalent. Like the other poly plastics, polystyrene and polyvinyl—and their sister, polyvinyl chloride—were in use commercially for decades before they found their way into home use. The durability of plastics made them popular with homemakers, as did their price. Their resistance to dirt was another check in their "plus" column. Polyvinyl chloride, or PVC as it became known, became a household favorite in the form of Gold Seal Vinyl kitchen flooring. Its appeal? Not only did it wear well, resisting scuffs and scratches, it also cleaned up well and it did not need to be waxed.

PVC's less-augmented relative, plain old polyvinyl, was another star in the American Kitchen of the fifties. The roll of plastic covering that would go on to carry the name Saran Wrap was made of the stuff.

Polystyrene had countless uses because the colorless compound was a perfect vehicle for dye. It was also the basis for another kitchen regular—Styrofoam.

Plastics were making the American Kitchen a more colorful room, as well as a safer one. Dropping a Tupperware container wasn't nearly as dangerous as dropping a stoneware casserole dish or crock or a glass jar. Science was once again living up to its promise.

If the combination of Tupperware and technology was a woman's ticket out of the kitchen (and out of the house) in the fifties, then the backyard barbecue and patio grill were the man's route *into* the American Kitchen.

The notion of a man cooking wasn't completely novel in the middle of the century. Restaurants had male chefs at their helms, many of whom became famous, and the history of the nation's Old West was seasoned with stories about campfires and cooking over open pits. As chef, cookbook author, and food expert Anthony Bourdain says, "There's the Jim Bowie, Davy Crockett frontier ideal: It's permissible to barbecue, and it's always been permissible to catch your own fish and cook it. In fact you were well thought of if you could do that." But, Bourdain points out, cooking as a means of survival was viewed quite differently than recreational or experimental cooking in the home or restaurant kitchen: "Even cooking professionally wasn't considered a masculine thing to do."

If a man was caught cooking, he had some explaining to do. In high school home economics books, teenage boys quickly clarified where they acquired their cooking know-how: "Why, when Dad and I went fishing a year ago . . ." They made it clear they'd received their education around a campfire, not while donning an apron in the kitchen with Mom.

The kitchen was the woman's domain, but that didn't necessarily mean that she had any rights or claim to the work done there. For instance, Thomas Jefferson was credited for turning his kitchen into the culinary marvel of its time, but there is no record of his having actually cooked in it. Likewise, it was W. O. Atwater's work in food chemistry that earned him the title Father of the Home Economics Profession in his obituary, despite the contributions of women to the burgeoning domestic-science movement. And it was Harvey Wiley whom the editors of *Good Housekeeping* turned to when searching for an authority figure to validate their publication's direction and tone with a regular column. Women may have done the cooking, but there was an underlying theme that they did so with the approval of the men, or under their supervision. In the *Good Housekeeping* story "A Masculine Solution," the man of the house, Mr. Copley, not only had to prepare meals for himself and his inept wife, he also had to give a cooking lesson or two to Otelia, their equally incompetent servant.

The idea of a man as the overseer of a kitchen's output was standard, even professionally. For example, restaurant critic Duncan Hines made a name for himself by praising, or undoing in some cases, the names of others. Hines traveled the country, assessing the quality of eating establishments in hotels as well as independent ventures. His reputation carried enough clout that when cake mixes with his name on the box began appearing in stores they made up for 48 percent of the cake-mix sales in the country within a month's time.

The kitchen's lack of a man's "inherent" organizational skills was sometimes lamented in ads or in the media. IF MEN WERE COOKS! exclaimed an ad for Stanley Tools in the late 1920s. "If men had to get the meals we venture the prediction that kitchen cabinets would quickly become as numerous as front doors!" The tone implied that a woman needed a man in the kitchen to help her keep her sphere in good order. The preparation of meals, however, was up to her.

Men did occasionally step up to the frying pan in America's kitchens, but it seems that a more eyebrow-raising set of circumstances prevailed if a man admitted that he *liked* to cook. However, by the mid-1950s men stood proudly over their barbecues, tongs in hand, while James Beard presided over a cooking school bearing his name.

Beard was an out-of-work actor looking to make ends meet when he opened a catering firm in 1935. He was soon getting more applause for his food than he'd ever received for his stage work so he devoted his energies to his business full-time. In 1940 he wrote *Hors d'Oeuvre and Canapes*. While finger foods weren't exactly the manliest of menu items, Beard came off more like a businessman sharing the secrets of his trade. Two years later, when he released *Cooking It Outdoors*, his career was made. The book was called "the first serious work on outdoor cooking" and legitimized the backyard fire and the man who built it. Other titles, like *Fowl and Game Cookery*, established Beard as a man's man in the kitchen. There weren't any doubts how the "game" of the title got from the woods to the dinner table; the host was assumed to be chef and hunter, provider for all. Or at least that was the idea. Beard published numerous other books in his long career, including tomes on how to cook fish and casseroles. By the time he was proclaimed "The King of Gourmets" by *Time* magazine there was no shame in being the bearer of that title.

Beard broke new ground in 1946 with his televised cooking show *I Love to Eat*. Beard relied on his background as an actor to provide a weekly televised cooking class. The show aired for a brief, Warholian fifteen minutes on Friday nights for its first eight months on the air. After that Beard was given a full thirty-minute time slot on Thursday nights for the remainder of the show's run. *I Love to Eat* ran for only ten months, but viewers loved to watch. Beard's on-camera style and enthusiasm for American recipes and ingredients helped earn him yet another title: "Dean of American Cooking."

James Beard wasn't the first male to write cookbooks in America, but he was the first to have such celebrity attached to his success. Beard legitimized a man's place in the kitchen, and even made it acceptable to delve into the cooking of foods that had formerly been considered dainty.

But tea sandwiches weren't on the menu when the man of the house took to the grill in the 1950s. Men were throwing steaks, beef kabobs, and spare ribs onto the fire with gusto—and doing so without shame. Even the simple act of grilling a steak carried with it an American sense of entitlement in the postwar kitchen.

In fact, after a long absence from the American Kitchen (and its dinner table), better cuts of beef were making a comeback in the fifties. One advertisement from the American Meat Institute shortly after the war's end carried the headline THIS IS LIFE! over a photo of a standing rib roast. "You may not find it every time you look for it in your store . . . but it's on its way back!" the ad promised.

As beef moved "back to the Home Plate" more Americans could now afford cuts of meat other than hamburger. Steaks were so popular that they were the topic of a story in *Life* magazine in 1955. Steaks were the symbol of the wealthy nation that the United States was becoming in the middle of the century.

Americans had had their fill of cooking ground beef during the thirties and forties, which might be why the idea of grabbing a burger on the run outside of the house seemed so appealing. Fast food was slowly becoming a popular alternative for the family meal by the middle of the 1950s. There was an of-the-era aspect to driving up to the hamburger stand in your new car and placing your order at the shiny counter. In just a few minutes you were out the door with dinner in a bag. Soon you didn't even have to drive very far, as franchises were opening up in convenient locations across America.

The idea that led to the numerous golden arches and drive-throughs that would sprout along American highways grew out of a lone hamburger stand the McDonald brothers of California had opened back in 1940. By the end of the forties they'd established a formula—and a franchise. By the end of the fifties, a man by the name of Ray Kroc—who became interested in the brothers' company in the mid-fifties—would personally own one hundred McDonald's restaurants. Another fast-food enterprise that opened at the same time was Burger King. Burger King creator James McLamore is credited with saying, "There are only two things our customers have, time and money—and they don't like spending either of them, so we better sell them their hamburgers quickly."

In McLamore's statement is the key to why fast food became such a phenomenal success in America: The foods were relatively inexpensive, and the speed with which they could be bought made Americans feel like they were benefiting yet again from all the new technology that was taking over American food production. If past generations in the American Kitchen could identify their cooking experiences in terms of precise science (the turn of the century) or sweetness (the 1920s) or deprivation (the 1930s and 1940s), then the fifties would be recognized by the way food production, and food preparation, had become a lightning-quick science. In fact, Harvey Levenstein, historian and author of *Revolution at the Table: The Transformation of the American Diet*, has called the 1950s "The Golden Age of Food Processing."

Frozen french fries were a perfect example of this processing, and they were being salted and bagged and sold along with countless burgers in fast-food joints across the country. They were also making their way into the American Kitchen.

Americans were starting to eat more potatoes in the fifties, but at the beginning of the decade the per capita consumption was only about six pounds per person per year. Fifty years later, at the beginning of the new millennium, the average American was consuming about eighty pounds of potatoes per year. And french fries constituted almost 40 percent of that total. The connection between the proliferation of fast-food hangouts and the emergence of the meat-and-potatoes combo as the all-American meal is a spurious one, but the popularity of french fries did bring about a boom for the potato industry.

Kids liked french fries and were more willing to eat potatoes cooked this way, as opposed to boiled or mashed or any of the other options available at the time. But moms in the American Kitchen faced the same problem as did the cooks in the fast-food shops: French fries were not the easiest food to make. Peeling potatoes and then cutting them into the matchstick-thin slivers was a tedious task, and to make matters worse, the kitchen could get pretty messy, and the splattering hot oil and grease into which the potatoes were dunked was dangerous. In the age of fast food, there was nothing speedy about this process. But the home cook, the short-order chef, and, to a degree, the potato farmers, were soon rescued by the efforts of an Idahoan by the name of J. R. Simplot.

John Richard Simplot became "America's great potato baron," as author Eric Schlosser refers to him in *Fast Food Nation*, by first servicing Uncle Sam's kitchen. Simplot was a successful potato farmer prior to the war, having built a strong business by planting the Russet potato, the variety perfected by Luther Burbank in the 1870s. This strain of tuber was a perfect match for the growing conditions in Idaho, especially since the government had begun financing irrigation of the arid Idaho land through the Snake River Reclamation Act earlier in the twentieth century.

In the early forties, Simplot's potato-processing plant was one of the American businesses awarded a contract by the government to keep the military fed. Simplot was charged with providing dehydrated potatoes for the army, and the money that he made from this venture allowed him to explore new food technologies, in particular frozen foods. By 1953 he'd established a facility for flash-freezing potatoes. By the following year, more McDonald's restaurants had opened. Burger King was open for business, too. Simplot saw an opportunity to be the frozen french fry vender of choice for these outlets, and he struck a deal with McDonald's.

The frozen french fry's entry into the American Kitchen was made easier thanks to Simplot because he had raised the bar when it came to flavor. While technology existed to dehydrate and freeze foods, the real challenge for science and for the laboratory chef was in producing a quality product that consistently tasted good upon reheating. Birdseye had found that flash-freezing freshly caught fish helped them retain their flavors when later thawed and cooked. But potatoes were another story, as companies had tried and failed to market a successful frozen french fry prior to Simplot's: A company from Long Island, New York, by the name of Maxson Food Systems, had tried their hand at manufacturing a frozen french fry product in the mid-1940s. The fries were sold at Macy's in New York City, but sales were dismal. (Maxson's timing could have been part of the reason for the fries' failure; in-home freezers weren't as common in 1946 as they would become within the next five years.)

Through a series of trial-and-error experiments, Simplot's on-staff scientists were able to perfect the flavor of their frozen french fries. With Simplot's innovation, the 1950s could also be called the Golden Age of the French Fry in America. Ketchup, the quintessential french fry accompaniment, was still made from fresh tomatoes, sugar, and vinegar (as opposed to corn syrup and acetic acid), and it helped to make the french fry *the* finger food of a new generation in the American Kitchen.

But not all Americans were rushing to chow down on fast foods and french fries. Calorie-counting became more popular than ever in the American Kitchen in the 1950s as dieting became more fashionable. But the diets favored by Americans in the fifties were different from the food-fad trends of earlier decades. For starters, more was known about the vitamin and mineral contents of foods. Dieters in the midcentury knew, for instance, that an all-grapefruit diet wasn't going to meet their nutritional or caloric needs. There were also new theories about the body's ability to absorb and utilize different types of foods. And Americans were now eating better for different reasons than they had before.

The diet reformists of the past were generally reactionaries. Looking back over the history of dieting in America, especially in the nineteenth century, most calls for tempered appetites were in response to a fear that maybe

Americans were indulging in certain foods, or even just too much food, that were exciting their carnal desires. Graham, Post, and Kellogg all preached a diet of abstinence in the hope that bland foods would keep physical urges at bay. Of course, good health was at the center of their thinking, but the distinction between what they considered to be good moral health and good physical health was irrelevant; they were one and the same.

But in the fifties, dieting was not only about physical health. It was more about physical image than ever before as the media helped Americans become more aware of their sex appeal. *From Here to Eternity*, the book and the movie, was wildly popular. The sight of lovers Burt Lancaster and Deborah Kerr, their limbs entwined as they rolled in the surf, was an iconic image of fifties sexuality. Marlon Brando's ripped T-shirt in *A Streetcar Named Desire* was another. *A Place in the Sun* and *Rebel Without a Cause* made the brooding and sensitive types like Montgomery Clift and James Dean appealing. Americans were becoming more open about issues of sex, if only slowly. *Sexual Behavior in the Human Female* by Alfred C. Kinsey became a best seller despite its somewhat clinical take on its subject. Americans wanted to know more and hear more. *Tallulah*, the memoir of the provocative movie star Tallulah Bankhead, and *A House Is Not a Home*, the behind-the-scenes story of life in a brothel by former madam Polly Adler, titillated Americans. *Peyton Place*, the racy tale of life in a seemingly subdued New England town, picked up where those other, real-life stories left off.

Americans now had movies, magazines, and television shows beaming images to them of what ideal men and women should be, and of what they should look like. The cult of celebrity is said to have started with Mathew Brady, as photography made it possible to duplicate an image (like the one of Ziegfeld's cigarette-thin dancers, which changed everything, circa 1907); but television came directly into the home, and as a result hit closer to the psyche. It was only a matter of steps from the front of the TV screen to the front of the bedroom mirror, where teenagers—and adults—could act out the performances and dances they'd seen on *American Bandstand* or *The Ed Sullivan Show*.

Dieting became a way to look good, and looking good was very stylish. Feeling good, however, wasn't always involved, as some new methods for getting thin deprived the body of more than just food. With science making advances in every other aspect of life, it's no surprise that some people turned to drugs as a way to keep off the weight. Dexedrine was prescribed as a diet aid, and Americans downed three billion of the amphetamines in

1952 alone. Americans lost their appetites, their waistlines, and their ability to sleep.

Other dieting methods of the time were more sensible. Calorie-counting was popular, and calorie charts appeared in cookbooks, cooking magazines, and even on tablecloths. Imagine the guilt induced by sitting down with a slice of chocolate cake, only to be informed—by the tablecloth, no less—that you're about to consume six hundred calories! Conversely, there could be a degree of self-satisfaction to be gained from biting into a plum and seeing that it contained only twenty-five calories. Calorie-counting carried even more weight in the American Kitchen when Metropolitan Life Insurance released their tables of ideal weights for men and women at the end of the fifties, and Americans who'd considered themselves reasonably fit saw that according to Met Life's calculations, they were seriously overweight. The company had adjusted its guidelines for the ideal weight of men and women, based on height and age, since their 1942 chart, and the new numbers were announced at a time when many people were already watching their figures. Image-conscious Americans were horrified to see that they were in some cases twenty pounds overweight. The table should have disclosed that the weights had been established at a time when there was less food in the American Kitchen's pantry, but it didn't.

For most dieting Americans, just the sheer volume of calories was bad. Where the calories came from—fat, sweets, or carbohydrates—didn't seem to be a concern for some scale-gazers. Cookbooks would label syrup-drenched concoctions like Broiled Oranges or Banana Freeze as "low-cal" foods. Flavor didn't seem to be taken into consideration, either, when calling a recipe low-cal. Cottage cheese was the vehicle of choice for a number of "healthy" or "diet" foods during the fifties; one recipe for low-cal cheese dip called for cottage cheese, anchovies, and poppy seeds to be stirred together and served with low-calorie crackers.

This attention to the caloric value of foods, driven by the attention to the growing American waistline, made the kitchen a scene of anxiety for some people. But there were more than enough resources to which they could turn when looking for an opinion regarding what they should eat. The Pennington diet, popularized in the forties by Dr. Alfred Pennington, championed a low-carbohydrate menu. Updated for the fifties and called the Eskimo diet because of its high fat and protein prescription, Pennington's suggestions were based on studies of overweight employees at the Du Pont plant in Delaware. Predating the Atkins diet by several decades, the high-protein/low-carb approach laid out by Pennington was echoed in other diets. One popular magazine urged its readers to cut down on their intake of starches and instead eat more protein, the logic being that protein built muscles and was processed quickly by the body. Starches took longer to metabolize and were thought to have a greater chance of not being burned off.

A health-food craze, based on the nutritional value of foods rather than merely their caloric content or their physical structure, began growing in the 1950s. *Prevention* magazine debuted in 1950. The magazine concentrated on the value of vitamin supplements while taking aim at food additives. In some cases, the editors were right on target: DDT, mercury, MSG (monosodium glutamate), and artificial sweeteners like cyclamates were all lanced as dangerous to the human body. In other situations *Prevention* sounded off against staples like wheat, sugar, and milk using data that was not applicable to the whole population and was in some cases altogether wrong. But just as J. I. Rodale, the man behind *Prevention* as well as *Organic Gardening and Farming*, raged against wheat, Gayelord Hauser was singing the praises of the "wonder foods" that he promised would help readers of his book *Look Younger, Live Longer*. Sales of wheat germ and Dannon yogurt shot up as a result of Hauser's endorsement. *Reduce and Stay Reduced* was another book that promoted a well-thought-out guide to weight loss. Written by Dr. Norman Jolliffe, the book approached dieting as a lifestyle change, not a temporary fix or fad.

All these choices were splitting dieting Americans into ranks, with the fad and fanatic dieters championing some doctors, diets, and foods, while other dieters favored more sensible, health-conscious approaches to eating right. *Let's Eat Right to Stay Fit* by Daisy Adelle Davis was, unfortunately, one of the books that appealed to the former by promoting itself as a source of good advice. Davis was able to rally millions behind her attacks on things like the pasteurization of milk. For those longing for the simpler way of life that the reformists of the previous century had championed, Davis's promotion of health foods preferred "natural" foods over anything that science's hand muddied up. Davis's opinions sat well with those Americans who felt betrayed by the years of the Depression and World War II, their opinion being that science and technology were not making the world a better place as they'd been promised. New discoveries, such as diet, sugarless soft drinks like No-Cal Ginger Ale, were not to be trusted. But neither were fruits or vegetables from the ever-expanding grocery store aisles: One could never be sure what types of pesticides, additives, or chemicals might be lurking on the surface of that carrot, or inside that apple.

But science and medicine were making discoveries diet-conscious Americans could use. The correlation between heart disease and diets that were high in saturated fats was conclusively made in 1957 by Ancel Keyes at the University of Minnesota. Americans learned that their diets could kill them, and in response to the fear this notion generated, some food manufacturers tried to eliminate unhealthy aspects from their foods without slipping dangerous additives in. Kellogg's unveiled Special K cereal, for instance, at a time when the prepared-cereal market was dominated by Sugar Smacks, Sugar Pops, Cocoa Puffs, and Cocoa Krispies. Cocoa Puffs, Cocoa Krispies, and Trix were comprised of approximately 45 percent sugar, whereas Special K contained only 4.4 percent sugar.

As the new style-conscious decade would reflect, caloric intake was cast as a lifestyle choice, and if science and medicine didn't give women cause to fret over their figures, Madison Avenue and the fashion industry did. For instance, how could a woman even think of eating one of those sugary-sweet kids' cereals and still hope to fit into her bikini while she read *Lady Chatterley's Lover* on the beach? If she needed extra help, *Better Homes and Gardens Diet Cookbook* and *Better Homes and Gardens Salad Cookbook* could surely give her some tips. Or, if she was craving a little sweet nothing, she could tear open one of those new little pink packets and sprinkle Sweet 'N Low on her cereal or grapefruit.

Saccharin was the new sugar substitute, and it was quickly becoming a star. Ben Eisenstadt and his wife, Betty, had run a cafeteria in a naval yard during the war. Afterward, they'd purchased a tea-packaging machine to earn a living bagging tea, as they no longer had the servicemen in and out of their eatery as they used to. Betty's disgust with open sugar bowls—all-you-can-eat venues for flies—on restaurant tables led Ben to wonder, aloud, why there wasn't a way to package sugar in individual servings. Betty reminded him of the tea-bagging equipment they'd just bought, and the rest is history. In 1957, the Eisenstadts' eureka experience led them to package a sugar substitute in similar packets for the new diet-conscious diners, and a year later Sweet 'N Low was sharing table space with the sugar, salt, and pepper.

Americans had improved their diets in the 1950s, and apparently the combined efforts of mass production and the government's Basic Seven campaign had bettered the nutritional quality of the average American's diet. A study conducted by the United States Department of Agriculture in 1955 reported that only 10 percent of the country's population now had inadequate diets. Compared to the findings during the war years, this was progress.

The American Kitchen had more options: Nearly four thousand types of food items lined the shelves, bins, coolers, and freezers of the country's supermarkets in 1952. More and more items entered the markets throughout the decade, for better or for worse.

Dinner was now easier to make than ever. Minute Rice, Green Giant canned green beans, and Mrs. Paul's frozen fish sticks were new convenience foods. And if someone wanted to give one of those new ethnic dishes that people were talking about a try, they could do so with the new boil-in-bag beef goulash and chicken cacciatore. Not only was the meal ready in a snap—less than a quarter of an hour!—there was plenty of time to make something else if the family didn't approve. For dessert there were new Pepperidge Farm cookies and Sara Lee cheesecakes. And everything could be washed down with one of the new "instant" beverages. Food technologists had brought powder to the people in their efforts to make the preparations of food less time-consuming. Kool-Aid, Carnation nonfat dry milk, White Rose Redi-Tea, and Lipton Instant Tea could be made with fresh water and a few good stirs of a spoon.

Meanwhile, Cheez Whiz was the new gee-whiz food. Anyone who longed for Welsh rabbit had a cheese sauce at the ready in a jar on the shelf. Choosy Moms chose Jif over Skippy, and Americans were buying more margarine than butter, willingly, for the first time since the product had been introduced. Casseroles were still a big hit. Homemakers were taking a can of tuna, a can of Campbell's Cream of Mushroom soup, frozen or canned peas, and some cooked egg noodles, plopping them together into their favorite baking dish, sliding the casserole into the Roper Double Oven—a post–World War II favorite—and in no time at all, the family had its one-pot meal, 1950s-style!

America's taste buds were also becoming more adventurous. Spaghetti sauces and pizzas continued to gain favor. Chinese foods—in cans—grew in popularity, too. And really brave Americans were taking their families and their guests on international culinary journeys to Russia, Scandinavia, the South Pacific, and France. Smorgasbords, from the fifties' perspective, were easy enough to create using Swedish meatballs. Put some cheese, flatbread or crackers, and pickled fish on a tray and you were practically in Stockholm.

Trader Vic's had made the pupu platter a hit with customers, and backyard barbecuers were grilling pork ribs in sweet sauces over the fire, trying to re-create a Polynesian atmosphere and exotic island flavors. The Russian Beef Stroganoff, the French Lobster Thermidor, and the American Chicken Divan were the choices of the "modern epicure," as Sylvia Lovegren describes culinary globetrotters in *Fashionable Food*. The appeal of these foods for the home cook was that these "gourmet restaurant dishes . . . were easy to make using convenience foods." In other words, preparing a meal merely required opening a few cans.

These bold new steps that Americans were taking into other culinary cultures were led by a variety of guides. In addition to the recipes of famous restaurateurs, upscale cooking magazines, movies, and television, Americans were learning things from their friends and neighbors. The country was becoming more integrated, with ethnic groups mingling and mixing in smaller towns across the country as well as in cities. The helping hand that neighbors lent one another in the Depression years had exposed them to different ethnic cuisines, as did the number of recipe collections that continued to pop up, like the *Portal to Good Cooking* cookbooks published by the Women's American ORT group. Like *The Settlement Cookbook* and *Joy of Cooking*, the *Portal* books contained recipes for family favorites submitted by housewives, passed down from one generation to the next. With the influx of new immigrants, the traditional foods brought to America by the first British settlers were now sharing shelf and table space with other cuisines as cooks attempted to duplicate the foods they saw their neighbors eating.

Large food manufacturing companies like Pillsbury were also broadening the horizons of the American Kitchen by holding contests, or bake-offs, and awarding prizes for the best new recipes. These contests and the resulting printed recipes exposed cooks to foods prepared by people all over the country. Closely guarded and prized recipes weren't always so secret anymore once there was big money at stake: The winner of Pillsbury's 1953 bake-off—the Turtle Cookie—earned its originator twenty-five thousand dollars!

And of course there were those soldiers who got to taste some of the foreign cuisines while stationed overseas during World War II. Those lucky few brought back with them fond memories of some of the delicious meals they'd eaten on the other side of the earth. In his *Food Chronology*, James Trager attributes the rise in oregano sales after World War II to the hankerings of these returning veterans, and while they may have played a part, there was also a high visibility for Italian culture after the war. Italian-American crooner

Frank Sinatra's star was rising in the early fifties, and films like *Roman Holiday* romanticized Italy.

New ideas continued coming into the American Kitchen from around the world through a variety of media in the fifties, and television was becoming the most influential medium of them all. TV brought life into the house and gave Americans new things to laugh at, cry with, and aspire to. When television first appeared in the late 1930s, there were only 150 sets in existence. By 1953 there were an estimated twenty million televisions in homes across America.

Cooking shows were exposing homemakers to new culinary ideas. Dione Lucas had taken to the air in the forties, and James Beard had also shared his talents on TV. But the American Kitchen was also being influenced by the action that occurred around the breakfast table of fictional families like the Ricardos and the Cleavers. The new consumer class that emerged in the postwar years was increasingly aware of what they did or did not have—appliances, furnishings, clothes, even the perfect family—and television was always adding something new to that list.

Barbara Billingsley's perfectly coiffed and perpetually composed June Cleaver was an ideal few moms could emulate in the fifties; still, the impression her kitchen made on Americans was a lasting one. Billingsley's kitchen became something to live up to, an ideal to achieve, and in some cases it became the quintessential model of the American Kitchen from the fifties. Its images were seen so often as to become iconic even if the fantastic depiction of the housewife and her home created unrealistic expectations.

June Cleaver's domestic excellence was just one of the ways television distorted American norms. Because women made up the majority of the television viewing audience, advertisers shifted focus and addressed them directly. Ad agencies knew that women ran the homes, if only domestically, and they crafted their sales pitches accordingly . . . most of the time. But a great deal of advertising presented women as barely having the aptitude of a child. "You mean a woman can open it?" an ad for Alcoa Aluminum incredulously asked. The "woman" in question held her fingers—with their perfectly manicured and polished nails, of course—next to the new twist-off cap featured on Del Monte ketchup, her mouth gaping open in astonishment. The ad answered her question: "*Easily*—without a knife blade, a bottle opener, or even a husband! All it takes is a dainty grasp." For the women who ran their homes during the Depression and the war years, this portrayal of themselves as helpless, brainless ditzes was insulting and degrading. But Alcoa's ad was nothing compared to the strange promotion for Chase & Sanborn coffee that warned, "If your husband ever finds out you're not 'store-testing' for fresher coffee . . . woe be unto you!" The reader of the ad saw the consequences displayed graphically beneath the ad copy: A man sat in a chair, his back to the viewer. He held his wife draped over his lap, and his flat palm was raised above her, ready to strike her backside. The woman, clearly guilty of one of the aforementioned coffee-buying offenses, raised one hand in protest as her legs dangled in the air.

This sort of twisted notion of women as servants, spankable for buying the wrong coffee, might have been intended as a joke, but it speaks volumes about the place housewives were believed to occupy in the American Kitchen of the fifties. After all the advances in technology to make housework easier, and all the style brought into the kitchen to make it a more inviting space, this was the sort of mind-set that was seen as acceptable: Men had worked for decades to make the kitchen a more user-friendly space for women, and woe be unto them if they were still so inept at housekeeping that they couldn't even purchase the right products.

With so many conflicting images bouncing in and out of the frame of the 1950s, is it any wonder that the American Kitchen started to feel the first rumblings of a cultural revolution as the decade came to an end?

The era was riddled with contradictions. Women were expected to stay in the home, but the kitchen was becoming nearly self-sufficient, with meals requiring more assembling than actual cooking. Most of the 1950s favorites, from tuna casserole to Lobster Thermidor, could be made using practically nothing but canned ingredients. Women had successfully held their families and their homes together during the war, only to see themselves portrayed as unable to survive without a man. Babies were being born in record numbers, yet to acknowledge sex was taboo. Alcohol flowed like tap water, but no one was ever too drunk to drive.

Americans embraced Norman Vincent Peale and the power of positive thinking, yet paranoia lurked underground: Escape hatches in backyards led to fallout shelters where two weeks of provisions were stored for the inevitable Soviet nuclear attack. *Popular Science* urged Americans to have a fourteen-day supply of "ready-to-eat food (dry or canned) and water (at least seven gallons per person)" on hand. Among the items found in an actual fallout shelter from the era were Velveeta processed cheese, Dinty Moore canned beef stew, dry milk mix, Shredded Wheat, and Metrical Weight Control Powder. Apparently, regardless of who would greet you aboveground once the coast was clear, you wanted to make sure you looked trim.

By the end of the 1950s, science, which had been relied on to increase the amount of food that could be safely produced and packaged all in the name of the sustainable future, was now being blamed for endangering Americans with deadly chemicals and life-threatening pesticides.

With so many mixed messages, the country was feeling at odds. The harmony and optimism of the era were out of sync with the discord of reality, and the unrest of the coming sixties was starting to resound.

CHAPTER SEVEN

Pop Tarts: 1960–1969

The technology movement of the fifties met the ecology movement of the sixties
as this plastic picnic set was made portable thanks to a macramé sling.
(Helen von Bosch. Bomba picnic set. Philadelphia Museum of Art:
Gift of Villeroy & Boch, New York, 2003.)

The optimism that soared through the fifties was grounded by a dispiriting reality in the 1960s. The country was involved in a war overseas that many Americans didn't understand, let alone support. And back home everybody was talking about the "isms." Racism denied African Americans their civil rights. Sexism restricted a woman's potential. Feminism rallied women to demand equality. Communism loomed as an unwavering threat. Transcendentalism promised to take everyone away from it all. Idealism envisioned equal rights for all. The generations were at odds. The youth were in revolt. Society went from controlled to chaotic in a few short years, and the American Kitchen went along for the ride as mealtime became a forum for debate.

As the 1960s began, Americans were becoming more divided as the recession that had slowed the postwar economy widened the gap between the haves and the have-nots. Industrial and economic growth had benefited some aspects of society, yet almost one third of the country lived at or below the poverty level. The government hoped that by reinstating the food stamp program (which had helped Americans during the Depression and early years of World War II), temporary assistance would prevent long-term economic dependence.

Cultural differences also separated Americans in the sixties, and a young politician by the name of John F. Kennedy proposed a vision for America that protected personal freedoms and guaranteed equality. As president, Kennedy's plan for national unity through his civil rights agenda faced staunch resistance from a separatist mind-set. Integrationists found another charismatic spokesperson for change in Martin Luther King Jr., who likewise demanded an end to the racist views that created division and hatred in the country. The civil rights movement had a significant effect on the American Kitchen as the rising visibility of African Americans sparked discussion and debate about their culture. It was becoming clear that the culinary practices of African slaves had helped define what was considered Southern cooking in America. Soul food became the haute cuisine in the sixties as white hipsters and food enthusiasts bragged about cooking up chitlins and black-eyed peas—that was, of course, when they weren't trying their hand at Boeuf Bourguignon. The interest in French cooking that had merely simmered in the fifties swept through the country with the intensity of a revolution in the sixties. Leading the charge was Julia Child, an unlikely advocate for the cuisine who conquered the American public with her endearing demeanor and DIY ethic.

More American men were moving into the kitchen as more women were starting to work out of the house. The role reversal was hardly universal, though, as society clung to its notions of what were acceptable positions for women to hold. Apron strings were proving to be strong tethers.

But women continued taking charge of their lives and toppling stereotypes. Marlo Thomas was America's independent *That Girl*, while Britain's supermodel Twiggy was the ultra-thin It Girl. The new "thin is in" mantra was a double-edged sword of a message: For a nation that was becoming increasingly overweight, practicing moderation was good advice. But for young girls who were already concerned about emulating the exaggerated proportions of the Barbie Doll, a preoccupation with losing weight was dangerous. Weight Watchers struck a balance for Americans who were unable to resist the temptation of having their fill of all of those new foods lining their kitchen's shelves. Americans had access to more food than any other country on earth, and their figures were starting to reflect that abundance.

Diet cookbooks continued to be best sellers. Fad diets promised quick results, while weight-loss gurus gave people false hope and wrong information that posed serious dangers to their health.

The country was being sold an image, via TV, movies, magazines, books, and advertisements, on how to dress, how to eat, how to act, how to live, and, most important, how to look. By the end of the 1960s, the American Kitchen was mirroring that sales pitch. And a lot of Americans decided they weren't buying it.

The food industry in America had been working overtime to meet the demands of the growing population, as well as to make good on its promise to eliminate drudgery from the preparation of meals. In the sixties, however, food engineers were determined to remove more than just hard work from the American Kitchen. The editors of *Food Engineering* magazine, circa 1963, stated that the "ultimate [achievement in the advancement of food technologies] is to take the homemaker from the kitchen and the cook from the restaurant." To make this type of a prediction a reality, meals would have to come into the kitchen ready to eat (which was already possible) and be able to heat themselves, a problem the British military had addressed somewhat successfully during World War II. A tiny pellet containing volatile chemicals was contained in a separate compartment of the soldier's ration. By pouring water into the chamber a chemical reaction between the water and pellet created enough heat to "cook" the meal.

With this kind of food technology bringing the prepared meal into the home, equally sophisticated methods would be needed to increase productivity in the fields and on the ranches and dairies where the foods were grown and raised.

The food industry in America had learned to adapt to the challenges that prevented it from keeping the American Kitchen well stocked, even overhauling nature's designs by rerouting rivers and streams to thirsty fields. Bugs had met their match in the pesticides that were doused on infested plants. Chemicals offered both a defense and a preventative measure in the war against crop-damaging insects. Declaring victory, however, was premature. What the scientists didn't figure into their equation was that nature would find a way to fight back. Insects began mutating, producing offspring that were resistant to the very chemicals that were supposed to annihilate them.

DDT, or dichloro-diphenyl-trichloroethane, as the chemical compound was officially known, was used to combat Colorado potato beetles that were destroying crops in Switzerland in the 1930s. By 1943, when the winning of the global war demanded increased production from American farms, it was being sprayed over fields in the United States. The pesticide helped create a greater harvest since fewer crops were lost to bugs, but what farmers didn't realize was that something else had started to grow in their fields: Within four years of its introduction, DDT had inadvertently helped spawn a generation of flies and mosquitoes that were now immune to its deadly effects.

Early environmentalists who warned that the full effects of the use of chemicals might not be seen for years to come had long attacked pesticides. They preached caution, but their admonitions often went unheeded. With the rest of the world moving forward into the brightly lit future, why would anyone listen to rants about the dangers of pesticides? Chemicals were science's way of moving forward. Returning to organic farming, as prescribed by J. I. Rodale in his magazine *Organic Gardening and Farming* and in his book, *The Organic Front*, was considered a move backward. Rodale's resistance was counter to the spirit of progress that had long ago ushered in the domestic-science movement and had, more than half a century later, kept the country's eyes focused on an era when the lean years of the Depression would be nothing more than a cautionary tale. But Rodale wasn't alone. *Our Plundered Planet* by Fairfield Osborne had issued similar warnings about the carelessness that typified the food industry's indiscriminate use of DDT at the end of the 1940s. By the end of the next decade, however, there were signs that Rodale's and Osborne's messages were getting through. In 1959 the FDA prevented a portion of the country's cranberry crop from going to market when traces of a weed killer were discovered in less than a quarter of one percent of the industry's output. That same year, the FDA clamped down on poultry farmers for using diethylstilbestrol (DES). The drug had been used in the poultry and cattle industries as a way to plump up livestock. Essentially, DES interacted with the body chemistry of the animals and, in the case of roosters, performed a chemical castration as estrogen overrode the birds' testosterone. About the time when the Food and Drug Administration yanked DES out of the poultry industry's hands, a rumor circulated that a man who had ingested chicken necks implanted with the chemical had started to display the drug's "feminizing effects."

The public was becoming curious, and rightfully paranoid, about the potential dangers chemicals posed in their foods. If chemicals that were supposed to be helpful were turning out to be harmful, what were some of the other consequences of advances made in the name of science? Hollywood had already picked up on the growing anxiety with *Them!*, a film about car-nivorous ants that had been super-sized by exposure to radiation. Stories were making their way into the news about Eskimos whose blood had traces of fallout from atomic testing. The Eskimos had eaten caribou that had eaten mosses and lichens. The lichens were heavy in cesium-137 because of the nu-clear particles that had entered the soil from rain. *Good Housekeeping* re-ported in 1963 that the Federal Radiation Council (FRC) had claimed "there were no immediate health risks to the public from fallout," though the maga-zine opted for caution, pointing out that "radioactive contamination of food supplies has increased substantially from nuclear tests."

This was just the sort of scenario that drove Rachel Carson to write *Silent Spring*. The book was released in 1962, almost in anticipation of future de-nials like the FRC's, and in the same year the Eskimos were testing positive for high levels of cesium. Carson's book cautioned that pesticides like DDT were going to damage more than just the insects they were intended to kill. Carson wrote that the chemicals threatened to disrupt the ecosystem as they were absorbed into the soil, where they could then be soaked up by other plants, which fed wildlife, or they could contaminate water supplies as rain caused the soil to drain into nearby rivers and lakes. "To adjust to these chemicals would require time on the scale that is nature's; it would require not merely the years of a man's life but the life of generations," she wrote in *Silent Spring*. She pointed to the unknown horrors that could be unleashed from the "almost five hundred . . . new chemicals to which the bodies of men and animals are required somehow to adapt each year, chemicals totally out-side the limits of biologic experience." Cautioning that the pesticides in use "should not be called 'insecticides,' but 'biocides,' " Carson leveled a somber reminder of science's responsibility: "Only . . . one species—man—[has] acquired significant power to alter the nature of his world."

Rachel Carson's admonitions made her the recipient of threats as well as praise. She even received the highest pop-culture honor of the decade when she became a heroine and role model for Lucy in Charles Schulz's *Peanuts* comic strip. Whether people loved, hated, or feared her, one thing was cer-tain: Carson's warnings were not going unheard. In what was a bittersweet victory, news would break before the sixties ended that her fears were justi-fied: Salmon caught in Michigan were found to have traces of DDT in their systems. The FDA determined in 1969 that nearly 90 percent of edible fish in the United States contained traces of the pesticide DDT. That same year, environmental watchdogs the Sierra Club submitted testimony before the

House Merchant Marine and Fisheries Committee, charging that breast milk from nursing mothers was found to have four times the levels of DDT allowed in cow's milk. Also in 1969, mercury poisoning had caused blindness and brain damage in children who had eaten contaminated pork. (A fungicide containing mercury had been used on seeds fed to the pigs.)

With reports like these making the news, a growing number of Americans were starting to believe that they couldn't trust the safety of the food that was coming into their kitchens.

What was happening? The country had progressed to the point where most Americans had, unwanted chemicals aside, a decent diet and ample amounts of food. And the U.S. economy was so strong that citizens spent less than 20 percent of their income on food. But what did it matter how much food someone could afford to buy if there was a chance that its consumption could seriously endanger one's health? How could homemakers be certain the food they were bringing into their kitchens was safe when poisons and chemicals had been spread to every corner of the earth? With pesticides in milk and millions of fish dying from the polluted waters of the Mississippi and Hudson rivers, many Americans felt they were left with no other choice but to take matters, and their next meals, into their own hands: The term *homegrown* was about to gain a broader meaning.

The Beatles' "Get Back," released in 1969, could have been a theme song for the movement that turned its back on the so-called progress of the American Kitchen of the sixties. Even before the news media began reporting stories about the new dangers pollution and nuclear testing posed to the environment, many Americans were choosing to adopt a simpler way of eating. Gayelord Hauser's book from the previous decade, *Look Younger, Live Longer*, had already created some wheat germ and yogurt devotees, and Rodale's books and magazines were attracting similar converts. White bread was usually one of the first foods to go as the new health-conscious generation tossed out items that were bleached or processed. In fact, most "white" foods were eschewed in favor of "brown" foods. White rice, sugar, flour, and bread were out. Brown rice, brown sugar, bulgur, and whole wheat were in. In addition to choosing natural foods over foods that had been adulterated by chemicals, these neo-earth mothers and fathers were also symbolically making a statement about the bleaching of society. Michael Pollan wrote in the British press that choosing brown foods also signified that one was expressing "solidarity with the oppressed non-whites." Even the use of honey and blackstrap molasses was a political statement. As this health-food movement tried to re-turn to the earth, they sometimes displayed questionable judgment: Raw-milk products, long considered a danger because of bacteria, were suddenly favored in this new American Kitchen.

As with any trend, the purveyors of the health-food movement had plenty of detractors who were quick to question the wisdom behind their choices. The benefits of health foods were dismissed as "nutritional quackery" by *Good Housekeeping* in September 1967, while *McCall's* warned of famine if commercial growers were to switch to organic farming methods. The inabil-ity to produce large amounts of food would drive prices up, and dwindling surpluses would create a dangerous scenario. Also, adapting to a new, chemical-free way of farming would be costly. Arrowhead Mills, one of the first of the new companies to begin manufacturing whole-grain products in 1960, actually lost revenue its first seven years in business, according to Trager's *Food Chronology*. It later became a huge success through sales to health-food stores.

One sign of Arrowhead's success was the opening of the Little Bread Company in Seattle at the end of the decade. More people were making the switch to whole-grain bread products, and like-minded bakers and entrepre-neurs were there to fill their orders. Food co-ops began to sprout, often in col-lege towns. The backyard gardener and the orchard owner were both welcome to sell, or trade, their harvests. Some shops allowed healthy alter-native snacks like brownies and moon bars, baked in unregulated home kitchens, with brown sugar, honey, unrefined flour, and a variety of seeds, fruits, or nuts, to be sold. It wasn't uncommon at the end of the decade to see tents or booths operated by local co-ops at Grateful Dead shows, and the hungry throngs at the three-day mud-fest known as Woodstock were able to chow down on vegetarian fare thanks to like-minded vendors.

The health-food craze was another way for the youth of the country to distance themselves from the so-called establishment, but it wasn't long be-fore certain foods were gaining popularity and crossing over from this new culinary underground into mainstream kitchens. If sprouts and whole wheat pita pockets were a little too gritty for the average person's tastes, items like zucchini bread and Bunny Burgers were more accessible. And flavorful. Tab-bouleh, one of the signature vegetarian dishes of the sixties, became com-mon restaurant fare over the next decade. Falafel followed close after. Dishes like these from the Middle and Near East were being discovered as headlines from both the political and pop-culture worlds brought news about Israel and India into the American Kitchen. The growing visibility of religious sects like the Hare Krishna also introduced meatless alternatives into the kitchen.

Vegetarianism was becoming increasingly popular as the environmental movement morphed into the ecology movement, complete with its own flag (designed by cartoonist Ron Cobb in 1968). While battling radioactive particles was next to impossible, cleaning up the littered piles of nonbiodegradable aluminum cans was an easier way to take action for those who wanted to make a difference; aluminum cans were widely used in the sixties, and prior to wide-scale recycling they posed a new environmental problem.

The growing concern for the environment and the emphasis on organic farming, which tended to be embraced by the younger set, were more than just manifestations of adolescent rebellion in the 1960s. The idea that the earth's resources were not limitless was starting to become a reality. Several species of animals had already been hunted to extinction, or close to it, for the sake of the American Kitchen. Passenger pigeons were once so numerous that black clouds of the birds used to darken the skies for miles. Dutch explorers had written of the populous dodo birds that appeared to have a safety-in-numbers mentality as they fearlessly approached humans—a personality trait that would only quicken their demise. And herds of buffalo, though still extant, likewise had once covered the landscape of the Midwest with their shaggy forms until their presence, and appetites, got in the way of would-be ranchers. While humankind had a direct involvement in reducing the ranks of those creatures, millions of others were now being killed indirectly, like the countless fish poisoned by pollution, as a result of man's disregard for the other inhabitants of the planet. As resources were lost or contaminated, the world's population grew. The deaths of pigeons and buffalo were immediate, while at other times, as with chemicals and atomic fallout being absorbed into the food chain, the damage done to the environment through man's disregard took longer to manifest.

The picture was coming into focus, and it looked rather grim. How were Americans going to feed themselves, in such large numbers, without the aid of science? The ability to produce more food was a sign of the culture's progress: The Powhatan were able to pursue the arts because their society had mastered the procurement of food. But the side effect of the twentieth century's progress was a greatly compromised environment. This posed a new challenge: The potential situation facing the American Kitchen was that more people had to be fed with fewer resources.

The alarm was sounded in 1965 when the Freedom from Hunger Foundation declared, "There is a global food catastrophe building up on the horizon which threatens to engulf the free world and the Communist world alike." The statement, issued by the foundation's Thomas Ware, was based on the observations over the decades since World War II as Meals for Millions, Freedom from Hunger's parent organization, had come to the aid of devastated as well as developing countries to combat famine. (The organization would later become famous for distributing a soy-based substance called Multi-Purpose Food, or MPF, an "instant food" manufactured by General Mills in Minneapolis. Freedom from Hunger provided assistance to people in need who were facing starvation due to war, drought, and crop failure.)

In the following year two reports came out that supported Ware's concern. *The World Food Problem* was a hefty one-thousand-plus-page examination of the world's food supplies. Sanctioned by the President's Science Advisory Committee, the tome addressed the problems being created by the expanding population. *Famine—1975!* came out the same year but was more direct, even panicked, in its prediction that the world would not be able to meet the needs of its inhabitants. The writers, brothers William and Paul Paddock, feared that limited resources would bring about inevitable famine, forcing the United States—which had come to the aid of countries facing starvation in the past—into the horrific position of having to choose between feeding the starving citizens of one country over another.

If natural resources couldn't support the swelling population, what could? Unnatural resources? Maybe the sci fi–sounding prediction of *Food Engineering* magazine of taking the "homemaker from the kitchen and the cook out of the restaurant" wasn't as far-fetched as it first seemed, especially if overpopulation led to the depletion of environmental resources. Alternative food sources would have to be considered.

Food technology had advanced to the point where nonfood items were already in use. Nondairy "dairy" products like Pream, Coffee-Mate, and Coffee Rich were being stirred into coffee cups all over America in the early sixties, and white peaks of Cool Whip, another nondairy item, were topping dessert dishes. With nondairy products like these sitting well with customers, why not go for broke and produce a nondairy milk? In 1967, the first imitation milk hit stores in Arizona. Carrying names like Moo and Farmer's Daughter, the faux milk was actually a mix of water, corn syrup, vegetable fats, and sugars, to name a few of the ingredients. While it relied on vegetables, one attractive aspect of imitation milk, at least from a conservation standpoint, was that its production didn't require the feeding of any live-stock. (Everything about raising livestock for consumption—the inhumane treatment the animals received to the methane gas expelled by their digestive systems—would soon come under fire from vegetarian activists, animal rights activists, and conservationists.)

Artificial sweeteners like saccharin had been used previously, but now the refrigerators of dieters across the country were stacked with Diet Rite cola and Tab, two beverages flavored with cyclamates instead of sugar. Cycla-mates were sold under a variety of names and in a variety of forms. There were powdered versions, granular versions, and even a liquid for Americans to sprinkle and pour into their foods. Sucaryl was one of the more popular brands. "You can save a lot of calories by sweetening with Sucaryl—and you can't tell the difference," announced one of their ads. Sucaryl was a favorite among dieters. President Lyndon Johnson, who'd been advised by his physi-cians to drop some weight before a surgery, confessed to reporters that his beloved tapioca "[had] less calories than any other dessert . . . and [had] great advantages when it is made with skim milk and Sucaryl."

Another of the nonfoods to arrive just in time for breakfast in the Ameri-can Kitchen during the sixties was Awake, a synthetic orange juice manufac-tured by General Foods in conjunction with Birds Eye. The beverage was apparently so close to the real thing in flavor that pitchperson Carol Chan-ning duped *Green Acres* actor Eddie Arnold, with some help from Eva Ga-bor, in their rural Hooterville kitchen.

Nondairy dairy products and artificial fruit flavors alone weren't going to sustain a hungry world for very long, however, and alternative sources had to be considered. The food of the future needed to be as low-maintenance as possible, which meant it had to come from a source lower on the food chain—if it came from the food chain at all. Michael Pollan writes that "future foods" were to be devised from "soybeans . . . algae . . . and petrochemicals" with "protein [being] extracted from fuel oil and spun into 'fillet steaks.'" The recipe Pollan mentioned, as frightening in its implications as it was, was still an improvement over futurist visions that condensed similar technology and RDA requirements into a pharmaceutical-like capsule. Food pills might have met a body's nutritional needs, but they didn't deliver any satisfaction in terms of taste, texture, or even chewing!

Petrochemicals as food sources were a hot topic in the sixties, in laborato-ries as well as in pop culture. In Harry Harrison's 1969 sci-fi classic, *Make Room! Make Room!*, one of the characters suspects his margarine is made from "motor oil and whale blubber." Andy Rusch, the book's protagonist, reminds him that "there's hardly any flavor at all to the fats made from petro-chemicals, and you know there aren't any whales left so they can't use whale blubber." Rusch then assures him the margarine is made from "good chlorella oil."

Harrison's book about an overcrowded world in which starvation is a daily reality and water supplies are guarded by armed police was the blue-print for *Soylent Green*. Though cannibalism and Charlton Heston's wail of "Soylent Green is people!" were both added to the story in the screen ver-sion, Harrison's bleak view of a nation unable to feed its huddled masses was nightmarish enough.

There was an interesting link connecting Harrison's science fiction, the food futurists' vision, and the health-food movement of the 1960s: They all turned to the ocean for a versatile and easily replenished food supply. The chlorella of Harrison's book and the algae used in future food are practically one and the same. Chlorella, a freshwater form of algae, is used in a number of supplements sold by health-food stores. And kelp was adding oomph to health shakes in the American Kitchen throughout the sixties. A somewhat unattractive brown seaweed, kelp was (and still is) a natural choice for any-one seeking a storehouse of nutrients, as it contains thirty-seven minerals and elements, including amino acids, carotene, niacin, and riboflavin. While it wasn't going to show up in any of the food-group charts any time soon, kelp floated into the sixties as one of the more exotic additions to America's kitchens in an era when strange and foreign foods were in no short supply.

American taste buds loosened up considerably in the sixties, as evidenced by people's willingness to eat seaweed and kelp. They'd also come a long way compared to the suspicious attitude with which foreign cuisine had been eyed and sampled in previous decades. Americans had a taste for adventure, and travelers were jet-setting their way around the globe. The American Kitchen was becoming more worldly, and the 1960s put a few more stamps in its pass-port. Swedish fondue pots were the It cooking gadget of the sixties. An up-dated version of the chafing dish, around which diners had gathered in previous decades, the fondue pot and its long-stemmed forks gave Americans a way to dip, dunk, swirl, coat, or drown just about everything edible into sauces made from cheese, cream, wine, ketchup, and chocolate, just to name a few. There was a similar appeal to the backyard barbecue and cooking food a la fondue.

At the start of the decade some dishes had become such everyday fare as to be included in the test kitchen pamphlets food manufacturers often sent out with their products. Crisco's "Praise for the Cook!" addressed the homemaker's daily quandary when facing the question, "What's for dinner?" Crisco sympathized, saying, "the main course for any meal presents the greatest challenge to your cooking imagination and ingenuity." Their solution? "A collection of main course recipes designed to bring a wide variety of delicious dishes to your table." And by "variety," Crisco meant "international." Pledging the authenticity of each recipe, they assured cooks "Whatever you desire—be it Veal Continental, Sukiyaki or Louisiana Seafood Pie—you can imagine yourself in the locales native to these dishes." The selections from their "Around the World" section included Hawaiian Pork, Casserole Parisienne, a dish called Musaca identified as being "inspired by a [Greek] import," and two Hungarian offerings: Beef Paprikash and Goulash.

The world of international travel was sexy and intriguing. And for those Americans who couldn't steal away for a quick jaunt to Acapulco, Rio, or Paris, there were plenty of ways to create a little global excitement in their very own homes. Columbia Records would give customers a chance to enjoy an evening abroad without leaving home: A recipe for a foreign dish, along with the essential spices and special utensils needed to create an exotic meal, would be sent in a package that also contained an album of music by an artist from that country.

It was the release of the Time-Life Books international cuisine series in 1968 that proved that foreign foods were in the American Kitchen to stay. *The Cooking of Italy*, *The Cooking of China*, *The Cooking of Provincial France*, and *Latin American Cooking* were some of the titles the publishing house released. Equal part cookbooks and travel brochures, these Time-Life books gave many readers the closest thing they'd ever get to a vacation abroad.

Americans also said *hola* to Latin American and Spanish dishes in the 1960s. While gazpacho offered cooks another excuse to put their new blenders to work, paella presented more of a challenge; the aromatic dish was a knockout and became quite popular dinner-party fare. Paella and other foods of Spain, in fact, were a big draw at the World's Fair of 1964.

South America was also simpatico as far as the American Kitchen was concerned in the sixties. *Time* magazine proclaimed in 1966 that "Latin fare has leaped into prominence," adding that the Venezuelan as well as Spanish embassies were the "chic places to go" among Washington's see-and-be-seen crowd. A popular cooking club at the time, Menus by Mail, featured a recipe for Peruvian ceviche, and First Lady "Lady Bird" Johnson was seduced by *esponjoso* when she tried the caramel treat at the Venezuelan embassy.

But the cuisine that signified a haute kitchen in the 1960s was French. The French cooking craze had started in the 1950s in America, when adventurous cooks had learned that wine could transform chicken into Coq au Vin and beef into Boeuf Bourguignon. The interest in the French way of cooking was popular enough that by the end of that decade, a hardware-store owner in California by the name of Chuck Williams had added French cooking utensils and instruments to his stock to create a West Coast version of Paris's famous cookware shop, E. Dehillerin. Williams-Sonoma, as the store was christened, became a mecca for food enthusiasts. French cooking got another boost in the early sixties when the stylish young first lady, Jacqueline Kennedy, stationed French chef René Verdon in the White House kitchen. Many Americans were smitten with the Kennedys' youth and charm, and it wasn't long before fashionable hostesses adopted French cuisine as the theme for their dinner parties. But the American Kitchen would find its premiere ambassador for French cooking in an unassuming public television show host.

The viewers who tuned in to *The French Chef* on Boston's public television channel on the night of February 11, 1963, may not have realized they were witnessing a revolution, but they knew they liked what they saw. In the thirty minutes it took Julia Child to demonstrate how to prepare and cook Boeuf Bourguignon, America fell in love with her. Child was no stranger to the American Kitchen; prior to her television debut, she'd coauthored *Mastering the Art of French Cooking* with her Parisian chums Simone Beck and Louisette Bertholle. Turned down by its initial publisher, the book had taken nearly seven years to write.

Julia Child, born Julia Carolyn McWilliams, was in her early fifties when her star began to rise. A self-described "late bloomer," Child discovered her life's mission after marrying Paul Child. The couple met while she was working for the Office of Strategic Services during World War II. The two formed an almost immediate partnership, though Paul's love of gourmet cooking presented a challenge for the unskilled Julia. When their jobs took them to France, Julia enrolled in the celebrated Le Cordon Bleu cooking school. The methodical instruction helped the novice cook learn her way around the kitchen, while her marriage to a gourmand allowed the husband and wife to explore recipes together. But when it came to the actual preparation of the meals, it was clear early on that Julia was in charge. Paul wrote to his brother, Charlie, that "she stands there [in the kitchen] surrounded by a battery of instruments with an air of authority and confidence." That confidence grew as Julia continued her studies and befriended chef Max Bugnard. Bugnard, who had studied under the legendary French chef Escoffier, would routinely browse the markets and butcher shops of Paris with Julia. These shopping trips reinforced her love and respect for the French way of cooking. This love was magnified again years later when she returned to the States, only to be frustrated to find that fresh herbs were in short supply.

The lack of herbs and ingredients like crème fraîche weren't the only things missing from the American Kitchen, Julia thought, according to her biographer Noël Riley Fitch. In her book *Appetite for Life*, Fitch notes that "Julia was astonished to learn how many Americans were letting Swanson do their cooking and eating on tin trays in front of the television." Fitch adds, "The country had turned to prepackaged quiz shows and prepackaged foods." But if Julia saw the television as an enemy of cooking in America, she would soon find a way to make the medium work to her advantage. Within three years of going on the air, Julia Child would become the first public television personality to win an Emmy Award.

Her influence on the American Kitchen of the 1960s was evident in dollars. Not only was her first book the number one cookbook in America in 1966, but *Time* magazine reported that same year that Julia's influence was such that any time she used a specific utensil or piece of kitchen equipment, brisk sales of that item would deplete store stocks. French chef knives, copper beating bowls, fish poachers, and wire whisks went flying off the shelves in Chicago, Pittsburgh, and New York City. "Let Julia Child so much as mention vanilla wafers, and the shelves are empty overnight," observed *Time*.

Julia Child tapped into the American DIY spirit at a time when can openers were being used more than measuring cups in the American Kitchen. By taking what was considered to be the loftiest of cuisines and breaking it down into manageable steps, she inspired millions to follow her can-do ethic. This was no small accomplishment. When Julia first began writing her cookbook, the consensus was that "Americans disdain[ed] home cooking," an outdated practice "which was being pushed aside by time-saving shortcuts," writes Fitch. According to *Appetite for Life*, Child's original publisher leafed through the recipes intended for *Mastering the Art of French Cooking* and told her "Americans don't want to cook like that; they want something quickly made with a mix."

Child had begun to understand the challenge facing her. In a letter to her coauthor, Simone Beck, she wrote that average American cooks "are not used to taking the time and care we are used to taking in preparing things . . . We shall have to emphasize in our introduction that LOVE is one of the big ingredients . . . and that the taste of food (not its looks, ease of preparation, etc.) is what you are striving for, and why some shortcuts won't work."

This awareness informed her on-camera approach. When viewers saw her dropping food, wrestling with a suckling pig, or trying to mold noncompliant ingredients with her hands they knew they had found someone to whom they could relate. Speculation was that "a sizeable portion of her following are people who wouldn't know a truffle from a toadstool," or at least that's what the editors of *Life* magazine believed when they featured Julia in their October 1966 issue. Yet part of her appeal to that crowd was the way she demystified French cuisine. "You can't turn a sow's ear into veal Orloff," she told *Time* in 1966, "but you can do something very good with a sow's ear."

After Julia won her Emmy, *The French Chef* went off the air, as its star preferred to wait until public television could afford to shoot in color. "I'm tired of gray food," she said. But Americans weren't tired of her. Her show was running on 104 public television stations when she announced her intended hiatus. Left with no other choice, these stations were forced to air reruns to satisfy Julia's fans (as were the additional outlets clamoring to add *The French Chef* to their lineups).

Julia Child might not have started the gourmet revolution in the 1960s, but she did wage war against culinary complacency, and especially prepackaged meals. She also helped show American cooks that French cooking and the preparation of haute cuisine needn't be a struggle. And apparently they were ready to follow her lead. Enrollments at cooking schools across the country were over capacity; supermarkets had to adjust their inventory to meet customers' demands. Said Ed Kiatta, the manager of a grocery store in Washington, D.C., at the time: "Today if you don't have at least fifty assorted, high-powered imported cheeses, you're not in business." More stores were starting to give the people what they wanted. As *Time* reported, supermarkets began to "carry more than 100 items" in their herbs and spices section. "Old stand-bys" like sage were "displaced as too strong, by such postwar newcomers as fresh tarragon, fennel, thyme, dill and coriander," the magazine said.

Julia Child initiated many Americans into more than just French cooking, however: She helped Americans realize that when the preparation of a meal wasn't rushed, the subtleties of culinary artistry could be appreciated. Furthermore, the nature of her marriage to Paul allowed couples to see that time spent together in the kitchen could be an enjoyable and fulfilling manifestation of their partnership. Maybe the kitchen wasn't such a bad place to be, after all.

The state of American cooking prior to the debut of *The French Chef* was more mechanized than ever, from the technology that helped package and process the foods to the kitchen appliances used to heat them. The preparation of these meals might not have required cookbooks, but they were responsible for launching a spate of fad diets, and those diets in turn inspired a slew of cookbooks and motivational guides for living a healthier lifestyle. The rush to put dinner on the table via frozen and prepackaged meals had an unwanted and possibly unforeseen side effect: Consumers might have saved a few minutes when they opted for a TV dinner instead of a home-cooked meal made with fresh produce, but while they were gaining more leisure time they were also gaining more weight during the sixties. As Fitch described the era in Julia Child's biography, "Processed food products and junk food led to unwanted poundage, which in turn stirred up a wave of dieting and diet books."

It seemed that at one point or another in the 1960s, everyone in America was dieting, or at least talking about dieting. When President Lyndon Johnson's doctors publicized their desire that he lose weight, reporters weren't above asking the leader of the free world if indeed he was following their orders. But undoubtedly the world's most famous dieter of the decade wasn't someone so accustomed to the attention from the media; she was just a determined woman from Queens, New York.

Jean Nidetch was the type of American woman who was supposed to benefit most from the advances in food technology and the streamlining of work in the American Kitchen. Unfortunately, those breakthroughs seemed to pay off in extra pounds for Nidetch. In 1963, weighing approximately 210 pounds, Nidetch went to a free clinic on dieting that was being sponsored by the New York City Board of Health. The program was structured for those individuals considered to be "critically obese." Nidetch found that she wasn't alone. Other women just like her, unhappy with their weight, had sought out the clinic's program, where they were given a prescriptive "meal plan for ladies" that had been written by a physician. The diet helped her lose eighty pounds, but did nothing for her morale. Jean Nidetch noticed that it was easier to keep off the weight and adhere to the diet when she could share her struggles and setbacks, as well as her successes, with other dieters. Inspired by the camaraderie that was established between her and her overweight friends when they gathered to talk about their dieting experiences, Jean began inviting others into her home. Realizing that dieters were reaching and maintaining their goal weights with the help of the support group, Nidetch decided to go public with her idea. After speaking in private homes around New York for a few months, the first official meeting of Weight Watchers was held in Queens. Four hundred individuals showed up, based on word of mouth alone.

Jean Nidetch's method helped people lose weight and keep it off, and the news of her success started to spread. In 1966 a Detroit woman by the name of Florine Mark became the first person to open a Weight Watchers franchise when simple logistics made it impossible for her to attend weekly meetings in New York. Under Nidetch's tutelage, Mark re-created the formula that had helped growing numbers of people reach their ideal weights. Two years later, in 1968, *The Weight Watchers Cookbook* would be on the best-seller list, along with *Better Homes and Gardens Eat and Stay Slim Cookbook* and *The Doctor's Quick Weight Loss Diet* book.

That three diet-related books held positions in the top ten best sellers of 1968 is very revealing about how Americans were looking at food—and at themselves. Research had already shown that too much of a good thing—in this case the abundance of food most Americans now had access to—could be a very bad thing indeed. Overeating and being overweight could lead to heart disease and diabetes, not to mention other health problems. In 1969, after a decade of increased dieting and in light of a growing national preoccupation with weight, Metropolitan Life—those same killjoys who'd published the controversial chart of ideal weights for adults that had them avoiding their bathroom scales during the 1950s—hit the airwaves with a Clio Award–winning commercial that was equally distressing. Set in a cemetery, the spot featured a procession of waiters and waitresses, butlers, maids, deli proprietors, and other food vendors advancing toward a fresh grave. The chilling voice-over warned viewers that "Someday all that beautiful food you put away could put you away. For good. Because too much food leads to fat, and too much fat can lead to heart disease and strokes and diabetes and high blood pressure. So if you'd like to live a little longer, eat a little less. It's a good life. Take care of it."

How did this happen? Americans now had access to healthy foods and plenty of convenient ways to prepare them. They also had more money and, in most cases, more time. But Americans weren't spending their extra time in the kitchen or engaged in physical activity. Many Americans were squandering their leisure time in front of the television, where, interestingly enough, they saw commercials cautioning them of the dangers of an unhealthy diet and a sedentary life. Unfortunately, from that same vantage point they also saw a lot of advertisements for the very foods that were ruining their health.

A study done by the U.S. Department of Agriculture in 1965 showed that the diets of Americans were already starting to slip in nutritional value from the postwar high of 1955. There was an increase in the quantity of food that was available and being consumed, but the quality of meals coming out of the American Kitchen had taken a significant turn for the worse. Americans were getting plenty of calories, as evidenced by the popularity of the controversial diet book *Calories Don't Count*, by Herman Taller. Taller advocated a diet high in fat, high in protein, and low in carbs. Taller's prescription wasn't new; diet gurus had been urging a reduction in carbohydrate consumption for decades. (Alfred Pennington and William Banting were two early proponents of the low-carb diet.) Unfortunately for Taller, his message got lost in a fraud scandal that had nothing to do with carbohydrate intake. Along with his eating guide, he also pushed a safflower capsule that he assured dieters would hasten their weight loss by stripping their body fat. He was convicted when his claims couldn't be proven. Taller's manual was followed by the above-mentioned *Doctor's Quick Weight Loss Diet*, written by Dr. Irvin Stillman. Stillman's book was released in 1967, the same year of Taller's arrest and six years after Taller's book first hit stores, and it likewise urged Americans to cut back on starchy carbohydrates. Foods with high carbohydrate counts were often high in calories. And this was something that the diets of poor and wealthy Americans were beginning to share. The USDA's 1965 study showed a rise in poor nutrition in American households, an increase of 6 percent, up from 15 percent in 1955 to 21 percent in 1965. The problem was that Americans were eating too much of the wrong kinds of food. Not only were these foods high in calories, they were low in the RDA's essential nutrients. In addressing this problem in his landmark book *Nutrition Scoreboard*, Michael F. Jacobson writes, "Millions of Americans suffer another kind of malnutrition: too rich a diet . . . which leads to obesity."

It has been said that the 1960s began America's battle with the bulge. *Men's Fitness* has called the 1950s "the last decade during which [the United States] still [wasn't] an obese nation." The access and abundance that had characterized the postwar American Kitchen and its food supply was shaping the future of American society, sending it right into super-sized territory, both in terms of serving portions and physical proportions.

Thus, millions of Americans had their eyes on their scales in the 1960s. And in a very popular commercial late in the decade, Diet Pepsi made a point of reminding—practically warning—American women that millions of American men had their eyes on them. The soft drink company admonished women that the United States was "a nation of sight-seers" as men craned and bent and stretched and swerved to ogle every woman who passed them by in the ad. If a girl wanted to be "the kind of girl girl-watchers watch," then drinking Diet Pepsi needed to be an essential part of her diet regimen. In the final shot, a slim, attractive girl walked past the White House, and the silhouette of a man appeared in one of the windows and eyed her as she passed by. Several Men-in-Black types outside followed suit. (So much for national security!) Messages like this weren't helping women in their cause to pass legislation like the Federal Equal Pay Act (advertised by a commercial that featured Batgirl demanding that "same job, same employer . . . means equal pay for men and women"), and they weren't helping to send women a healthy message about their bodies. Preoccupations with weight, measurements, and body image were common enough to be pop-culture fodder. Magazine spreads and runways were full of stick-thin young women. The wispy British model Penelope Tree admitted that her ultra-thin figure was the by-product of her anorexic condition, while the popularity of her compatriot, Twiggy, made American girls believe that there was no such thing as too thin. In comparison to the ample curves of fifties pinup girls like Marilyn Monroe, the hype and fuss over the slender lines of Twiggy and Tree served as validation for young girls who were far from voluptuous. "Thank you, thank you, thank you!" effused a letter to the editors of *Time* from nineteen-year-old Monica Cloutier in 1966 after the magazine printed a feature on Twiggy. "[H]aving always been shaped like a board, I now have the satisfaction of knowing that I'm not alone in my malady. If Twiggy can do it, perhaps there is still some chance for me," the young Ms. Cloutier concluded.

Thin was in, but women weren't the only ones who were getting this message. Metrecal, a ready-to-mix powdered "meal" popular with dieters, was advertised by a TV commercial in which fit men and women cavorted on a yacht in revealing swimwear by day, yet feasted on sumptuous, rich meals by night. "How can they eat a meal like this?" the voice-over asked. The answer was, by not eating anything else solid the rest of the day. "Drinking one for breakfast and one for lunch" would "help keep you sleek as a seal," the campaign promised. The powder mix soon had a prepared, single-serving can for the "Metrecal for lunch bunch" to help them keep off the weight. The appeal of a ready-to-drink meal in a can held a powerful appeal for Americans since it was "convenience food" and "diet food" all in one: Within two years of its introduction, Metrecal was raking in sales of $350 million.

Metrecal, and the other diet foods that made their way into the American Kitchen in the 1960s (especially diet colas), owed a good deal of their success to the increasingly powerful instant image-maker—TV. Nearly every house in America had at least one television set, and advertisers had a rapt audience. The middle class continued to grow and become more affluent. More of the hallmarks of the proverbial good life—better home, better car, better clothes, even a better body—were within the financial means of a larger segment of the population. Television commercials as well as TV shows gave Americans a preview of life as it could be lived.

The reflection of the American diet and American Kitchen in the television screen of the sixties was a mirror of what was happening culturally in the country, to a lesser or greater degree, depending on the circumstances being viewed. In the case of the growing visibility of African Americans in the United States, television shows finally began depicting blacks in starring roles. *Julia*, starring Diahann Carroll, was a weekly sitcom devoted to the life of a widowed nurse who just happened to be African American. NBC began airing the program in September 1968, four years after the Civil Rights Act was signed, promising constitutional protection from employment discrimination "based on race, color, religion, sex or national origin," and five months after the assassination of civil rights leader Dr. Martin Luther King Jr.

The arrival of a show starring a black woman playing a professional, in prime time, on a major network, was late in coming but was evidence of the dissolution of segregation in America. With issues of race on the nightly news and in the morning newspapers, the food community began to acknowledge the influences of African Americans on the American Kitchen.

New York Times food columnist Craig Claiborne penned an essay in the November 3, 1968, issue of the paper titled "Cooking with Soul." Claiborne's power as a food writer and cookbook author was evident in the number of white food-fiends who began prowling through black neighborhoods looking for restaurants where they could order authentic soul food. These newbies often found themselves competing for table space with the "displaced Southerners," and Claiborne was empathetic, being Mississippi-born himself. So intent on finding the real thing were these "soul-food devotees," as Claiborne called them, that complaints arose "that the food in most soul-food restaurants is more Southern than soul. The menus [of these restaurants] mostly feature such typical Southern dishes as fried chicken, spareribs, candied yams and mustard or collard greens. One rarely finds trotters, neck-bones, pigs' tails and chitterlings."

An article in *Time* magazine the following year titled "Eating Like Soul Brothers" called out the poseurs among the black-eyed peas and hog maws: "Today, as 200 years ago, the true 'stone soul' dish is chitterlings, pronounced 'chitlins.'" As Doris Witt noted in *Black Hunger: Food and the Politics of U.S. Identity*, "The elided syllable evidently distinguished genuine 'insiders' to black culture from less sedulous fellow travelers." Witt's comment points to the ownership that some whites were starting to claim over a type of food that, there's little way of ignoring, developed because of the poor food rations given to slaves by their white owners; in the politically charged sixties, attempts to assuage white guilt took many forms.

But what Claiborne called Southern cooking still owes an enormous debt to African Americans, especially since yams were a vegetable indigenous to the African continent. The arrival of foods like yams and watermelon to North America is filled with tales of slaves storing seeds in their hair and ears as they made the crossing to North America. But as John T. Edge, director of the Southern Foodways Alliance, points out, this is an incredible notion: "You are captured and the last thing you think about is grabbing a few okra seeds and stowing them away in your ears?" he asks rhetorically, and incredulously. Edge points out the harsh reality of the slave traders' mind-set, which included provisions, as meager as they were, on the boats for their captives. "If you were looking upon your captured human as a resource, and you think enough to provision them with foods they were accustomed to for the passage, then you would think enough to stow away seeds for when they land," he suggests.

The influence of soul food on what is considered Southern cooking is inescapable, not only because of the types of foods—okra, sesame, and yams—but also because of the way they were prepared. "Because so many blacks were in Southern kitchens, what we think of today as Southern foods were originally black people's food," says Barbara Haber, author of *From*

Hardtack to Homefries. Even barbecue has been attributed to African Americans. In his book *Southern Food*, John Egerton calls it "a cultural gift from black men."

The fact that the foods of black America were even being discussed in the 1960s was progress. The American Kitchen had acknowledged and welcomed foods from other cultures through its doors, but the acceptance of so-called soul food had been slow in coming. The migration of blacks from the South into the more industrialized cities of the North during the war years had spread the formerly regional cooking of African Americans into other parts of the country.

Of course, the overt images of African Americans in the culture of the American Kitchen were often limited to bottles of Aunt Jemima pancake syrup or the blackface canisters and salt and pepper shakers that had been popular prior to the civil rights movement. So while the acceptance of soul food as a contributing cuisine to the American menu wasn't about to end racism as the sixties ended, as with other instances of cultural integration, it started to promote appreciation and understanding.

As the 1960s came to a close, the fallout from the decade's events lingered everywhere, especially in the American Kitchen itself. Despite their differences, people wanted to be near one another. The kitchen was becoming the only room in the house where the paths of the increasingly busy family ever crossed. Pass-through spaces between the kitchen and the dining room became larger, with shutters or folding doors that were now being left open more than they were closed. The kitchen began to expand, slowly, into the rooms adjoining it as some brave souls removed whole walls. With the family unit threatened, barriers of any sort were too risky to leave in place.

As the American Kitchen became more visible from the rest of the house, its makeover continued. Appliances were getting dipped in fashionable colors and Whirlpool was "edging" its dishwashers in "decorator colors"; "avocado, sapphire blue, fawn and copper" were appearing alongside the ever-popular white. Radar love was in the air as the flashy Amana Radarange debuted in the homes of the lucky few who could afford the new microwave oven. The idea of the beautified, upgraded kitchen came with less of the gee-whiz element of the forties and fifties, and with more of a sense of entitlement and control for the homemaker. With television showing Americans all the wonders that science and technology could bring them, even cartoon kitchens reflected the emphasis on civilized domesticity, from the prehistoric spray faucet (an elephant) and garbage disposal (a small dinosaur) of *The Flintstones* to the pancake-emitting machine and food pill of *The Jetsons*.

If the microwave was the white-hot—yet costly—appliance at the end of the sixties, the deep freezer was the coolest. The purchase of large, refrigerator-sized units to be used exclusively for freezing was becoming so popular that cookbooks were adding specific recipes for meals that could be frozen and eaten later. The makers of these freezers promoted them as yet another convenience making housework easier for the harried modern woman.

Women began looking for more satisfying lives outside the walls of their kitchens during the 1960s, and what they were looking for didn't always have to do with employment. *Hints from Heloise* might have been scintillating reading for some women, but *Sex and the Single Girl* by Helen Gurley Brown became a best seller because of its frank attitude toward that formerly whispered question about what a girl wants. Attitudes toward sex were changing. Annette's bikini gave way to Peggy Moffatt's topless bathing suit, which was in turn replaced by the total full-frontal au naturel look in the musical *Hair* (which, by the way, contained its own ode to the glories of soul food).

Gender roles for men continued to change, albeit slowly, but attitudes toward a man in the kitchen had altered enough that *Time* magazine featured a spread with photos of Vice President Hubert Humphrey, St. Louis Cardinals' Vice President William Bidwill, and actor Burgess Meredith all showing that they knew the difference between a saucepan and a soufflé pan.

Americans were reminded of their differences in the sixties, and even food preferences could spark debate. As the seventies were about to begin, many Americans were realizing that the nation needed to come back together. And the American Kitchen seemed as good a place as any to start.

CHAPTER EIGHT

Salad Days: 1970–1979

Michael F. Jacobson's Nutrition Scoreboard *held a mirror, and a scale, up to the American diet, and warned the country's citizens, "You are what you eat." (Courtesy of Center for Science in the Public Interest.)*

When the 1970s began, Americans didn't need the proverbial revolution to be televised. It had been unfolding in front of their eyes, playing out right in their very own kitchens, for nearly a decade. The counterculture of the 1960s moved from the social fringe into the mainstream. Food became more politicized in the seventies, as did domestic duties, and America's kitchens were the stumping grounds. The anxiety over the healthfulness of the foods Americans were eating became a point of activism for the newly formed Center for Science in the Public Interest (CSPI), just as those concerns became the catalyst for a lifestyle choice for the growing number of Americans who favored organic and vegetarian foods in the kitchen.

New standards for food labeling were introduced, and government-sponsored studies were published showing the ill effects of the American diet upon the health of the nation. The number of obese Americans escalated sharply beginning in 1976, while the overall percentage of overweight

Americans increased only slightly. That same year marked the first time Americans purchased more soft drinks than milk.

Processed foods, like soft drinks, were in abundant supply in the seventies. The food-technology industry had developed new packaging and preserving methods aimed to improve the quality of American life, even if they didn't always enhance the quality or flavor of food. With a sluggish economy forcing both parents out of the house and into the workforce, time, rather than taste, became a determining factor for some families when considering what to have for dinner in the 1970s. There were plenty of new prepared foods in grocery stores to help frazzled moms and dads put meals on the table in a fraction of the time required to cook meals from scratch. Frozen dinners were piled high in family freezers, as that must-have vanity appliance of the sixties became the can't-live-without necessity of the seventies. TV dinners had come a long way since their aluminum-tray inception, and new, "oven-able" paper and ovenproof plastic trays were developed, lowering the cost of packaging frozen entrées in thin metal compartments. When it came to prepackaged and instant meals, food manufacturers started to think outside the box; ready-to-eat as well as just-add-water meals were now coming in bags and cups.

Food manufacturers also gave busy homemakers time-saving products like Hamburger Helper and Hunt's Manwich. These products stretched dollars as well as ingredients at a time when the economic outlook was less than bright.

The American family was feeling the pinch of time and money in the seventies in a way they hadn't since the thirties and forties. The nation wanted to forget about its troubles, and more families found themselves congregating in the kitchen, as mealtime seemed to be one of the only occasions when all family members were present. The great room concept of the blended TV room/dining room/kitchen was in its formative stages in the seventies, but signs of its inevitability were everywhere. On TV, *The Brady Bunch*, *The Odd Couple*, and *The Mary Tyler Moore Show* all featured kitchens that had shuttered pass-throughs that were left open so that family members could interact with one another without barriers, regardless of which room they were in. The "fire" of the kitchen stove was becoming more like the old hearth that family and friends had gathered around centuries earlier.

The political and social turmoil that had shaken the American population in the sixties had spilled into the seventies, and now the looming political and economic uncertainty of the new decade was leaving people feeling even more disillusioned. When the economy began to slide, the climate darkened further. *Inflation* became the buzzword, and not only in the United States. Around the world prices were soaring, spirits were falling, and the economic outlook seemed grim. Optimism was in short supply at the beginning of the decade, with the country at war and the generations battling on the home front. The future as envisioned in the fifties and sixties wasn't materializing; in fact, the forecast projected by the book *Let Them Eat Promises: The Politics of Hunger in America,* by Nick Kotz, appeared particularly bleak. The book, published in 1969, investigated the problem of hunger and starvation in the United States and came up with some surprising figures. Kotz's Pulitzer Prize–winning report showed that, coming on the heels of one of the country's most dramatic growth spurts, there were more than a million Americans who didn't have enough money to pay for food stamps, let alone put meals on their families' tables. The concern raised by Kotz's book was one that senators Robert Kennedy and Joseph Clark had previously helped to publicize in 1967, when they'd visited poor families in the Mississippi Delta region. But things hadn't improved since then.

The plight of the impoverished in America was being ignored by the very institutions and programs the U.S. government had created to address their needs. In 1970, a year after Kotz published *Let Them Eat Promises,* a report by the Consumers Union pointed to an unsettling disparity in eligibility factors, as determined by each state. Scores of needy Americans, living below the poverty line, were not receiving food stamps because the states in which they lived did not recognize their financial situations as being particularly dire. By the mid-seventies, Congress had established a minimum and uniform eligibility requirement for food-stamp assistance, and every county in every state participated. By 1977, recipients no longer had to purchase stamps.

The lean years and troubled assistance programs made government economic advisors, as well as food companies and their advertisers, nervous. Still, their anxiety could not match that of the average American family.

Advertisers began positioning themselves as sympathetic to homemakers' concerns about the economy and rising food costs. An ad for Campbell's soup tapped into this nervousness by using the parlance of the times. Above a photo showing three cans of Campbell's soup, including Chicken with Rice, Chicken Noodle, and Chicken and Stars, a headline advised BEAT IN-FLATION. PUT YOUR MONEY IN TWO CHICKEN STOCKS. Underneath the photo, a tag line read "for about 7 cents a share." Budget-stretching ideas dominated food ads. Makers of Minute Rice, for instance, suggested that mothers could make meals go further by adding a cup of cooked rice to a can of vegetable soup; it was the one-pot meal, 1970s-style.

The growing apprehension in the country was palpable. In 1970, the United States' already shaky stock market plummeted to its lowest point in eight years. Things were bad: The U.S. Consumer Price Index rose 8.8 percent between 1972 and 1973, and then jumped up an additional 12.2 percent by 1974. Food prices continued to climb. A loaf of white bread, which had cost fewer than 20 cents at the beginning of the decade, now cost a family 34.5 cents on average; the cost of a pound of rice rose from 26 cents to 44 cents per pound; and a pound of sugar nearly doubled in price. By 1976, the federal government was looking for additional options to help needy families stock their kitchens, and a grant was given to John Van Hengel of Phoenix, Arizona, to duplicate his successful food-bank formula in cities across the country. Van Hengel had created the St. Mary's Food Bank, the first food bank in America, in 1967. Van Hengel actualized his vision of helping the hungry by collecting foods that local businesses such as restaurants, bakeries, and grocery stores were about to throw out. In a donated warehouse space, Van Hengel was able to set up a distribution center. Word of his success led to the formation of food banks across the country, and it was only a matter of time before the government took notice.

Despite such efforts, in the early half of the seventies the scene from the American Kitchen was bleak, and things were about to get worse. The collective of oil producing countries, known as OPEC, placed an embargo against the United States, Japan, and several countries in Eastern Europe in 1973. Their motive was to voice their discontent with the pro-Israel stance taken by these nations over the turmoil in the Middle East. As a result, gas and oil prices skyrocketed, and an energy crisis was born.

The cost of putting food on the table was already frighteningly high, but now Americans were facing another threat in their kitchens: The energy crisis made the prospect of feeding a family even more costly. Gas and oil fueled the distribution of foods across the country, and shipping costs were reflected in rising grocery bills.

The American palate had become accustomed to new, adventurous tastes in the two decades prior to the seventies, but the country's current economic situation was making it difficult for many Americans to continue eating in the ways to which they had grown accustomed. As author Greg Critser writes in his book *Fat Land: How Americans Became the Fattest People in the World*, the high price of foods, coupled with the sudden dearth of certain grocery store staples, led Lester R. Brown of the Overseas Development Council to observe, "Like it or not, Americans are sharing food scarcity with Russia." For decades the United States had prided itself on having a diet superior to that in the Soviet Union, and as a *Life* magazine spread from the 1950s boasted, unlike the Russians, Americans could eat steak as often as they liked. In 1971, beef consumption in America hit a staggering 113 pounds of beef per capita, up almost 20 percent from 1960, and nearly twice as much as would be consumed twenty years later, in the early 1990s. It wasn't long before the consequences of that old enemy of the consumer—supply and demand—hit the American Kitchen. A beef shortage, precipitated by a corn fungus that hit feed supplies in 1972, caused meat prices to soar. The slowing economy made it harder for the average family to fit beef into their budget. Clearly this was a problem for Americans because beef was not only a dietary staple, but for those who remembered the rationing during World War II, its availability was a source of national pride. Food technologists had to start finding ways to give customers more budget-stretchers, and products like Hunt's Manwich Sloppy Joe mix, with the tag line "A sandwich is a sandwich but a Manwich is a meal," started to appear. It wasn't long before General Mills followed suit with an economical solution of its own: Hamburger Helper.

Hamburger Helper was introduced at the perfect time. Financially strapped families who were having trouble with their food budgets could now stretch one pound of hamburger into a meal that could easily feed a family of five.

In the positioning of Hamburger Helper to the general public, Madison Avenue capitalized on a number of issues weighing heavily on the American Kitchen of the early 1970s. Hamburger Helper was quickly prepared, an asset in busy households in which both parents worked; an added bonus was that its preparation didn't require the dirtying of numerous pots and pans. A deep saucepan, a measuring cup, and a spatula were all that was required to take the meal from the stove to the table. For any homemaker feeling the pinch of inflation, Hamburger Helper was relatively cheap. It was also something of a novelty at a time when Americans, though they might have come to expect "instant" foods, were still fascinated by the ways in which technology was changing their eating habits.

General Mills had found a way for Americans to continue their love affair with beef, despite rising costs that could have made struggling families look for alternatives. Furthermore, Hamburger Helper allowed all Americans to participate, even if only in a freeze-dried way, in the ethnic food fad that had begun sweeping the country in the sixties. A number of different flavors were introduced to grocery stores that were meant to resemble Italian and south-of-the-border cuisines.

Hamburger Helper's success led General Mills to roll out boxes of Tuna Helper barely two years after the hamburger variety's debut. Canned tuna was comparatively inexpensive at the time, and Tuna Helper became another way to stretch a household's budget.

Of all the company's marketing maneuvers that relied on the Helping Hand, General Mills' shrewdest move was the placement of a clock on the "face" of their product's mascot. This further emphasized the quick-fix nature of the product, a message that was well received by busy American home-makers in the seventies. The ready-in-minutes aspect of the meal helped families who were juggling hectic schedules to hold on to the notion that they were still sitting down to dinner as a cohesive family unit. Making it all the more attractive was that it was a dish either parent could easily prepare.

In 1970 the United States Census reported that for the first time in history, women outnumbered men. A quick survey of pop culture at the time could lead some to argue that maybe Tom Wolfe should have christened the seventies the "She Decade" instead of the "Me Decade." Groups like the National Organization of Women and political issues like the Equal Rights Amendment had galvanized women in the sixties, and by the seventies women were on the move politically, socially, and economically. A record number of women entered the work force between 1960 and 1970, increasing the number of women employed outside the home from 45 percent to 60 percent in ten years. With all these women stepping out of their homes and into careers, advertisers, marketers, manufacturers, designers, and television programmers had to keep pace with the demands of the new feminist attitude.

The kitchen was definitely viewed as one battleground in what would become the war between the sexes. Women had been determined to break free from this domain for decades, and as Terrence Uber and Shirley Wajda both suggested, the changing role of women helped create the new look that was sweeping through the American Kitchen.

"It used to be that the kitchen was like a scullery, a work closet," adds Joan Kohn, host of HGTV's *Kitchen Design*. And for the newly liberated female, being stuck anywhere—let alone a closet of any type—was undesirable.

Freedom from the kitchen was an idea that advertisers worked hard to spread, sometimes with mixed results. There was a strong contrast between the 1965 ad for Pillsbury's "Busy Lady Bake-Off," which featured a woman in an apron wearing kitchen whites and hovering over her stove, and the young mom in tennis whites who appeared in a 1976 ad for Stouffer's Green Pepper Steak and Chicken Stuffed Shells frozen entrées. A headline declared, THE JOY OF NOT COOKING, above the photo of the young mother on the tennis court, as she was clearly in no hurry to get back to her kitchen. She could now feed her family with a convenient Stouffer frozen entrée that could be heated and served in minutes.

Advertisers weren't the only ones picking up on the kitchen exodus. Television shows were depicting a different kind of American Kitchen than the ones kept by Harriet Nelson and June Cleaver, or even Samantha Stevens. Women were no longer presented as domestic goddesses, as evidenced by Mary Richards's culinary undertakings on *The Mary Tyler Moore Show*. (One classic episode centered on Mary's attempts at serving Veal Saint Olaf to her dinner guests; the evening was marked by one faux pas after another.)

Just as women were proving they could make their way in the world outside the kitchen, men were learning that they could take care of themselves in the American Kitchen. The idea of a man cooking for himself had become increasingly acceptable ever since the gold rush era, when the western United States was populated by single men, all seeking their fortunes in the hills of California. But a man cooking for his family? That was a notion still hampered by the idea that the kitchen was a woman's world. But with the changing roles and additional sharing of responsibilities that the tough times of the seventies required, more men were tying those apron strings around their own waists and turning up the flames inside the house as well as at barbecues. Television audiences of the sixties had no trouble accepting Bub O'Casey, and then Uncle Charley, as the chief cook and bottle-washer on *My Three Sons*. Aside from the fact that the death of Steve Douglas's wife left the home without a woman to assume those duties, Charley's galley stint in the military had given him plenty of experience in running a kitchen. The gourmet kitchen run by Felix Unger in the apartment he shared with Oscar Madison on *The Odd Couple* was also considered acceptable: Both men had been married, after all, and still lamented their lost loves. It was ABC's *Three's Company* that finally challenged the portrayal of traditional roles in a nontraditional home during unconventional times. Debuting in 1977, *Three's Company* easily slipped into the groove of the decade as it followed the high jinks of three sexy young singles who shared an apartment in sunny California. The twist in the show's storyline was that two of the roommates were working women who couldn't cook their way out of a box of Stove Top stuffing. Jack Tripper, the male roommate, handled the cooking duties ably and willingly. A man freely engaged in workings of the American Kitchen was still considered suspicious by some members of the public as more conventions were challenged and the seventies rolled on. But as *Time* magazine stated in 1977, "The feminist movement has helped open minds and kitchens to the notion that men can be at home on the range," and increasing numbers of men began commandeering the ranges in their homes.

With both parents being pushed out the door and into the workplace in the seventies, homemakers looked for ways to maximize their family time and minimize their cooking time. Products like Hamburger Helper and Stouffer's frozen entrées catered to tight schedules as well as tight budgets, but a slew of new countertop gizmos and gadgets also came to the cook's aid in the kitchen during the 1970s. Mr. Coffee invented a drip coffeemaker for the home, while Cuisinart crafted a small food processor that sat easily on the counter. The Cuisinart processor, fashioned after the French Magimix by Robot Coupe long used by Julia Child, would transform Americans from gourmands into "foodies" by the decade's end. In-the-know cooks credited Cuisinart with stirring up "the new French revolution." La Machine was another popular food processor that shared its ancestry with the Magimix.

Americans were smitten with the novelty of cooking appliances that were not only portable, but which whirred, stirred, sizzled, and sliced. Two of the *Better Homes and Gardens* cookbooks, *Fondue and Tabletop Cooking* and the *Blender Cook Book*, became best sellers as a result of this trend. But the most popular and seventies-significant debut in the American Kitchen in the first half of the decade, at least as far as working families were concerned, came from Rival in the form of their Crock-Pot.

Rival didn't invent the Crock-Pot; in fact, they bought the rights to a pre-existing electric slow cooker called the Beanery in 1970. The Beanery was a ceramic pot that was used to slow-cook its namesake—sort of a twentieth-century version of the Puritans' long-simmering bean pot. When the technicians at Rival began to modernize the idea behind the Beanery, they formulated a new double-wrap system of heat-bearing coils to encase the barrel, which in turn enabled the food inside to be cooked more evenly, and more slowly, for hours at a time. In 1971, Rival unveiled the revamped slow-cooker and christened it the Crock-Pot. It was an instant success. Homemakers liked the convenience of the one-pot meal, and the Crock-Pot's timer gave them new flexibility with their menu-planning, not to mention their workday. Once the pot was filled with the meal's ingredients and its timer was set, folks could head off to work for the day confident that their dinner would be perfectly and safely cooked by the time they returned home. Rival even capitalized on the appeal the Crock-Pot had for families with hurried lifestyles. One popular slogan used by the company to advertise their product said it all: "Cooks all day while the cook's away!"

Another advantage of having a slow cooker managing the kitchen duties in the seventies was that for most families, the parents were not the first ones to arrive home at the end of the day. The children were; a whole generation of latchkey kids was fending for itself. Crock-Pots ensured that a hot meal was ready when they got home, even if Mom or Dad weren't there to serve it.

The PrestoBurger was another alternative for the busy household that made meal preparation quick and easy. Like the Crock-Pot, the PrestoBurger was a hit. The economic recession of the seventies had made ground beef a popular mealtime choice for families on a budget. Many homemakers bought it in large quantities, opting to make hamburger patties at home that could be then stored in the family freezer. With hamburgers already formed into single-serving portions, kids could come home from school, place the thawed, ready-to-cook burgers in the PrestoBurger, and make dinner for themselves without any adult supervision.

Presto, the manufacturer of the PrestoBurger, had had earlier success in the American Kitchen with its other countertop appliances. The company, which had originally fashioned large, commercial-sized canners for food manufacturers, turned its attention to the workings of the family kitchen with its saucepan-sized pressure cooker in 1939. At a time when household budgets were as strapped as they would be in the 1970s, Presto's home-canning cooker allowed homemakers to preserve their own foods rather than rely on store-bought items. Presto pioneered another new trend in cooking when they created the first immersible electric skillet for the home kitchen in 1956. A stainless-steel, completely immersible coffeepot followed.

In the 1970s, Presto tapped into the American infatuation with no-muss no-fuss cooking gadgets. Their burger-frying machine fit on the counter and, like its ancestors, was easily cleaned. The company followed up the success of the PrestoBurger with the FryBaby, a small, countertop deep fryer, in 1976. The larger FryDaddy, and the even bigger GranPappy, hit the stores in

1977 and 1978, respectively. When the home popcorn craze swept through America, Presto introduced one of the first countertop air poppers, the Pop-CornNow machine. The company's inventions closely followed the country's eating habits, and in the 1980s, when Americans began to move away from the fatty food choices of the seventies, Presto would be ready with another kitchen gadget to help change the way family meals were prepared.

Appliances had been the avatars of all that was new and cool in the postwar kitchen, but by the seventies technology allowed for smaller displays of hipness. The Crock-Pot, for example, might not have seemed very cutting-edge, especially when compared to the sleek plastic dinnerware designs of the Vignellis, but the very idea of a burnt orange or avocado-colored cooker, small enough to sit on the kitchen counter, was a reflection of the stylistic decisions popular in the 1970s.

Visually, the American Kitchen underwent one of its most significant changes during the 1970s, the largest, in fact, since the appliance boom of the late 1940s. The desire for a more "natural" kitchen might not have been prevalent in all the food choices Americans were making, since Hamburger Helper and other prefab or dinner mixes were helping families who were short on time and cash, but the environment inside the American Kitchen was beginning to take its cues from the environment *outside* its windows. Baby Boomers who had been spurning the foods of their parents' kitchens since the sixties were now building nests of their own, and this new generation of homemakers was opting for a kitchen that reflected their sensibilities. Coffee, paprika, and avocado were no longer just foods in the American Kitchen—they were the colors in which appliances, countertops, dishes, coffee mugs, tabletops, and even paper towels were dipped. This new trend toward warm tones mirrored the growing interests of the ecology movement. Earth tones were the, well, natural choice for a generation that had become distrustful of not only its government, but also of technology and its unfortunate by-product—pollution. The gleaming plastics and space-age shapes of the sixties were out as a back-to-nature aesthetic began to sprout in kitchens across the country. Even microwaves, in homes that could afford them, were coming wrapped in faux-wood paneling to give them a more natural look, as Joan Kohn, points out. Kohn also notes that the offbeat colors of the 1970s American Kitchen "matched a youthful, fresh approach to things."

Manufacturers hopped on the trend. Not only did the introduction of the new colors make the older, all-white or pastel appliances seem out-of-date, they also played into the changing role occupied by the woman in the American home. The June Cleaver kitchens and the ideology that once kept a woman tethered there were not being remembered with fond nostalgia by the current generation.

"The liberation of women and their changing role in the household may have influenced the design of kitchens by attempting to make [the room] less of a workplace and more of an integrated part of the house," comments Professor Terry Uber of Kent State University, adding that the earth-toned appliances were more "warm and inviting" than their sterile all-white predecessors. The kitchen's design scheme had to coexist with the look of the rest of the house. Orange, brown, green, and yellow were all popular palate choices during the earthy seventies, and as Dr. Shirley Wajda, professor of material culture, suggests, the colors reflected the nation's growing fascination with one particular state in the union.

"It was California," she says of the umber and verdant tones used in the American Kitchen of the 1970s. "It really was about leisure culture, popular culture, and trend-setting. Los Angeles, in the sixties and seventies, became that place that you dealt with when looking for [those trends.]" Like Uber, Wajda sees the colorful revolution as being another example of how the kitchen adapted to the woman of the 1970s leaving the house and going to work outside the home. "With the warm colors, you're re-creating the new notion of home," she says. Since the fire of the stove no longer burned all day long, the feelings of security and hospitality that its warmth once generated now had to come from other sources.

The American Kitchen of the seventies brought the outdoors in with its use of harvest gold and burnt orange refrigerators and stoves, but the desire for an all-natural look didn't stop at appliances. Wood-grain cabinets replaced their metal-clad ancestors, and Formica, maker of countertops since the 1920s, jettisoned its signature atomic- and space-age designs of the 1950s and '60s and instead of decorating surfaces with boomerangs and spangles began offering customers colors like Sliced Avocado. The long, unadorned countertops echoed the green of long stretches of fields, or the orange and yellow sunset of that Pacific horizon line.

The colorful revolution also found its way into the American Kitchen of the 1970s through a very unnatural material. The popularity of plastic kitchenware had already been established in the sixties with the marriage of pop art and new technology. Plastic dishes were no strangers to the kitchen, and neither were plastic furnishings. The Eero Saarinen–designed tulip chairs and round table that held court in Carol Brady's kitchen on *The Brady Bunch* were a groovy symbol and icon of the early seventies (even though they'd been designed in the fifties).

But the novelty of the plastic wasn't the allure this time. The resilience and fortitude of the material endeared plastic dishes and furniture to homemakers of the 1970s. Cleanup was now a snap—important for a nation that was becoming too busy to be bothered with the worrisome task of carefully washing, drying, and stacking ceramic, china, or porcelain plates, cups, and saucers. It wasn't long before the American Kitchen had plastic dishware, which appealed to homemakers who were looking for a sense of style without sacrificing plastic's convenience. Italian architect and designer Massimo Vignelli was hired by the American manufacturing company Heller to create a line of dishes for more style-savvy consumers. Vignelli's talent for fashioning eye-catching and functional pieces resulted in a durable, stackable line of plates and mugs that were soon on as many museum shelves as kitchen shelves.

In another shift, the ecology-conscious youth of the sixties were becoming the activist-minded adults of the seventies. In the decade's first year, the inaugural celebration of Earth Day was observed and the Environmental Protection Agency was established. Being concerned about the environment was no longer a trend or fad; it was a burgeoning way of life for Americans who wanted a less disruptive approach to coexisting with the world around them. This meant farming and gardening without harmful pesticides, chemicals, or fertilizers. Cookbooks like *The New York Times Natural Foods Cookbook* taught homemakers how to rely on whole grains and organically grown fruits and vegetables when preparing their meals. *Organic Gardening and Farming* magazine, along with guidebooks on organic gardening like *Living on the Earth* by Alicia Bay Laurel, sold well in the 1970s, just as *The Whole Earth Catalog* continued to be popular since its inception in 1968. *Whole Earth*, the brainchild of Stewart Brand, was an ecologist's guide to the universe that was inspired by the work of R. Buckminster Fuller. Fuller's 1973 book, *Earth, Inc.*, contained his prescription for a more environmentally sensitive approach to living. Fuller was one of the earliest conservationists to propose that renewable energy sources, like wind and wave action, be harnessed as an alternative to pollution-causing fossil fuels. "There is no energy crisis," he would state, "only a crisis of ignorance." Fuller also proposed that modern science, along with ecologically sound practices, could wipe out world poverty and hunger by the year 2000.

Another champion of the au naturel movement of the seventies, Euell Gibbons, had made a name for himself in the 1960s. Gibbons's role as pitchman for Post Cereal's Grape-Nuts had made him an icon of a generation. His books, like *Stalking the Wild Asparagus*, were manifestos for Americans who longed for the challenge of eating, living, and even surviving in the wild. Gibbons endeared himself to many through his books and television commercials, and through his appearances on network shows. When he received an award for his environmental activism on CBS's *The Sonny and Cher Show*, Gibbons proceeded to demonstrate his "everything natural is edible" philosophy by sinking his teeth into the wooden plaque he'd been given.

Gibbons was one of the purveyors of eco-sensitive thinking who made the idea of natural foods seem less threatening and less radical to the general public. Soon the mainstream in America began following the lead of what had been considered by some to be an underground movement. In 1971, Hunt's Tomato Sauce boasted that the only added ingredients in its sauce were "real bits of onions, green peppers, tomatoes, and celery," assuring consumers that the product did not contain anything artificial. The health-food craze that had started in the fifties and caught on in the sixties was, by the seventies, a viable lifestyle, complete with a target audience at whom marketers could take aim. ALL AMERICA'S CATCHING THE WHEAT GERM, heralded one ad, and most Americans could identify Columbo and Yoplait as brands of yogurt. The crossover success of Quaker Oats 100% Natural Cereal was an example of how mainstream food manufacturers could co-opt the idea of healthy eating. With Quaker's 100% Natural it was official: Granola had made its way out of trail-mix bags, shaken off any associations with its ninth-century sanatorium origins, and landed in cereal bowls on America's breakfast table.

For Quaker Oats, their timing for marketing the new cereal, initially, couldn't have been better. The year before their cereal was introduced the Center for Science in the Public Interest was established in Washington, D.C. The goal of the CSPI was to raise the awareness of the American public about the nutritional content of the food they eat; sort of a full-time monitor of what the Pure Food Act in the United States had always tried to enforce. Within a year's time, the CSPI would popularize the terms *junk food* and *empty calories* to describe foods that were unhealthy, yet prevalent, in the

American Kitchen, like candy, snacks, and soda. Obviously the American public listened: Consumption of candy dropped by 24 percent in the early 1970s.

Meanwhile, just two years after it first appeared on store shelves, Quaker Oats 100% Natural Cereal became one of the top-five-selling cereals in the country. Unfortunately for Quaker Oats, however, it wouldn't take long before the high fat and sugar content of its "healthy" cereal became public knowledge. In 1973 the Food and Drug Administration standardized a system for labeling the nutritional breakdown of foods sold in grocery stores. The number of calories, plus the carbohydrate, fat, sodium, and cholesterol contents, would be listed on the product's packaging. Armed with this information, the CSPI blasted Quaker Oats 100% Natural Cereal for having more saturated fat per half-cup serving than a McDonald's hamburger.

If comparing the grams of fat and sodium was too taxing of a proposition for the average consumer to undertake, the CSPI came to their aid with the 1975 publication of the *Nutrition Scoreboard*. The *Scoreboard* ranked nationally known and readily available products according to their nutritional value, from highest to lowest. As a shopping guide, the book was a powerful ally for homemakers who wanted to be sure they were feeding their families healthy foods.

The publication of CSPI's *How Sodium Nitrite Can Affect Your Health*—which called attention to the unregulated use, and the dangers, of the preservative that appeared in wieners and other meat products—led the U.S. Department of Agriculture to call for a reduction in the use of nitrites in packaged meats in 1977. With kids across the country wishing they were Oscar Mayer wieners, moms no longer had to guess whether the hot dogs they served their families contained dangerous amounts of nitrites or other preservatives: Beyond listing the recommended daily allowance of vitamins and minerals, these labels also itemized chemical substances like sodium nitrite and other preservatives that might be contained in the foods. Across America there was a growing desire for the truth. In an era when mistrust of the government could be justified, consumers wanted honest answers to many questions, and in regard to the foods they ate, Americans wanted to know "What *was* 'in there.'"

Madison Avenue and corporate advertisers quickly picked up on the buzzworthy issue and began steering their clients toward ads that promoted the healthier aspects of their products. Even as early as 1971 a print ad for Kellogg's Corn Flakes turned a bowl of the breakfast cereal into a

Venn diagram with arrows pointing to the vitamins, minerals, and nutrients contained within.

More Americans began taking a more thoughtful approach to their diets and their purchases. With the growing awareness about the unhealthy things they should be stripping *out* of their diets, several diet-conscious entrepreneurs started opening grocery stores where they could market healthy, all-natural, and organic products so Americans could find the types of food they wanted to put into their pantries. This trend wasn't limited to óne particular city or region of the United States, though. San Pedro, California, was where George Mateljan started Health Valley Foods in 1970, while the Whole Foods Company, a grocery store that stocked health foods and organically grown produce, got its start a few years later in New Orleans, Louisiana, showing that the new approach to healthier eating wasn't limited to one region.

As a grocery store, the Whole Foods Company was devoted to carrying "good, wholesome food" in its aisles, rather than "pills and potions," as the company's history states. Many so-called health-food stores commonly carried powdered supplements and additives in pill forms. Whole Foods wanted to give its customers something they could actually sink their teeth into and enjoy the taste of. The similarly named, but independently owned, Whole Foods Market opened in 1980 in Austin, Texas, and was the cornerstone of what would later become the Whole Foods Market supermarket chain. At the time there were fewer than half a dozen natural-food supermarkets in the United States. Bread and Circus, which had first opened its doors in Brookline, Massachusetts, in 1975, would later become part of the Whole Foods Market chain. Wellspring Grocery, Fresh Fields, Mrs. Gooch's, Bread of Life, Amrion, and Food for Thought were all independent organic and/or natural food stores that would later be gathered under the Whole Foods Market umbrella as the American hunger for healthier choices grew.

The organic markets of the early seventies got a boost from a ready-made public relations campaign when the Environmental Protection Agency banned the use of pesticides like DDT, long a concern of Rachel Carson's, in 1972. Two years later, the EPA added other lethal insecticides to their banned list, including those containing chlorinated hydrocarbons. There was a slight backlash from some biochemists, who argued that the benefits of pesticides far outweighed the risks because the use of pesticides on fruits and vegetables produced a higher crop yield since less food was damaged, thus lowering the cost for consumers. Eventually farmers agreed to limit their use of carcinogenic sprays and fertilizers.

The idea that less was more when it came to chemicals and tampering was trickling down. Even tea drinkers became concerned about the amount of processing that went into the bags containing their tea leaves. Morris and Peggy Siegel, Wyck Hay, and Lucinda Ziesing heard their call. Using herbs picked in their native Colorado mountains, they started a different kind of revolution with their tea party. Marketing their teas under the brand name Celestial Seasonings, the foursome created brews with names like Sleepy Time, Morning Thunder, and the more traditionally named Mandarin Orange. With so many homemakers curling up with a cup of one of their teas, the Celestial folks garnered 10 percent of the tea-drinking market within ten years of the debut of their line. They became so popular that leading tea giants like Lipton and Tetley introduced herbal teas of their own to win back some of the customers who might have switched to Celestial Seasonings.

Overall, more Americans were trying the herbal and organic alternatives that were now firmly rooted in their grocery stores' aisles. For those times when health-conscious Americans of the 1970s wanted to eat fresh, organic foods, they had an increasing number of alternatives to which they could turn. As *Time* magazine reported in December 1977, "Farmer's markets and small vegetable stands are sprouting like mung beans—which they also sell." The same article stated that the amount of money Americans were spending on "specialty foods"—which included gourmet as well as organic fare—had increased 20 percent since the early seventies. And, it seemed, American cooks knew what to do with those new foods they were eating, especially the vegetables. Gone—well, almost—were the heavy white blankets of sauce that tucked asparagus, broccoli, and cauliflower onto dinner plates during the heyday of Fannie Farmer and the turn-of-the-century cooking schools. There were also fewer salads being drowned in heavy oily dressings in the American Kitchen than in years past. And fewer green beans were reduced to mush as more Americans began to appreciate the crisp snap delivered by a properly cooked legume. "Crisp vegetables, which used to be as scarce as lap-wings eggs, have become a mainstay of any well-planned menu," *Time* stated. "At their best, the vitaminiferous vegetables are lightly steamed, or stir-fried Chinese-style, or tossed raw in oil and vinegar."

How did the American Kitchen become so savvy in the ways of bok choy, brussels sprouts, carrots, and cucumbers? Television shows like Julia Child's continued to school the growing number of Americans who where intrigued by food, and most newspapers carried a food column, if not an entire dining and food section. Cookbooks were selling as briskly as Jacqueline Susann's and Peter Benchley's latest sizzlers. And dining out was becoming as much of an educational field trip as it was a night off from kitchen duties.

By the mid 1970s, the American Kitchen routinely experienced nights when the refrigerator wasn't the only appliance in the room that remained cool. Busy families were firing up their ovens and stoves less now that fast-food stands, deli counters with prepared foods, take-out, and restaurants dotted streets and highways across the United States. At the beginning of 1978, Americans were spending nearly 25 percent of their food budgets on meals in restaurants or instant, prepared foods they brought home. As with the foods that were becoming more readily available in grocery stores, so the foods in some restaurants were beginning to mirror the desire for healthier dining alternatives. Health-food restaurants began to pop up on college campuses, in larger urban areas, and even in suburban towns. Two restaurants that opened in the 1970s, one in New York, the other in California, established trends that would go on to shape the way Americans shopped for food and cooked at home for the rest of the century.

Mollie Katzen, who in 1973 opened her now famous Moosewood Restaurant in Ithaca, New York, found herself facing a dilemma many vegetarians of the twentieth century encountered: Where were all the flavorful meatless recipes? Katzen began collecting the best recipes she could find when she worked in a small macrobiotic restaurant in San Francisco in 1970. Her search for quality vegetarian recipes, which resulted in dishes and meals that actually tasted good, led her to start writing and illustrating her own cookbooks. At the time when Katzen began her search, vegetarianism wasn't the full-fledged movement it would later become. Many carnivores who were pro-ecology were experiencing a crisis of conscience and laying down their steak knives. But the problem for these former meat-eaters was that they didn't have experience preparing meatless meals, and many attempts at constructing a vegetarian diet were built upon the idea that as long as it didn't have any animal products it was okay to eat. But there weren't many guidelines for budding vegetarians who were looking to prepare healthy and tasty meals at home. The 1964 World's Fair had resulted in a slow infusion of Indian cooking into the American Kitchen, and by the mid-seventies savvier cooks were familiar with the use of exotic spices and rice dishes. Curry powder had "become a kitchen commonplace," as *Time* magazine observed in 1977. Tabbouleh was also becoming a staple of the vegetarian American Kitchen of the seventies. Still, the vegetarian meal option at restaurants and functions was often an oily pasta salad with dismal chunks of iceberg lettuce and beefsteak tomato served on the side.

One of the first resources to come to the rescue of American vegetarians was Frances Moore Lappé's cookbook *Diet for a Small Planet*, first published in 1971. Lappé's book became a platform for those whose political views had led them to become vegetarians. *Diet for a Small Planet* made a strong case, from an ecological viewpoint, as to why more of the world's population should start adopting a meatless diet. While Lappé was not a vegetarian herself, she claimed that eating meat was becoming unconscionable because of the cost and, more specifically, the waste of grains required to feed livestock. Lappé argued that the planet could not sustain this type of farming and ranching lifestyle for much longer. Corn as the principle food for cattle was particularly costly; not only did cows require antibiotics to be able to digest corn, but the resulting gastrointestinal distress caused by that corn and other grains created enough methane for environmental activists to consider cows major polluters: According to the Environmental Protection Agency, livestock and their manure are the second-highest producers of methane in the world. (Methane is characterized as a greenhouse gas that contributes to global warming.)

If Lappé's book was too heavy on agenda for some Americans, the 1973 publication of *The Supermarket Handbook*, written by husband-and-wife team David and Nikki Goldbeck, would offer more of a how-to, rather than a why-to, guide for burgeoning vegetarians when it came to stocking their kitchens. The Goldbecks worked their charm on talk shows like *The Phil Donahue Show* and were invited back on three separate occasions during the 1970s.

As Lappé and the Goldbecks were busy promoting their books, Katzen was still at work on her own collection of vegetarian recipes. Finally, in 1977, Katzen debuted *The Moosewood Cookbook*. It was an immediate smash. The simple language of the recipes and Katzen's hand-drawn instructions were revolutionary compared to the more technical cookbooks that had previously anchored bookshelves in the American Kitchen. The fact that Katzen's book became a crossover success—appealing to vegetarians and carnivores alike—was a sign of just how significantly the American approach to dining had changed.

Even if all Americans weren't becoming vegetarians in the 1970s, more and more were hearing and heeding the message that going green was good. Salads became wildly popular. Salad bars were introduced in restaurants, and produce departments in grocery stores began offering more varieties of salad dressings—which were now stocked above the new varieties of lettuce and fresh vegetables. Sales of salad dressings had nearly doubled from the 17.5 million gallons sold in 1960, to 34.3 million gallons sold in 1970. That number continued to rise throughout the seventies and the eighties, and it doubled again in the nineties.

The notion of what comprised a salad was drastically changing, too. In most homes across America, a salad with dinner meant a bowl of iceberg lettuce tossed with tomatoes, along with carrot and cucumber slices. (At least the American Kitchen had liberated the salad's vegetables from the gelatin cells in which they had been trapped during the first part of the twentieth century.) By the mid-seventies the vegetarian movement had made most Americans familiar with alfalfa and bean sprouts, and even tofu, as toppings for salad. The credit for tossing out the salad of old and beginning with fresh, in-season ingredients goes to chefs Alice Waters and Jeremiah Tower. Both had established a new benchmark in their restaurants for what were considered "fresh" vegetables. Relying on the locally grown bounty of organic seasonal vegetables, Waters and Tower introduced diners to varieties of lettuce that sounded as foreign to their patrons as the most exotic French or Asian dishes had once seemed. Arugula and radicchio rose from obscurity and became superstars among the salad set. Waters continued choosing only seasonal, regional vegetables for her trend-making restaurant Chez Panisse in Berkeley, California, while Tower went on to open the sensation-causing Stars in San Francisco. The food sense and food philosophies of the two chefs soon spread across the California border and headed into kitchens across America.

As the books by Mollie Katzen and the Goldbecks proved, no matter what type of diet Americans chose to follow in the 1970s, there were guides available to offer them instruction. *Better Homes and Gardens* continued to offer solutions to their readers, no matter what their dietary needs, and the *Better Homes and Gardens Low-Calorie Dessert Cook Book* became a best seller in 1972 among Americans who wanted to have their cake and look good eating it, too. That same year, a cardiologist by the name of Robert C. Atkins published a dieting guide that proposed a radically new approach to the American meal. *Dr. Atkins' Diet Revolution* lived up to its title, causing a ruckus in the medical community. Atkins's prescription of a high-fat, low-carbohydrate diet went against everything new studies were showing about the links between heart disease and diet. Meanwhile, also in 1973, Jean Nidetch continued to win converts with her highly successful Weight Watchers support groups, and *The Weight Watchers Program Cookbook* flew off the shelves.

The popularization of the term *junk food* in 1971 by the Center for Science in the Public Interest had given Americans an identifiable enemy to combat in their kitchens, and the last half of the decade saw the publication of an arsenal of cookbooks and lifestyle guides ready to help the country's growing over-weight population fight their battle against obesity. And with the sexual revolu-tion still transforming the nation's social mores, Americans were learning that eating right during the day meant that they looked better in the mirror at night. Scores of adults were taking one last look at themselves as they headed out the door to the new "singles bars." But Americans wanted more than just to look good in the seventies; they wanted to feel good, too. Dr. David Reuben's *Everything You Always Wanted to Know About Sex, But Were Afraid to Ask* was soon joined by well-worn copies of *The Sensuous Woman* and *The Sensuous Man* on nightstands in bedrooms across the country.

The seventies also saw the return of the grapefruit-as-miracle-food phe-nomenon in the American Kitchen, this time as espoused by Dr. Herman Tarnower in his *Complete Scarsdale Medical Diet*. Tarnower called for fol-lowers of his regimen to start each day with grapefruit. But with so many different approaches to eating showing up in bookstores every week, dieters who were dissatisfied with the Scarsdale approach had plenty of others to choose from. *The Pritikin Program for Diet and Exercise* was on the best-seller lists at the same time as Tarnower's book. Named after its proponent, Nathan Pritikin, the Pritikin diet came as close to endorsing vegetarianism as any mainstream diet book ever would. Pritikin's protocol also ran contrary to the Atkins diet in that it favored low-fat, high-fiber eating habits and made no allowances for animal fats. At a time when many busy American families were struggling to share even one meal per day together, the Pritikin formula recommended that six to seven smaller meals be eaten throughout the day, rather than the traditional meals of breakfast, lunch, and dinner.

As the American approach to losing weight continued to grow more sophis-ticated, looking for the new next thing, so did the American pursuit of new gourmet heights. Two popular cookbooks of the 1970s helped them in their endeavors. Julia Child's *Mastering the Art of French Cooking II* was the long-awaited sequel to her sixties debut, and Craig Claiborne, whose *New York Times Cookbook* had appeared in the early 1960s as well, likewise published a companion piece: *The New York Times International Cookbook*.

Child continued to raise the consciousness of the American Kitchen with her second book on French cooking, assuring Americans that they weren't merely tourists in the land of this foreign cuisine; Claiborne's book, on the other hand, provided an atlas for the increasing number of Americans who were looking to explore beyond their culinary boundaries.

Three cuisines that defined cooking in the seventies the way French had in the sixties were Chinese, Greek, and Italian. These cuisines became nearly as common as meat loaf on restaurant menus and in home kitchens in the 1970s as Americans continued learning that international culture could be very tasty.

In April 1971 an American Ping-Pong team traveling to China on a good-will mission was received by Chinese leader Zhou Enlai. This table-tennis diplomacy, as the visit was called, opened up the door for President Nixon's arrival in China in 1972. With Nixon lobbying for restored trade relations with China, as well as for a United Nations seat for the country, the leader of the free world was inadvertently providing some pretty good PR for chicken lo mein.

The American Kitchen had begun flirting with Chinese cuisine in the early 1920s, and began again after World War II, in the forties and early fifties, especially in urban areas. But the visibility of Chinese Americans and their culture in art, movies, and television shows was on the rise in the 1970s. Andy Warhol began silk-screening stylized portraits of Mao Tse-tung in 1972. Peter Bogdanovich's madcap movie *What's Up, Doc?* and ABC's television series *The Streets of San Francisco* both premiered in 1972 and relied heavily on San Francisco's Chinatown, almost making the neighborhood a character in their stories.

With so much free advertising from the media, anything that seemed remotely associated with Chinese food or even San Francisco's Chinatown—such as La Choy's canned chop suey or Rice-A-Roni's boxed side dishes—played into the country's growing interest in the Asian cuisine. Americans were getting into the swing of things by trying their own hand at "authentic" Chinese cooking. Wok sets, complete with wooden steaming racks and recipe booklets, were now being sold at that purveyor of all things domestic, Sears. Soy sauce, duck sauce, and canned chow mein noodles could be plucked off the shelves at the local A&P as "stir-fry" became the hot new answer to the question "What's for dinner?"

In the world of restaurants, Szechuan and Hunan cuisines were newcomers to Chinese menus in America. In Manhattan, "new ancient" Chinese dishes like General Tso's Chicken, Orange Crispy Beef, and Crispy Sea Bass were coming out of the kitchens of Chinese restaurants. Carry-out boxes from Chinese takeout stands were even appearing on kitchen tables in the American suburbs. The reason for the proliferation of all things Chinese was that more Chinese immigrants were landing on American shores than in previous years thanks to the Immigration Act of 1965. Although it was not fully implemented until 1968, the Immigration Act increased the number of visas given to Asian countries and allowed more Asian people the opportunity to enter the United States to seek citizenship than had ever been permitted before. The rush of Chinese immigrants into the United States after the passing of the act resulted in more Chinese-owned businesses in all parts of the country. The Nixon administration's warm attitude toward the Chinese government helped remove barriers that might previously have prevented some Americans from embracing Chinese cuisine. But the Chinese food that had become popular in the United States was not exactly authentic.

"We don't eat sweet and sour, we don't eat egg rolls," says Shirley Fong-Torres, cookbook author, tour guide, and ambassador of Chinese cooking—real Chinese cooking, that is—in San Francisco's Chinatown. Fong-Torres says that the dishes on many Chinese menus across the United States, and in many cookbooks and prepared in many home kitchens, are more American than they are Chinese.

"I call it the Disgusting Dinner for Two Syndrome," she says. "It's Egg Drop Soup, Sweet and Sour Pork, Fried Rice and Egg Foo Young, or Broccoli Beef."

But the average American can't be blamed for thinking these dishes are authentic Chinese cuisine, especially since the person responsible for helping to popularize this style of cooking was a Chinese man by the name of Sammy Louie. At Sammy Louie's Chinatown American Cooks School in San Francisco, Chinese immigrants in the sixties and seventies were taught by Louie, an immigrant from China's Guangdong Province, how to prepare "sweet-and-sour sauce so that they could [make] those popular Chinese dishes that only Americans ate," Fong-Torres wrote in an article for the *San Jose Mercury News*. The graduates from Louie's school then moved across the country, becoming chefs at restaurants and hotels.

"It was easy for Americans to think that Chinese food was sweet-and-sour cooking, because most Americans liked it," Fong-Torres admits. It was also easy for most Americans to think that this type of cooking was Cantonese, since the majority of Chinese immigrants in the United States had emigrated from China's coastal areas of Canton and Shanghai.

The American Kitchen of the 1970s was becoming sophisticated enough that cooks wanted to move past the "Cantonese" recipes, and when immigrants from the Chinese provinces of Szechuan and Hunan began entering the United States, Americans became fascinated with the fiery cuisines they brought with them. *Gourmet* magazine did its part to help culinary explorers travel beyond Peking Duck with dishes like San Hsiang T'ang (Duck and Winter Melon Soup) and Li Tzu Pan Huo Ya (Duck Salad with Litchis and Green Peppers). In the late seventies the magazine devoted a monthly column to Chinese cooking, offering a social-studies course along with each recipe. In one issue, an explanation of the Chinese custom of gifting new mothers with eggs, sometimes dyed bright red, introduced recipes for Tea Eggs and Cold Bean Curd with Thousand-Year-Old Eggs. Americans now enjoyed being able to serve a side dish of cultural relevance along with their meals.

Even with more Americans warming up to Chinese cuisines in their own kitchens, the 1970s were still more about the pasta pot than the Mongolian pot. The American Kitchen continued to be romanced by the flavors of Italy, and many cooks began moving past the traditional tomato sauces and trying their hands at a variety of dishes. Among food aficionados, as Sylvia Lovegren writes in *Fashionable Food*, "Spaghetti was In, but only with . . . white sauces." The heavy, creamy sauces that accompanied Spaghetti Carbonara, Fettuccine Alfredo, and even the Italian-like Pasta Primavera were the new favorites among adventurous cooks. But the red sauce poured on top of that old stand-by, Spaghetti and Meatballs, was still popular in most American kitchens. Lasagna, also made with tomato sauce, remained a popular budget stretcher during the seventies' recession as well.

Italian cuisine was also a big moneymaker for companies like Chef Boyardee (named after Italian-born immigrant Hector Boiardi), as food technologists worked overtime to put flavor and convenience into affordable food items for busy parents.

The visibility of Italian culture had been high in America since the seventies began, though presentations of the culture weren't always considered acceptable, flattering, or accurate, in the opinion of many Italian Americans. A popular commercial for Alka-Seltzer, for instance, featured an actor portraying an Italian immigrant who, after exclaiming "Mama Mia!," kept botching his lines about the "speecy-a-spicy meat-a-balls" his wife was serving him, in take after take. On the other hand, the huge, Academy Award–winning success of *The Godfather* and *The Godfather, Part II*, in 1972 and 1974, re-spectively, increased the American appetite for all things Italian.

Americans were as taken with the red, white, and green as they were with the red, white, and blue during the 1970s. Food companies elbowed one an-other out of public favor as they tried to assure shoppers that their pasta sauce was more authentic than the competition's product. In television ads, skeptics who tasted Ragu's sauce exclaimed "*That's* Italian!"—discrediting any other heat-and-serve sauces as impostors.

Italian food was one of the staples in America's kitchens by the mid-seventies, but another Mediterranean cuisine was beginning to woo those who were looking for a new kind of kick. Some of those seekers found what they were looking for in foods from Greece.

The popularity of Greek food wasn't going to threaten the sales of pasta noodles or jarred spaghetti sauces during the seventies, nor was it going to cut into the market for La Choy's canned Chinese foods; but for the growing portion of the American population that identified itself as vegetarian, the Greek menu was a godsend. Because the religious observances of Greek Or-thodox Catholics regularly required abstaining from meat and even dairy products, meat alternatives were not only common in the average Greek household, they were delicious. Through other cuisines, the growing vege-tarian movement in the United States had already become familiar with chickpeas, lentils, and eggplant, all of which were ingredients in many Greek dishes. Yogurt and pita breads were also more available in American grocery stores than they had been in previous decades. Moussaka, which resembled lasagna in its cakelike, layered density, was one Greek dish sliding in and out of ovens in kitchens across America during the seventies. For most Ameri-cans, however, the sweet dessert pastry baklava was the Greek food of choice.

The end of the 1970s saw the American Kitchen turning its attention closer to home even as international cuisines began gracing its table. In 1977 *Time* magazine noted "born-again American cooks . . . have rediscovered the glo-rious raw ingredients and inimitable provincial dishes of their own country." With the celebration of the American Bicentennial in 1976, and with the elec-tion of Georgia's unassuming Jimmy Carter to the office of president of the United States, Americans were finding a wealth of gastronomical delights in the "down-home" cookbooks and recipes of their hometowns. Southern cooking in particular came into its own as President Carter's penchant for fried chicken and peanuts helped American gourmands return to their roots. After the disruption and discord of the first half of the decade everyone needed some reassurance—and what better place to find it than in the soothing, filling comfort foods of America? Interested cooks found that they had an appropriate library waiting for them to peruse: Time-Life Books published a six-volume series of cookbooks celebrating the cooking of the "Eastern Heartland," "The Northwest," and "The Great West," along with the Creole and Acadian cooking of the Mississippi Delta region.

By the latter half of the seventies Americans were looking for authentic regional dishes, recipes written out of necessity and experience, and *The Taste of Country Cooking* by Edna Lewis became a must-read. Lewis had grown up in Freetown, Virginia, a community settled by free slaves. In her memoir-cum-cookbook she detailed the plain but thoughtful approach her mother took to cooking mutton, greens, and shad caught fresh from local waters. After enduring years of inflation, many Americans could relate to the sometimes lean existence described by Lewis in *Country Cooking*. Similarly, the popular 1970s television show *Little House on the Prairie*, based on the books by Laura Ingalls Wilder, told the story of a simpler time when the bonds of family and friends made what little food that was present seem so much more enjoyable.

Even as the cultural upheaval of the sixties and early seventies created rifts in some households, the American Kitchen remained a place where those divisions could be mended. Julia Child said, "The family that cooks together stays together," while British designer Terence Conran declared that "the kitchen is, once again, the heart of the home. It really ought to be renamed the living room, because that is what it is."

Regardless of whether the food they were eating was Chinese, Italian, freeze-dried, or organic, Americans at the end of the 1970s loved to eat, loved to cook, and loved doing so with others. Of all the movements that staged food-related fights during the seventies, the real winner was the American Kitchen. As journalist Michael Demarest wrote in 1977, "The sexual revolution is passé . . . We have gone from Pan to pots. The Great American Love Affair is taking place in the kitchen."

CHAPTER NINE

Let's Get Physical: 1980–1989

*Phillipe Starck's orange juicer looked like an alien in the sleek kitchen of the
1980s, and that only served to make it all the more desirable. (Phillipe Starck.
Juicy Salif. Philadelphia Museum of Art: Gift of Alessi SpA, 1997.)*

When the ball dropped in Times Square on New Year's Eve 1979, in the
eyes of many Americans, it marked the symbolic end of years of
uncertainty and upheaval and the beginning of an era of hope, if not confidence, in the future. As the New Year was ushered in, complete with *1980*
displayed in a futuristic cyber-font, it was clear that the eighties were going
to be different. And it wasn't long before Americans had reason to feel optimistic again. When the new decade was only a few months old, the U.S.
Olympic Hockey Team defeated the invincible Soviet Union en route to
winning the gold medal at the Lake Placid Olympic Games. This "Miracle
on Ice" rejuvenated the energy of a country whose spirit had been deflated.

The eighties also began with a slight improvement in the U.S. economy.
The seventies had ended with one in twelve Americans on food stamps, and
with generic food products for sale in grocery stores. Selling at a price up
to 30 percent below nationally advertised brands, the foodstuffs behind the

generic product's austere white label and black lettering were a godsend for some families and an embarrassment to others.

With the new decade came a new interest in fitness. In gyms across America, new sleek machines by Universal, Nautilus, and BowFlex pumped muscles into shape. At dance studios people lined up to hustle off those unwanted pounds as the disco craze of the seventies became the aerobics phenomenon of the eighties. And jogging? That was so seventies; people *ran* in the eighties, in newly designed performance gear that turned the humble sneaker into an aerodynamic slipper.

There were also new cookbooks and diets in the exercise-driven eighties. Along with these new diets came new spokespersons. Weight Watchers' Jean Nidetch continued to inspire those desperately seeking sleekness, but now the metabolically challenged had a new source of inspiration in the form of a bouncy fitness-and-food advocate named Richard Simmons.

In the new decade, Americans eliminated some foods from their diets while continuing to assimilate others. On their way out were foods heavy in saturated fats and cholesterol. In place of the banished foods, fish, skinless cuts of chicken, light salt, fat-free cheeses, and oat bran were all welcomed into America's kitchens. New cooking techniques, exciting spice combinations, and the introduction of other foreign cuisines made eating smart more flavorful than before. The veggie-heavy condiment salsa found a prominent place in the American Kitchen of the 1980s, eventually nudging ketchup off many shelves as Mexican food became incorporated into the mainstream of American cooking.

Two of the earliest American hybrid cuisines, Cajun and Creole, also became popular in the American Kitchen during the eighties. Paul Prudhomme was the larger-than-life ambassador of Louisiana-based cooking who cast an impressive shadow on the notion that diet foods were taking over the country. Prudhomme's cable-television appearances turned him into a celebrity in much the same way that Julia Child's show had made her a star. Chefs became rock-star hot in the 1980s; they were trendsetters and social directors who were tempting more and more Americans to take a bite out of life. At a time when AIDS cast a somber pall across the nation, the enjoyment of food was one sensual pleasure that remained relatively safe.

Frozen, microwaveable meals may have been the talk of the seventies, but consumers were left speechless in the early eighties with the arrival of shelf-stable boxes of milk—which didn't require refrigeration. In other techie news, scientists had discovered how to splice genetic material, leading to the development of pest-resistant crops by 1987. *Recombinant DNA* became the highly trafficked phrase of the decade. The foods of the future had arrived; meanwhile, the look of the future was to be found in the smooth, black, mirrorlike surfaces of the American Kitchen of the 1980s.

From their new muscular physiques to their sexy sleek appliances and countertops, Americans were turning to the kitchen in the 1980s as the place that made them feel shiny and new.

The decade would end, unfortunately, on a note less optimistic than the one that rang it in. The glamour and opulence that had characterized the Reagan White House were replaced by the hard reality of another economic downturn when the stock market crashed in October 1987. The ritzy champagne-wishes-and-caviar-dreams world of Robin Leach, TV's ambassador to the rich and famous, were out. The working-class reality of *Roseanne* and her cluttered kitchen were in.

In 1980 at the outset of the new decade, the Senate Select Committee on Nutrition and Human Needs published the final installment of their *Dietary Goals for the United States*. The committee had already unsettled the country in 1977, when their preliminary findings showed that the state of the nation's diet and health was poor; the conclusion of their study showed that it was pathetic. According to their report, Americans were an unhealthy bunch, favoring fatty foods and sweets. The committee urged an immediate change in the country's eating habits, most notably a 10 percent reduction in fat intake. Whole-milk drinkers were told to switch to skim; eaters of red meat were informed they'd better learn to like chicken and fish; fans of salt and eggs were warned to cut their consumption by half; and sugary sweets were to be passed over in favor of fresh fruits. For a country that was falling in love with food, *Dietary Goals* delivered heartbreaking news. Changing eating habits, at a time when cuisine in America was just starting to come into its own, seemed like a lot of work, not to mention deprivation, especially in an era when busy schedules and hectic lifestyles had created a demand for fast foods and ready-to-eat meals.

Food technologists in America had created an entire industry out of understanding the needs of the hungry public for decades, and the eighties were no exception. "Low-cal!" became the battle cry of dieters across America, and food companies were quick to help consumers with new products aimed at fighting their war. Stouffer's, whose frozen entrées had become staple items in the freezers of the American Kitchen, debuted their Lean Cuisine line in 1981 to instant success. That same year, the Food and Drug Administration gave food manufacturers the green light to use aspartame as an alternative to sugar in soft drinks and other products. NutraSweet became the brand name by which aspartame was marketed to the public. Like Stouffer's Lean Cuisine, NutraSweet was quickly welcomed into American homes. Stouffer's took the guesswork out of what constituted a low-calorie meal, while aspartame could be used, guilt-free and in abundance, in coffee, tea, or on breakfast cereals without leaving a synthetic or chemical aftertaste. For a body-conscious nation preoccupied with its self-image, these new convenient items made the prospect of dieting more appealing. Americans could now have foods that were quickly prepared and that tasted good (or at least didn't taste so different from the foods they were giving up). *Low-calorie* became synonymous with *healthy*, as did *light*. Light mayonnaise, light yogurt, and light beer were soon available as was light microwaveable popcorn.

The difference between the diet news of the eighties and that of previous decades was the message that reducing caloric intake alone was not enough to lose weight or ensure better health. The unholy trinity of salt, cholesterol, and fat became the new targets in the American Kitchen. With eggs identified as an early culprit in the *Dietary Goals* report, food technologists introduced lower-cholesterol egg substitutes called Scramblers and Egg Beaters.

The Senate Select Committee on Nutrition and Human Needs likewise targeted whole-milk dairy products that were high in fat. While the dairy industry raced to market fat-free, or skim, ice creams and yogurts, a man by the name of David Mintz set out to create a dairy-free, soybean-based ice cream in 1981. Mintz got the idea after he'd successfully created dishes like kosher Beef Stroganoff, in which he used tofu instead of sour cream. He called his ice cream alternative Tofutti. With upscale ice cream imprint Häagen Dazs as its distribution mentor, Tofutti became somewhat of a niche-market novelty. By the time Ann Magnuson's Cigarette Girl gave it a name check in Susan Seidelman's 1985 film *Desperately Seeking Susan*—"Cigars, cigarettes, Tofutti . . ."—the dessert was synonymous with the quirkier side of the eighties' preoccupation with health foods.

In addition to these new healthy alternatives to old favorites, the American Kitchen had armloads of new diet books cracked open on its counter. In the first half of the decade Richard Simmons—who'd fought his own battle with obesity—bounded onto the scene with his *Never Say Diet* book, Weight Watchers landed four cookbooks on the best-seller list, including the Weight Watchers' *Fast & Fabulous Cookbook*, and people were buying up copies of

Judy Mazel's *Beverly Hills Diet* hoping that if they couldn't live like the Holly-wood elite, maybe there was a chance they could at least look like them.

Hollywood was also providing some great examples when it came to keeping fit. Actress Jane Fonda released a series of best-selling aerobic-workout videotapes and self-help books, all geared at raising people's heart rates and lowering their blood pressure. Television star Victoria Principal also got into the act with *The Body Principal: The Exercise Program for Life*. Personal struggles with diet and fitness even became fodder for memoirs. Hollywood icon Elizabeth Taylor had a best seller on her hands with *Eliza-beth Takes Off*, her tell-all book about her struggle to lose weight.

Far from being a place of comfort for all, the American Kitchen presented a different source of anxiety and depression now as some dieters, like Taylor, tried one weight-loss program after another without success.

Americans who were trying to lose weight received a message in the 1980s that was as unwelcome for some as the news about the dangers of their fa-vorite foods: Health experts began stressing the importance of exercise, along with a sensible diet, in the battle against obesity. In a country where a segment of the population defiantly took pride in being called "couch pota-toes," this was the most depressing news yet. Though *The Official Couch Potato Handbook* by Jack Mingo and Robert Armstrong was meant as a send-up of the ways of the sedentary, there was some truth behind their lampoon-ing of a nation that had become reliant on ready-to-eat meals and super-sized servings. Calling the couch potato's way of cooking "Squeezine," Mingo and Armstrong not only poked fun at the "foodie" movement but also at the laziness of a culture whose constant search for the easy way out of every-thing, especially cooking and food preparation, had resulted in products like Parkay Squeeze Margarine and similarly packaged bottles of Hershey's Chocolate Syrup. Aerosol-propelled Cheez Whiz served double-duty as a Squeezine staple; not only was it a processed food, but it was dispensed, ready to eat, with the simple push of a button.

Despite the good-natured, self-mocking tone of *The Official Couch Potato Handbook*, the growing girth of the nation and the health risks involved were nothing for Americans to take sitting down. Americans' food choices were making them fat, and there were more factors working against them in their battle to lose weight than they'd previously thought. Fat was everywhere. Prior to a call from the Center for Science in the Public Interest to disclose the nutritional content of their foods, McDonald's and Burger King were giving customers the beef in more than just their burgers. Vats of oil for french fries were commonly filled with beef fat, and beef tallow was often added to frozen french fries as a flavor enhancer. Both fast-food companies set out to prove they could keep in step with the rest of the nation's new health-conscious attitude by adding salads to their menus.

With all this talk about fats, cholesterol, calories, and health, attitudes toward food were changing in the American Kitchen. According to James Trager's *Food Chronology*, a survey showed that the main concerns among Americans shopping for groceries in 1986 compared to shoppers in 1980 were the desire to eat foods low in fat, low in calories, and low in cholesterol. The old fears about pesticides, preservatives, and chemical additives in foods had fallen several points in the six years since the decade's start.

Fats was *the* four-letter word in the 1980s. As nitrites were to the seventies, and DDT was to the sixties, fat was the potential killer in the diet of the eighties. Everybody was weighing in on the topic. In July 1987, a stern admonishment came from United States Surgeon General C. Everett Koop, who cautioned Americans that they were eating entirely too much saturated fat. What made the news of the potential health risks lurking in foods so annoying was that denial, restraint, and even moderation ran contrary to the ideas of freedom, surplus, and choice that were an identifiable part of the American experience, especially in the kitchen! Throughout the centuries the American Kitchen had endured starvation, famine, drought, war, lack, and even poison. The benefits of a capitalist and industrialized society were access and abundance. As the financial picture started to improve for a portion of the population in the mid-eighties, Americans returned to living life with gusto. In a decade when excesses were celebrated, and even encouraged, who wanted to exercise personal restraint? Television shows like *Dynasty* and *Lifestyles of the Rich and Famous* idolized and idealized the, well, lifestyles of the rich, famous, and infamous. Donald Trump and John DeLorean were moguls to emulate (and, later, revile). Gordon Gekko, Michael Douglas's ruthless character in Oliver Stone's film *Wall Street*, summed up the motivation of the eighties with three words: "Greed is good." When everything surrounding them was telling Americans to reach for more, more, more, no one wanted to hear a message about eating less, less, less.

But the country was finding a way to have its (fat-free, sugarless) cake and eat it, too. The health and fitness trend that kicked off the decade fortunately had more endurance in American culture than did the headband fad—as demonstrated by Olivia Newton-John in her video, and album-cover art, for her 1981 hit "(Let's Get) Physical"—that went along with it. The nation was encouraged to peddle, paddle, and run, jump rope, or pump iron along with their caloric and fat reduction. The American Kitchen became an annex of the health club as more Americans recognized, and began to accept, the partnership between exercise and a healthy diet. The reduction of diet-related health risks turned out to be the secondary motivation to exercise, though, as more Americans learned the upshot of watching their figures—other people, in turn, watched them, too. By 1987 exercise had become a regular part of the country's routine. In that year 17.4 million Americans maintained memberships to health clubs.

Clearly, the American Kitchen's menu received an overhaul in the 1980s when the country's eating habits began to change. Beef had been the mainstay of the all-American meal since World War II, when transportation and technology had combined to assure that fresh cuts appeared in meat cases across the country. When someone was described as a "meat-and-potatoes kinda guy" there was no question what was on his plate. But now questions were being raised about the wisdom of eating so much red meat. With studies suggesting that beef's fat and cholesterol were artery-clogging enemies capable of shortening a person's life span, Americans began eating more chicken, turkey, and fish. By the end of the 1980s the American Kitchen cooked 50 percent more chickens, nearly 70 percent more turkeys, and almost 25 percent more fish than it had at the beginning of the decade. Beef consumption during those same years, however, dropped by nearly 10 percent, to levels that marked a twenty-five-year low.

The growing popularity of poultry and fish in the American diet was an unlikely success story given that both were once foods eaten out of necessity rather than choice, the rations of the have-nots as far back as colonial times. Fish could be put on the dinner table for the cost of an afternoon spent by the stream, and with so many Americans raising their own chickens, dinner was often within arm's reach, just outside the back door. Beef, however, required a trip to the market or grocery store and, depending upon the chosen cut, a significant output of cash. The eating of fish and chicken had always been an economic, rather than gastronomic, matter, even until the 1950s.

In 1956 poultry farming became a less risky venture when an effective treatment was finally found for coccidiosis, one of several diseases that could wipe out a farmer's entire chicken flock. Marek's disease, spread through the dander in a chicken's feathers, could also destroy large numbers of birds if it happened to infiltrate a farm. These illnesses made raising chickens on a large scale cost-prohibitive since an epidemic could destroy all the birds. Coccidiosis, for example, could potentially wreak more havoc in the warmer months when the coccidia parasites had longer lives outside the bodies of their hosts. Since they live in the intestines of chickens and are passed through the feces, the cold, frozen winter earth was an inhospitable environment, whereas the warm weather allowed them a better chance of survival. Because of this vulnerability in the parasite, farmers had more luck raising chickens through the winter and sending them off to market before the warm weather broke. Hence the term *spring chickens*. With the arrival of Nicarbazin and other medicines to treat these diseases, however, chicken-farming could become more of a year-round venture.

The new treatments to combat diseases in chickens resulted in the creation of poultry empires like Perdue and Tyson who could now house tens of thousands of chickens in the same facility with less risk of infection. By 1958 the American Kitchen was benefiting from this technology as the price per pound of chicken fell by a third. In the 1960s, there was more good news for the consumer. The use of soy proteins in poultry feed turned ordinary chickens into plump ready-to-roast birds in a third less time than it used to take to fatten the flock for market. The proteins also reduced the amount of food farmers had to buy because the chickens were maturing and leaving the nest so quickly.

The per capita consumption of chicken in the United States rose by nearly 50 percent from 1950 to 1960, and then nearly doubled between 1960 and 1970. Shake 'N Bake fried chicken coating mix, Tyson's Rock Cornish, and Perdue's Oven Stuffer Roaster were just some of the ways Americans were enjoying the birds.

The biggest change, though, to how Americans eat and buy chicken, and the way poultry farmers raise chickens, all stemmed from a simple request made by Fred Turner, chairman of McDonald's fast-food chain, in 1979.

According to Eric Schlosser's book *Fast Food Nation*, Turner set in motion a revolution when he challenged vendors, saying, "I want a chicken finger food without bones . . . Can you do it?"

Turner's request led Tyson to develop a chicken with a plumper breast, perfect for the meaty strips McDonald's would coat with breading, deep-fry, and call McNuggets. Within a few years Americans wouldn't have to pull up to the drive-through window of the fast-food joint to see how far Turner's idea had gone. The advent of the chicken strip resulted in prepackaged chicken tenders and boneless chicken breasts in grocery stores across the country. With poultry farms like those of Perdue and Tyson now developing birds with meatier breasts, Americans were less interested in wings, thighs, backs, and drumsticks for recipes and meals. Grocers began selling fewer whole birds, and instead packaged cut-up chicken parts. Chicken breasts were perfect for stir-frying and stuffing, and the skinless, boneless presentation made them more appealing to busy homemakers. On top of that convenience, chicken—especially skinless white meat—was being proclaimed a healthier alternative to beef. But the ultimate sign of chicken's new affordability and status as a budget stretcher was the appearance of Chicken Helper, Hamburger Helper's newest shelf-mate, in 1985.

Turkey also got a makeover in the American Kitchen during the 1980s. Savvy poultry farmers realized that, as with chicken, the health benefits of turkey could prove to be a selling point among the health-conscious consumers of the eighties. The larger bird was also more versatile than its smaller counterpart and could be used in less conventional ways. Turkey-breast luncheon meats were reminiscent of the sandwiches Americans made from the leftovers of their Thanksgiving turkey, and ground turkey could be formed into patties, just like ground beef. Most important, turkey was priced lower than choice cuts of beef. Turkey consumption, per capita, nearly doubled from 1980 to 1990, as Americans began to view it as another cost-effective way to eat healthy.

The new emphasis on leaner cuisine also made fish a more attractive meal choice in the 1980s. While Americans ate less fish in the mid-fifties because of their love affair with beef, the mid-sixties saw an increase in the consumption of fish, per capita, which gradually continued through the early eighties, with only some minor setbacks. Even the November 1966 repeal of the law requiring Roman Catholics to abstain from meat on Fridays year-round didn't sink fish sales in America. The tuna industry had new money backing the StarKist brand of canned tuna after the Heinz corporation scooped it into its net. The cartoon mascot Charlie the Tuna began appearing in television commercials at about the same time. Increased visibility, and a likeable spokes-fish, led to increased sales.

Americans were fond enough of fish during the 1960s that Shake 'N Bake was originally released with two recipes—one for chicken, the other for fish. Even the fear of pollutants in the world's oceans, lakes, and streams didn't discourage people from eating salmon, tuna, trout, haddock, and cod. The pollution issue did, however, bring about the start of catfish hatcheries in the South, where fish farmers could monitor their gilled charges by controlling their diets and filtering the water they lived in. The catfish farms were so successful that they sparked a trend of other, similar facilities. Even clam hatcheries began opening, supplying markets and restaurants with another fresh source of seafood.

By the beginning of the 1970s Americans, along with the rest of the world's inhabitants, were eating enough fish to cause some concern among environmentalists that natural resources were being depleted. Farm-raised fish continued to be a viable solution to the problem, as the Arkansas catfish farmers had proven, and soon farm-raised trout and salmon were appearing in America's grocery stores.

Unfortunately, that trend didn't make it into the early 1980s; fish sales slumped from 1978 until 1984. Helping to spark some of the new interest in fish in the mid-eighties were the spicy flavors of the hot Cajun and Creole trends. Chunks of fish and bits of shrimp and other seafood swam through molten pots of gumbo, and fillets of catfish and red snapper were encrusted with an armor of spices and then blackened in cast-iron skillets.

The National Fisheries Institute also did its part to capitalize on the nation's new interest in healthy eating; the organization sponsored a campaign to hook more of the public into making the switch. "Eat Fish and Seafood Twice a Week," the institute advised, and Americans listened, increasing their per capita consumption by about 25 percent from the decade's start to its end.

As more plates of poultry and fish were served in the American Kitchen of the 1980s, less beef was being eaten. In 1985 beef consumption in the United States reached its per capita high for the decade—an average of nearly seventy-nine pounds. After that peak point, sales figures began to decline steadily. Statistics from the USRDA and the USDA seemed to provide all the damning evidence a consumer would need: If fat and cholesterol were potential contributors to the development of heart disease, diners had to look no further than the nutritional breakdown of a hamburger, for instance, to see that maybe they could make healthier choices when it came time to eat or cook a meal.

Farmers and ranchers who raised cattle and dairy cows were hit twice as hard in the eighties. Sales of milk and dairy products dropped by 20 percent in 1983 compared to sales and consumption in the 1950s. Americans especially turned their backs on whole milk, due to its higher fat content, and sales sank over 50 percent. With the plain hard facts in front of them, more

Americans were switching to a healthier lifestyle. And beef and whole dairy products were not part of their plan.

What was making things more difficult for the beef and dairy industries—as if the medical reports weren't bad enough—was that now there were more alternatives available to red meat, and even to dairy products, in grocery stores across the United States. Chicken, turkey, fish, and even vegetarian foods were easily obtained, and they were often cheaper than dairy. There were more options in the American Kitchen than ever before.

The beef industry had to do something to prop up its slumping sales figures. In 1987 the Beef Industry Council launched an advertising campaign featuring statistics of its own. If the American public was so attuned to the fat content of the foods they ate, the beef industry's tactic was to use those very same figures to promote their product. The campaign, "Beef. Real Food for Real People," was designed to show Americans the healthier side of red meat. Using visually stunning print ads that appeared in the likes of *Gourmet* magazine, the beef industry made its case for the inclusion of beef in a low-fat diet by focusing on "The Skinniest Six": the cuts of beef that had the lowest fat and calorie counts. Top round, top loin, round tip, eye of round, sirloin, and tenderloin slabs of meat were low in fat, once any visible flab was discarded, and they were also high in the U.S. recommended daily allowances of protein, zinc, and vitamin B$_{12}$. By using government-set dietary guidelines, the Beef Industry Council also called attention to the "wonderfully average" cholesterol levels in a three-ounce serving of beef.

The "Real Food for Real People" campaign was meant to reassure fans of beef that they weren't inching a step closer to the grave with each bite of red meat they forked into their mouths. But the use of the phrase *real people* was also a way to disparage the eating habits of those who might have made a choice to switch to healthier foods, deciding to avoid beef altogether. The print campaign blasted the health-food movement from the start: "If your taste buds are not altogether excited about a future of organic fiber flakes, the beef industry would like a few words with you." Later, another swipe was taken at the American Kitchen's growing haute cuisine trend, as the ad promised cooks that beef was one meal that required "no sauces, no fussing, no frou-frou."

The National Dairy Board was likewise facing its own share of bad PR as the fat and cholesterol contents of milk and cheese products branded both foods with an unhealthy stamp. Like the Beef Industry Council, the Dairy Board decided to shift public attention toward what was healthy about their foods. America's dairy farmers had already found an effective way to combat the loss of sales they might have endured as "lactose intolerance" became a much talked about health issue in the eighties by formulating lactose-free milk and ice cream. But the National Dairy Board discovered that by focusing on osteoporosis, another hot medical topic of the decade, they had the means to lure back certain customers, particularly women (since women were more likely to be affected by the degenerative bone disease than were men). Milk products are full of calcium, a necessary element in the building of strong teeth and bones, and in a series of ads aimed at women, the Dairy Board reminded consumers of the one-stop-shopping aspect of keeping dairy in their diets. At a time when orange juice companies were beginning to fortify their breakfast drinks with added calcium—one way to attract lactose-intolerant types who were concerned about brittle bones—America's dairy farmers fought back by reminding their customers that calcium occurred in milk "the way nature intended." With words like *natural* and *organic* still being descriptors associated with a healthy lifestyle, the Dairy Board was able to keep the attention on why milk and cheese *should* be in the American diet. And the board made sure that homemakers knew their foods could be part of every meal and snack break. "It's as easy to add more dairy foods to your diet as it is to enjoy them," the campaign urged. Frothy steamed milk was the magic element that not only turned coffee into cappuccino, but created an all-new, calcium-rich delivery system. Taste did not have to be sacrificed in the name of cutting fat and calories, either: "Stay on a diet and have your carrot and celery sticks with a cottage cheese, yogurt, green onion and dill weed dip," the dairy industry urged.

The beef and dairy industries weren't alone in the struggle for a place on the table. Pork was soon christened the "Other White Meat" as a way to remind homemakers that chicken wasn't the only substitute for beef. "If you think you have to serve fish or fowl to get the light, wholesome nutrition and easy convenience that today's lifestyles demand, take a fresh look at pork— the *other* white meat," the ad from the National Pork Producers Council and National Pork Board implored. Meanwhile, the American Egg Board had been trying to enact some damage control of its own since the late seventies by repositioning its namesake with the "Incredible Edible Egg" campaign. Fears about the high level of cholesterol in eggs made consumers more apt to reach for a carton of egg alternatives like Scramblers or Egg Beaters. Regardless of the campaigning, though, per capita consumption of eggs began to slide in 1984 and continued to do so into the next decade. But as Americans concentrated on what was being taken out of their diets, something else was sneaking into their kitchens that had the potential to be just as harmful to their overall health.

Americans may have been cutting back on some of their favorite foods in the eighties, but they were hardly ready to give up all of their vices. In fact, as beef consumption was on the decline, sugar consumption was soaring. Candy sales were booming. Chocolate was one indulgence Americans didn't want to turn their backs on, and high-end "designer" confectioners like Godiva were more than happy to deliver the fix. In true eighties fashion, the mind-set of "the higher the price the sweeter the reward" applied to everything, even ice cream. Luxury labels like Häagen Dazs and Früsen Gladjé could be found in grocers' freezers across the country, and slick ad campaigns for rival brands capitalized on the growing culinary awareness in the American Kitchen. Dove Bars were promoted as being "Haute And Cold," whereas Häagen Dazs tried to entice consumers with ice cream bars "tastefully wrapped" in "imported Belgian chocolate."

Americans were on a sugar high, but the climbing price of the sweetener was enough to bring that high to a screeching halt. A cheaper alternative was already making its way into the American Kitchen and diet. In 1980 Coca-Cola replaced part of the sugar content in its formula with high-fructose corn syrup. Companies had been using high-fructose corn syrup since the last half of the seventies because of its economical versatility. Coke's switch came about at a time when a surplus in corn in America—the Russian invasion of Afghanistan in 1979 prompted President Jimmy Carter to enact an embargo against grain sales to the Soviet Union—had made it the cheaper choice for a sweetener. With an abundance of corn in the U.S. market and with sugar on the world market climbing to prices 50 percent higher than the previous year, replacing sugar in products with high-fructose corn syrup seemed like the natural, and smart, choice.

At first the benefits of replacing sugar with high-fructose corn syrup were obvious. The product was a life-saver for a company's bottom line, as it was 25 percent cheaper to use than cane sugar. It was also six times sweeter than regular sugar, and that meant a food manufacturer could use even less high-fructose corn syrup than sugar. But the reward-reaping didn't stop there. With more food manufacturers beginning to use high-fructose corn syrup in their products, the demand for corn resulted in farmers planting from fence post to fence post. Such unrestricted production had been discouraged in the past.

There were only so many uses for the crop, and a surplus could tip an already teetering economy too far by driving prices too low, hurting the farmer, or too high, affecting the consumer. But the development of corn as a basis for a sweetening agent made its presence in the market nearly irreplaceable.

For the consumer, the widespread planting and uses of corn manifested in the form of savings on their grocery bills. With the grain being so readily available, meat and poultry became more affordable, as did dairy products. Beyond functioning as a sweetener and as feed for livestock, corn, in the form of high-fructose corn syrup, made the foods it was used in less perishable. According to Greg Critser, in his book *Fat Land*, high-fructose corn syrup not only protected products from developing freezer burn, it also kept foods destined to be sold—and stored—in vending machines fresher, longer. Even baked goods, like rolls, were given an oven-browned glow.

While additional corn yields were great for the economy, the effects of high-fructose corn syrup on the human body were quite detrimental. High-fructose corn syrup doesn't get broken down by the body the same way as other sweeteners like dextrose or sucrose. The by-product of this reaction is that the body burns sugar, rather than stored fat, for its energy. And the extra calories, courtesy of the high-fructose corn syrup, settle into the body and eventually turn into additional pounds of fat.

The fallout from the widespread use of high-fructose corn syrup was clearly visible by the end of the eighties, as the obesity trend in America continued to balloon.

Of course, not all corn consumption in the American Kitchen during the 1980s was as potentially harmful as was its high-fructose corn syrup derivative. The continued popularity of Mexican food, along with the buzz over America's own Southwest cuisine, returned corn to the American menu in style.

By the 1980s the foods of Mexico had been popular in America for at least a decade. Tacos, for instance, were already as ordinary as spaghetti by 1979. On the other hand Chiles Rellenos, the stuffed pepper of the Mexican kitchen, was still exotic enough in the late seventies that a reader in search of a recipe for the dish had to write in to *Gourmet*'s "You Asked for It" column. Nearly ten years later, much had changed. Sales of Mexican foods in grocery stores had reached the billion-dollar mark by 1987. Shoppers could now find jicama and yucca with relative ease in the produce section, and frozen burritos in the freezer aisle. American food manufacturers were even trying to find their niche in this growing market, stocking jars of jalapeño Cheez Whiz on supermarket shelves.

America's love affair with south-of-the-border cuisine received an additional spark in the mid-eighties when a large influx of Mexican immigrants settled in the United States. With so many great new recipes being brought into the country along with these new arrivals, the American Kitchen began venturing deeper into Mexican cooking. Quesadillas were the hot new appetizer. Tamales tested Americans' mettle as they tried working with cornhusks. Potato chips and onion dips were out; tortilla chips, guacamole, sour cream, and salsa—both red and green varieties—were in.

Mexican foods retained their authenticity once they arrived in the American Kitchen; with Mexican Americans creating such large, close-knit communities in various parts of the country, Mexican immigrants were assured that the legacy of their culture and cuisine remained intact. In addition to the markets in cities like Miami, Los Angeles, and Washington, D.C., which were now carrying vegetables and herbs like tomatillos and cilantro, kitchen-supply stores owned and operated by Mexican and other Hispanic immigrants were peddling items like tortilla pans. Americans of all ethnic backgrounds who wanted to remain purists and grind corn into their own tortillas could now get a feel for *hecho a mano*—"made by hand"—authenticity.

Refried beans and fajitas were now readily available by the can and at fast-food counters, but the American Kitchen didn't stop at Mexican foods when it came to embracing Hispanic culture in the 1980s. Spanish cuisine had another burst of popularity, as it had in the sixties with paella, but this time tapas became the hot menu item. The small tapas plates of olives, anchovies, and mushrooms fit nicely into the eighties' nouvelle cuisine notion of less-is-more. And like in the sixties, when artists such as Miró, Picasso, and Dalí ushered in a cultural exchange, the eighties had the work of another Spanish maverick whose art was capturing the attention of Americans: The films of director Pedro Almodóvar appealed to the arty sensibility of the eighties postmodern movement. American film-critic groups, like the New York Film Critics Circle, honored Almodóvar in their annual awards ceremonies. While the director's cult favorite *Women on the Verge of a Nervous Breakdown* might have given American audiences who missed *Law of Desire* their first glimpse at Spanish star Antonio Banderas, it was the blender full of sedative-laced gazpacho that created the film's most memorable moment.

Gazpacho, like salsa, was another tomato-based food with Hispanic ties the American Kitchen had accepted, mastered, and then experimented with by the decade's end. Restaurants served it with islands of crabmeat, or sub-stituted yellow or green tomatoes and peppers for the traditional red. But for home cooks, the fun of creating the soup came from the no-cook, no-fuss recipe; all the ingredients could be thrown into the food processor, and after several minutes of slicing and whirring, a tasty and sophisticated dish was ready to serve. Gazpacho was also one of the dishes that had crossover ap-peal between the Spanish, Mexican, and Southwestern food trends of the eighties, the latter being a phenomenon unto itself.

While Southwestern cooking relied on some of the same ingredients of its Mexican ancestor—corn, beans, chili peppers—it set itself apart with the strong and distinctly American presence of beef in its recipes. Even though beef consumption in the United States had begun to drop in the eighties, red meat experienced a small revival thanks to dishes like Black Bean Chili with Sirloin and Asiago, Spicy Beef Tartare, and Enchiladas of Filet Mignon and Chanterelles and Sorrel Sauce. This trio of recipes, taken from Ellen Brown's *Southwest Tastes*, the companion cookbook to the *Great Chefs of the World* public television series, was a good example of the fusion mentality Ameri-cans were adopting in their kitchens. Regional offerings, like the bean and corn dishes of the Southwest, were now viewed as canvases, prime outlets for other forms of culinary expression. Chefs and home cooks alike were discov-ering that the foods of the Southwest provided great tools for experimenta-tion, as the smoky and peppery flavors lent themselves well to a variety of ingredients. With this kind of adaptability, this homegrown American cui-sine was destined to remain popular. Besides, Southwestern accents were everywhere in the eighties. The spirituality of the Native Americans of the region was a draw for the decade's New Age enthusiasts looking for alterna-tive ways to express and explore their metaphysical sides.

As the U.S. economy came back to life in the eighties after the recession in the seventies, the world was once again wide open for Americans with the fi-nancial means to explore it. As they had in the postwar years of the fifties, throngs of American tourists packed their bags and headed overseas. *Time* magazine noted in April 1985 that "millions [were going] abroad on the greatest sight-seeing and shopping spree ever." The strong market at home had made the U.S. dollar even more powerful abroad, and just as they had in the past, Americans brought home stories and, in some cases, recipes of the exotic foods and extravagant meals they encountered in their travels.

Travel had made the world smaller for many Americans, but when it came to dining experiences in the eighties, so had immigration. More foreign cuisines were now represented in restaurants throughout the country than ever before, and more exotic foods were popping up in produce sections of supermarkets across America. For instance, of the half-million-plus legal immigrants who entered the United States in 1984, Vietnamese arrivals comprised the third-largest group. Before long, pork snouts and pickled banana buds, staples of the home kitchen in Vietnam, were just an aisle over from Vienna sausage and iceberg lettuce in the grocery stores of suburban California. Soon Vietnamese-owned storefront restaurants and carry-out shops started to appear in cities like Minneapolis, selling delicately crisp spring rolls and soul-warming bowls of noodle soup called *pho*. Vietnamese cuisine didn't conquer the American Kitchen the way other Asian foods, like Chinese, had in the past or, like Thai, would in the future. As Sylvia Lovegren writes in *Fashionable Food*, "Americans who were getting bored with Chinese food were intrigued by the new flavors of Vietnamese cooking [and its] . . . sweet-sour-salty-fresh tastes," and that "Vietnamese restaurants became a fad for a while in the early Eighties." Lovegren also notes that Thai food received a warmer welcome in the American Kitchen than did its Vietnamese counterpart during the same decade. While some food historians would agree that one of a nation's best cultural ambassadors is its cuisine, the initial indifference among Americans to Vietnamese cuisine probably had less to do with the actual food and more to do with the lingering unease due to U.S. military involvement in Vietnam and its divisive impact on the United States home front. Thai food, however, had no such strikes against it.

Thai food might share some ingredients with Vietnamese dishes, but it is the bolder of the two cuisines. Fish sauce, for instance, is a favorite condiment in both cuisines, but the Vietnamese version tends to be less pungent than the Thai. While chili peppers heat up dishes in both countries, Thai recipes tend to be more scorching, and if there was one thing Americans loved in the eighties, it was extreme food. The spiciness of the Thai cuisine offered a new high for foodies who were no longer wowed by hot Hunan dishes or sizzling Mexican fare. For the home cook, Thai dishes were also easy enough to approximate. A passable version of Spicy Thai Noodles could be whipped up with staples that lined the shelves of most American kitchens—peanut butter, angel hair pasta, and soy sauce. More authentic recipes could be found in magazines like *Gourmet*, which in the late eighties printed recipes for Thai Chicken Salad with Cellophane Noodles with only the slightest explanation that said noodles were "bean threads, available at

Oriental markets and many supermarkets." Such a footnote, even a few short months prior, would have read "and *some* supermarkets." Between January and June 1989, availability had become less of an issue.

The one international cuisine that opened the American Kitchen's doors even wider for other foods, particularly Asian, was Japanese sushi. Chef and best-selling author Anthony Bourdain says, "When Americans suddenly decided they could and would eat sushi, and they liked it, it changed everything." Bourdain explains, "Once you're willing to eat a quivering raw piece of fish, or to eat fish roe or octopus, suddenly you're open to everything. You've crossed the Rubicon."

Bourdain, the author of *Kitchen Confidential* and host of the Food Network's *A Cook's Tour*, credits sushi with allowing chefs of other ethnic cuisines to serve the traditional foods of their own cultures. "Suddenly the threshold for seafood and products that are part of traditional French and Italian menus changes," Bourdain says of sushi's impact on the American palate. "Suddenly we can serve mackerel, anchovies, sardines, squid, tuna. . . ." Italian restaurants in the United States, took advantage of that opportunity, adding additional seafood dishes to their menus. Fish markets began carrying more than the standard haddock, cod, perch, and tuna; meaty slabs of mahimahi and swordfish steaks were now for sale. Items that once seemed exotic, like fried calamari, were now less threatening if for no other reason than that they were cooked. The same went for black strings of fettuccini. Black pasta, made with squid and octopus ink, began appearing on restaurant menus, and even in some gourmet shops. Spanish tapas, which had chilled dishes featuring marinated baby octopus and squid, also got a lift from the sushi wave. Sushi was one food, however, that cooks were not rushing to try at home. Kits for making rolls, which included sheets of seaweed and bamboo rolling mats, were primarily put to work making "safe" sushi like smoked salmon and avocado rolls. Americans might not have had any trouble eating raw fish, but preparing it in their own kitchens took some getting used to. Ceviche, sushi's Hispanic cousin, seduced some cooks during the eighties with its promise that the acid in lime juice "cooked" the fish flesh. Once news of this spread, raw tuna eventually gained clearance in America's kitchens with recipes that relied heavily on the powers of acidic lime juice, and *Gourmet* featured several such recipes in the late eighties, like Raw Tuna with Preserved Vegetables and Ginger.

Sushi, as an emissary for Japanese cuisine, helped Americans become acquainted with other elements of the Japanese kitchen. Items like miso, pickled ginger, wasabi, and daikon were soon available for the American home cook through mainstream outlets like A&P or Giant Food.

In its role as culinary ice-breaker, sushi also made the idea of eating raw beef fashionable again. Sixties fave Steak Tartare, served with potent chili peppers and wedges of the trusty "bacteria-killing" lime, made a comeback in the 1980s. Similarly, Beef Carpaccio, sliced thin enough to read a newspaper through, became the Italian representative in the raw-food trend.

As the flirtation with Beef Carpaccio proved, the American Kitchen was not ready to say *arrivederci* to Italian food. In fact, Americans in the eighties fell even deeper in love with Italy's cuisines, and were now able to make distinctions between cuisines of the northern and southern regions of the country. Americans had become more comfortable with the ins and outs of Italian cooking since the 1950s, having moved past the al dente test of throwing partially cooked pasta against the wall to see if it would stick. There were more options than spaghetti in the pasta section of most supermarkets, even though homemade pasta-makers were the gift of the moment. And as for boxed risotto . . . not in the eighties. With Arborio rice readily available in most grocery stores, Americans who were interested in eating bona fide ethnic meals were rolling up their sleeves, and in the case of stirring-intensive dishes like risotto, flexing the necessary muscles to achieve that authenticity.

Then, as the eighties came to a close, it was all about pesto in the world of pasta. Pine nuts and basil were on gourmands' grocery lists across the country. Pesto would go on to become so popular that in an early episode of the 1990s sitcom *Seinfeld*, Jason Alexander's character, George Costanza, groused about the now-ubiquitous nature of the sauce. "Where was pesto ten years ago?"

One reason for the popularity of pesto during the second half of the eighties was its ease of execution, thanks to the ubiquity of the food processor in the American Kitchen. The once costly Cuisinart food processor and its imitators could be had for less than forty dollars, *and* they came with variable speed switches. Pine nuts for pesto could now be ground with the flick of a switch. Food processors now had to fight for favorite appliance status with the other new gadgets available on the market. Microwaves were in enough kitchens that *Gourmet* had a monthly column devoted to "Microwave Mastery," in which the machine's convenience was as important as the cuisine. Shrimp salad, for instance, could be made in the microwave in the cool of a summer's morning and refrigerated until dinnertime. (The column disappeared toward the decade's end as more people came to rely on their microwaves for popping corn or heating water for tea rather than for actual cooking.) Braun introduced a handheld blender that slipped easily into a drawer when not in use. The wandlike instrument whipped up a small storm in a cup or bowl and was perfect for those times when the power of the KitchenAid mixer was more muscle than the job required.

When it came to big kitchen "machines," bulky cappuccino and espresso machines were holding court on countertops in some American homes. The role of coffee in American life was beginning to change, and Braun and its German compatriot Krups were changing how Americans thought about the automatic-drip coffeemaker and seducing java junkies with the cylindrical forms and cone-shaped drip baskets of the European machines. Krups also made its machines more enticing by occasionally offering gold-plated reusable basket filters and compact electric coffee-bean grinders with the sale of one of their coffeemakers. Vegetable juicers were also hot in the eighties, with both the haute and health-conscious crowds.

Best of all, this new equipment could be had without a trip to Europe, or without placing an order from a pricy catalog or kitchen specialty store. The kitchenware department at Macy's department store, known as The Cellar, was making acquisition of these new toys as easy as a trip to the mall. Brands like Braun, Krups, and T-Fal (makers of sturdy pots and pans) were not only readily available, they were reasonably priced. Even electronic appliances like VCRs were being used in the kitchen; in Susan Seidelman's *Desperately Seeking Susan*, Rosanna Arquette's character, Roberta, relies on her Julia Child videotape and her countertop VCR to coach her through dinner preparations.

Technology and the healthy economy were responsible for changing the way Americans cooked in the eighties, as both had done in the past. The difference in the latter part of the twentieth century, however, was that cooking had gone from an arduous task done out of necessity to a leisure activity pursued for the sake of cultural exploration, personal enjoyment, and status. Americans were not cooking now because they *had* to; there were plenty of prepared frozen and canned foods, and even shelf-stable foods, that could go from the fridge or pantry to the dinner table with a few simple pushes of a button. Americans were now using their kitchens because they *wanted* to. While this hardly would have been viewed as a victory for the domestic scientists and food technologists whose mission had always been to take the fuss out of cooking, those lab-coated types from the first half of the century had the last laugh, since the American Kitchen of the 1980s resembled the stark but sanitary laboratories where they toiled. The eco-conscious colors of the American Kitchen of the 1970s, like avocado and paprika, were as unwelcome in the sleek kitchen of the eighties as bell-bottoms and platform shoes were in the decade's wardrobe. Earth tones were no longer chic, and the American Kitchen began to fade to black: black-clad appliances, black-tile backsplashes, and black-granite countertops.

"Everything went black in the eighties," says Walter Gagliano, interior designer at G&G Arte in Washington, D.C. "Black just felt great and techie. Black was very cool. Cars were purged of wood trim, and stereos and TVs stopped being wood-grained and went black."

Black was the new harvest gold. By stripping away the seasonal shades and the earthy hues, the look of America's kitchens echoed the assumed automation of the decade. Black also felt more in line with the eighties' synthetic vision of the future. Popular bands like New Order, Soft Cell, and Depeche Mode made music that often sounded cold and robotic. Television shows like *Max Headroom* and *Knight Rider*, movies like *The Terminator* and *Robocop*, and books like William Gibson's genre-defining *Neuromancer* predicted an era when the line between humans and computer-machines would be blurred. And in some kitchens of the eighties, the human touch was noticeably, and intentionally, lacking. "The room looked like nobody was home," Gagliano says. "Everything was hidden. There were appliance garages where everything was tucked away. There were big, long, sleek horizontal bands of cabinetry where you weren't quite sure where to grab or touch to make them open."

Gagliano also points to these high-tech labs as the beginning of "vanity kitchens." The state-of-the-art, high-design kitchens of the 1980s were on display, like a work of art. "When you can see the kitchen from the living room sofa, you want it to look different than it did when it was behind a door," Gagliano says.

The clean, linear designs and black finishes of the eighties kitchen were the perfect dramatic backdrop for countertop appliances like the well-designed Krups coffeepot—when it was allowed out of its hiding place—but the items that really made an impression in this severe setting were the new arty trophies Americans were bringing into their kitchens, often for no other reason than display. The Whistling Bird Teakettle, designed by American architect Michael Graves in 1985 for Italian company Alessi, became such an unparalleled success both in style and sales that it became known simply as the Teakettle. The vessel was the It item of the American Kitchen during the eighties and has been called "one of the most influential objects of the post-modern style that typified the 1980s."

Around the same time that Graves's Teakettle was making its auspicious debut in America's kitchens, French designer Philippe Starck began working with Alessi. Starck was known as the enfant terrible of the international de-sign world; the items he went on to produce for the Italian manufacturer be-came as iconic as Graves's. Starck's Juicy Salif Lemon Squeezer showed his genius for tweaking expectations when it came to form and function. Most citrus juicers were handheld gadgets that were small enough to slip into a drawer when they weren't on the job. But the Juicy Salif, standing nearly a foot tall and looking more like an alien spider than a kitchen utensil, de-manded attention—which is precisely why it was another must-have item in the American Kitchen of the eighties.

Graves and Starck were giving the increasingly status- (and style-)conscious consumers of the 1980s what Russel and Mary Wright, Eva Zeisel, and Arne Jacobson had given homeowners in the past—well-designed objects that re-flected their own aesthetic and the times in which they lived.

When the stock market crashed in October 1987, the joyride that had been the 1980s came to an abrupt end. The extravagant worlds that Americans had seen on TV—from the lavish lifestyles of the rich and famous to the over-the-top glamour of the Carringtons and Colbys of *Dynasty*—were now more of a fantasy than ever. Even the upwardly mobile white-collar Keatons and Huxtables of *Family Ties* and *The Cosby Show* lived beyond the means of most Americans. The blue-collar reality of Roseanne and Dan Conner, on the other hand, was one way of life many Americans could relate to.

Based on the comedy of stand-up comic Roseanne Barr, *Roseanne* por-trayed a side of America the media had long neglected. As Steven D. Stark writes in *Glued to the Set*, "TV has traditionally ignored anyone who can't afford to buy a five-bedroom home."

What made Roseanne's television stardom unique was that there was nothing upper-middle class, or even classy, about the Conner household. Compared to the other people, events, trends, and shows that defined the de-cade, *Roseanne* was the antithesis of the eighties—or at least the media's por-trayal of it. At a time when aerobics classes and Slim-Fast diet drinks were a national obsession, Roseanne and her husband Dan were hefty, and for the most part seemingly happy with their size. And there was nothing state-of-the-art about the Conner family kitchen; not only were there no sexy European coffeemakers or designer teapots anywhere in sight, Roseanne barely had the essentials. (In one episode she joked about trading in one of her kids for a dishwasher.) And come mealtime, the food was more likely to be inspired by one of the institutional-sized cans of baked beans or vegetables that were in plain view on the pantry shelves, than by a recipe from Julia Child or an issue of *Bon Appétit*.

The honesty of *Roseanne* lay in its depiction of a family for whom bulk foods, shift work, and periods of unemployment were a way of life. Roseanne's television character didn't have the luxury of being able to worry about having it all; getting by was struggle enough.

Roseanne became known in the eighties for deadpanning that she preferred the term *domestic goddess* to *housewife*. The joke, of course, was that there seemed to be nothing domestic or godlike about her. She might not have been an image worthy of worship, but she was sovereign over her domain. And despite the wisecracks about using her kids as bartering chips for appliances, like other working moms in America, Roseanne's sitcom character gathered her family into the kitchen at mealtimes.

Needless to say, not everyone was carried along to a better way of life on the wave of prosperity that rose in the eighties, but regardless of the economic circumstances, appliances, or cuisines that defined them, kitchens across America were very much the same. The large, well-appointed kitchens of the Huxtables and the Keatons might have been something to aspire to, but the Conner kitchen was still very much the center of family activity despite its humble provisions. *Roseanne*'s kitchen definitely had more heart than haute, and the slight was intentional. As Stark writes "Barr called the show an attempt to create 'a comic vocabulary of material resentment,'" and with the conspicuous displays of wealth in the eighties, the Conner family had plenty, if they so chose, to resent.

If Roseanne was at one end of the eighties spectrum, another TV diva, Martha Stewart, certainly held down the position directly opposite her. Stewart's book *Entertaining* debuted in 1982 and altered the course of the American Kitchen with her distinctive do-it-yourself approach to the good life. At a time when all the things that symbolized the proverbial "good life" could be bought, and the ability to buy them was a sign of status in itself, Stewart changed the rules of the game by cooking, canning, baking, sewing, building, designing, arranging, and making things herself and—here was the real kicker—encouraging other American women to do the same. In this regard, Martha Stewart was no different from Julia Child twenty years earlier. Child appeared on the scene presenting recipes that required the type of attention to detail Americans had been trying to liberate themselves from in their kitchens. The workings of the American Kitchen at the time *The French Chef* premiered in 1962 were being quickly revolutionized as prepackaged, prepared, and instant foods were taking the place of the home-cooked meal. Likewise, in the eighties, when having the buying power to afford a lavishly catered event was one way of saying "I have it all," Stewart's hands-on approach applied an overachiever's sensibility to that mentality and upped the ante by adding "and I'm in control."

Through television appearances and subsequent books, Stewart established a cult following in the eighties, eventually attracting admiring legions of fans. It was hard not to be astounded by the way she made the nearly impossible seem everyday and ordinary. Tossing out comments like "I set my Thanksgiving table this year with an antique, twelve-piece Tom Turkey decanter set I found in the attic—and you can, too," she encouraged viewers to think past the limitations of their routines; never mind that not everyone had an attic where hidden treasures like an heirloom serving set were waiting to be discovered! Critics of Martha Stewart ridiculed her seeming ignorance of how much free time most Americans had to actually devote to one of her labor-intensive crafts or recipes—and as anyone who's ever tackled her approach to a simple dish like macaroni and cheese can attest, Martha Stewart's way of doing things requires a significant investment of time, not to mention a whole cabinet's worth of pots and pans. There are no such things as shortcuts or one-pot meals in her kitchen. But what her detractors didn't understand was that by investing the time in making something the Martha Stewart way, and in surrendering to the machinations involved, Americans were creating a new sense of home.

While this preoccupation with beautifying one's surroundings at first glance may have seemed like another symptom of the greed and vanity of the eighties, it soon revealed itself to be a much-needed remedy to the decade's excesses. As the 1990s drew near and the economic tide began to ebb, Americans began looking for things that had more lasting value. The instant nostalgia of Martha Stewart's approach helped families create new traditions in their homes. And for the American Kitchen, this was a good thing.

*   *   *

The rise in popularity of Martha Stewart as the eighties ended reflected the attitude of ownership that pervaded the American Kitchen throughout the decade. *Cook's* magazine, the ancestor of *Cook's Illustrated*, approached cooking in much the same way as Stewart did. Christopher Kimball, *Cook's* editor, began producing the journal-like publication in 1980. He ended the magazine's run in 1989, only to reinvent it as *Cook's Illustrated*, which combined *Cook's* observational notes on recipes with a *Consumer Reports*–like comparing and contrasting of ingredients. Like Stewart, Kimball addressed those food enthusiasts who derived an almost Zen-like pleasure by being mindful of the moment in the preparation of a recipe, no matter how detailed or involved.

The relationship between diet and lifestyle became more symbiotic in the eighties. The fitness craze had Americans breaking a sweat as they went in search of the ultimate exercise to help bulk up their muscles and the perfect diet to slim down their waistlines. As *GQ* magazine reported in 1983, "New fad diets are being served to our fitness-hungry society with the regularity of fresh fashion trends." Americans heeded the message that they could gain control over their health by making better choices at mealtime and in the supermarket.

And in the tech-driven world of kitchen gadgetry, there was always something new on the market in the 1980s to make food preparation exciting. Hi-tech vegetable juicers transformed carrot sticks and red beets into vitamin-rich drinks, and the handheld Salad Shooter by Presto tossed out round slices of cucumber as if they were poker chips. Both gizmos cashed in on dieting Americans' love affair with veggies and salad. In fact, some Americans began planting their own gardens. In their attempts to get back to basics, more Americans began to look no farther than their own backyards. Home gardens allowed people to have complete confidence in the foods they were serving their families, and to cater to their own tastes.

Looking through the rows of green sprouting across the country, the gardens at the end of the eighties were playing host to foods the Powhatan and even the first British settlers would never have imagined. The original trio of corn, squash, and beans had long ago made room for the likes of okra, carrots, and cauliflower, and now Americans were welcoming new arrivals like purple Peruvian potatoes, bitter Asian melons, and green-hulled tomatillos into their gardens.

Of all the transplants into the American Kitchen over the centuries, however, the 1990s would see the introduction of the strangest foods yet.

CHAPTER TEN

The Warmest Room: 1990–1999

The pots and pans, and the woman, who taught a generation of Americans how to cook were immortalized in Julia Child's wall of copper cookware. Donated from her original kitchen, part of the wall is in the Smithsonian Institute in Washington, D.C. This portion resides at COPIA, the American Center for Wine, Food, and the Arts in Napa Valley, California. (Courtesy of Faith Echtermeyer.)

The American Kitchen found itself on familiar but not so hospitable ground as the eighties ended and the nineties began. Once again, after a period of prosperity, the nation slid into an economic slump. Comparisons between the nineties and the seventies, and even the thirties, were inevitable, and not completely unjustified. Like the decades preceding those eras, the 1980s had been a time when living the good life no longer meant having the finer things but having the *finest* things. Armani became a household word, Trump became an adjective, and *Lifestyles of the Rich and Famous* became a precursor to reality TV for the wildly ambitious.

When the stock market crash of 1987 led to the recession of 1990, the trappings and excesses of the eighties looked empty and cold, and America's kitchens felt the chill in more ways than one. Those black-clad appliances, which were once white-hot, now felt icy and impersonal. Making a fuss over exotic cuisines seemed pretentious, and paying a fortune to enjoy them edged toward the perverse.

But this didn't mean that Americans were any less enthused about cooking or feeling at home in their kitchens. As it had during difficult times in the past, the American Kitchen turned to food as a source of comfort in the early 1990s. Dishes like macaroni and cheese, meat loaf, chili, and roasted chicken were popular again. *Taste of Home*, a magazine that featured the everyday recipes of its working-mom readership, debuted in 1993 and rapidly became the most-read cooking magazine on the market. Foreign foods were still welcome in the American Kitchen, but now the emphasis was on a culture's traditional fare, or, to quote the jacket of Jeff Smith's best seller, *The Frugal Gourmet on Our Immigrant Ancestors*, the "recipes you should have gotten from your grandmother."

Bioengineered foods were definitely not part of your grandmother's kitchen, but "Frankenfoods," as they came to be called, had been coming out of labs and growing in farmers' fields since the 1980s. In the 1990s, genetically altered vegetables were approved for sale by the United States Food and Drug Administration.

A less controversial addition to the kitchen to come from the decade's technological progress was online grocery shopping. With computers becoming more affordable in the nineties, Americans could now shop for their groceries without leaving their homes. (The online ordering and subsequent delivery of foods wasn't much different from the midcentury practice of telephoning the local grocer to place an order; direct human contact was the only thing missing in the cyber version.)

The emergence of e-commerce in the American Kitchen of the second half of the 1990s was one sure sign that the nation's financial prognosis was healthier; the proliferation of the Viking Stove was another. Now that income levels were on the rise again and new jobs were being created—in part because of the cyber explosion of dot-com commerce and investing—the trophy stove became the new must-have item for home-cooking aficionados. In some ways the restaurant-quality appliance actually fit right in with the comfort-food and homey trend of the early nineties; few things warmed up a kitchen like the tens of thousands of fiery BTUs coming from the multiburner Viking Stove.

For those who couldn't afford a professional stove, the terra-cotta garlic roaster was a more humble, but just as hot, kitchen must-have in the nineties. Garlic enjoyed a turn in the culinary spotlight as the It ingredient in restaurants and home kitchens. Garlic mashed potatoes were on menus coast-to-coast, and ramekins of roasted-garlic purees and spreads began accompanying breadsticks and crudités on the dinner table. Soon wasabi replaced garlic, as the versatile powdered Japanese horseradish wasn't just served with sushi any more: It gave mashed potatoes a new kick, and it teamed up with sesame seeds to encrust fish steaks, beef, and even meat loaf.

Americans also took the drinks accompanying their meals very seriously in the nineties. Microbrews became popular, and it wasn't long before would-be beer-meisters were fermenting a wild assortment of ingredients like hops, wheat, barley, oats, honey, and raspberries in their basements as they tried to bottle their own brews. For those who didn't have such a pioneering spirit and preferred to leave beer-making in the American Kitchen's distant past, the cocktail craze was a better bit. Hipsters sank garlic-stuffed olives into martini glasses big enough for Dean Martin to swim in. Tracks by Esquivel and João Gilberto became the music of choice for the crowd that wanted to zoom-a-zoom-zoom back to the days of swingin' chicks and space-age bachelor pads.

But martinis weren't the only blast from the past shaking and stirring things up in the nineties. Midcentury nostalgia gave the American Kitchen a design makeover as furniture by the Eameses, Saarinen, and Jacobsen were in demand. The works of Russel and Mary Wright were again en vogue, and whimsical New York designer Jonathan Adler created a sensation with the retro-spin of his sugar bowl and creamer sets and salt and pepper shakers.

The optimism associated with midcentury design and the post–World War II era permeated America's kitchens at the end of the twentieth century. In their final year, however, the nineties suffered from a slight case of new-millennium jitters. Kitchen cupboards, pantry shelves, basements, and garages were filled with bottles of water, batteries, Coleman lanterns and stoves, and nonperishable foods. Necessities were stockpiled by the nervous and the practical: Predictions that the dreaded Millennium Bug would bite the elaborate computer system that kept the water flowing and the lights burning in kitchens across America cast a pall over the last days of the nation's longest era of peace and prosperity.

By January 1991 food prices were on average 34 percent higher than they had been when the nation had last transitioned out of an economic slump, not even ten years earlier (in the years between 1982 and 1984). Refrigerator staples like milk and eggs were especially vulnerable since both were products of industries that relied on feed corn, and the corn industry had in turn endured setbacks due to droughts and infections by a fungus known as aspergillus.

By 1993, one in ten Americans was receiving government assistance through food stamps. With some Americans having less money to spend on food, the U.S. government picked the perfect time to revise the dietary guidelines formerly referred to as the four basic food groups. Malnutrition often occurs because people who otherwise might be able to afford to eat healthy make the wrong dietary choices in an attempt to eat foods that are more filling. So, in 1992, the United States Department of Agriculture unveiled its Food Pyramid, which assigned numeric and positional quantifiers to the amount and types of foods that should be eaten. Doing away with the four basic food groups, the Food Pyramid showed Americans that the foundation of their diet should be several servings of grains. Using the suggestions of breads and grains as a solid base, the Pyramid then recommended three to five daily servings of vegetables and fruit. Protein followed, and was to come from dairy, poultry, and meat. Finally, at its peak, the Food Pyramid made allowances for limited use of fats and sugars.

Another noticeable sign of the economic instability of the early nineties was the reappearance in television commercials of the Hamburger Helper Helping Hand mascot. Since the creation of the TV spokes-hand in the late 1970s, General Mills had trotted the animated kitchen helper back into its advertisements at times when homemakers might be having trouble making ends meet. In a press release from General Mills' public relations group, the food manufacturer explained that Hamburger Helper itself was "introduced [in 1971] in response to economy-minded consumers' demand for convenient ways to use hamburger," and with the country in a recession in the early nineties, most Americans were again counting their pennies. With this advertising campaign, reminiscent of the tough economic times of the 1970s, and with the previously mentioned drought recalling the 1930s, the American Kitchen was facing a set of circumstances similar to the ones that had triggered the Great Depression. But this time around, breadlines wouldn't be threading through city blocks. Food production had developed significantly since the first half of the century, and the concerns that had beleaguered human survival from the very beginning—the production, preservation, and storage of sufficient food supplies—were no longer the threats they'd once been. Agricultural methods had changed, too. The problems of erosion and depleted soils had been addressed as farmers learned about crop rotation. The government, likewise, had learned from the recession of the 1970s that a safety net of welfare assistance has to be in place for citizens who come upon hard economic times. The promise of the food technologists that Americans would have an abundance of food to guarantee their subsistence had been kept, and the U.S. food industry could now withstand natural disasters and economic uncertainty and still have food to spare. Pesticides battled vermin, irrigation brought water to dry or drought-parched fields, and methods of food preservation—from frozen meals to shelf-stable ready-to-eat canned goods— all helped to create a surplus of provisions. Soon, science would undertake new efforts in its attempts to improve upon nature by developing new varieties of engineered crops.

In the year 2073, when Miles Monroe, Woody Allen's alter ego in his film *Sleeper*, awakes from a two-hundred-year-long cryogenic nap, he finds himself in a world where fruits and vegetables grow on electrode wires instead of vines, and chickens, twice the size of a grown man, are walked on leashes. After wresting a banana the size of a canoe, and a towering stalk of celery out of the fields in which they were growing, Monroe deadpans, "I still can't believe the size of these vegetables. I'd hate to see what they use for fertilizer."

Allen's vision of the gardens of the future, as seen in his 1973 film, emphasized a single plant's output. In this case tomatoes, strawberries, onions, bananas, and celery all grew to gigantic proportions thanks to a lifeline that fed them über-growth hormones. The movie was science fiction, of course, but as time would tell, *Sleeper*'s vision of futuristic food was closer to reality than the dinner-pill-as-diet-of-the-future depicted in other forms of entertainment.

Seven years after Woody Allen's film was released, food technology was about to boldly go where no crop had gone before: In 1980, gene-splicing went from science fiction to laboratory reality. In the nineties, the resulting bioengineered foods would make it to America's kitchen table.

A whole new world of possibilities was created when the genes from one organism were successfully spliced with the genes of another. Food-technology and food-engineering literature are fond of comparing what goes on in the fermentation process of bread and cheese to the manipulation of organisms that results from gene-splicing. But there *is* a difference. As Dr. Michael Ambrose explains:

Fermentation is simply the normal biological action of the yeast. In the case of beer and bread, the yeast eats the sugars and through their metabolism of this energy source, carbon dioxide is created. And in the case of beer, alcohol occurs as well. This is simple bio-energy conversion: life. But in rDNA [recombinant DNA] work, the splicing of foreign genes into the genomic material of the host species is done in such a manner that the host will duplicate and express the foreign gene as its own.

Dr. Ambrose's example is best illustrated by two bioengineered foods that were generated during the 1990s—Insect-Resistant Corn and the Improved Ripening Tomato. "The *biological function* of those foreign genes"—the ones being spliced into the host—"are specific to the gene in question: In the corn, it is resistance, in the tomato, it's the aging process."

Prior to the breakthroughs in gene-splicing, genetically modified fruits and vegetables were fodder for science-fiction plotlines. But once this know-how became a reality, the full potential of its applications was quickly considered. It was one thing to better the quality of preexisting enzymes and proteins; but what about moving beyond the specimen under a microscope, into the rest of the world? On one hand, gene-splicing could produce new varieties of vegetables that are resistant to different types of natural pests, like the above-mentioned corn; on the other, new microbes that nature never intended to roam the earth could be created. Evolution and natural selection could be by passed all together. What would be the consequences?

In the 1980s, food engineers waded into these new waters cautiously. One of the first applications of the gene-splicing technology was the creation of rennin, a substance needed to coagulate cream in the cheese-making process. Rennin is an enzyme, the natural by-product of rennet, which in turn is an extract from the lining of a cow's stomach. Then, in 1990, the FDA approved the use of chymosin, a clotting agent used in the manufacturing of cheese, as the first bioengineered food product. This was relatively small stuff, however, compared with what was to follow.

If synthetic rennin could be created to accelerate the ripening of cheese (which resulted in significant savings for manufacturer and consumer alike, since nearly one third of the processing time was eliminated thanks to the engineered rennin), what could be done to address the vulnerability of certain types of crops, not only to pests but to any aversion a plant might have to the poisons used to eradicate those pests? What about developing vegetables that were resistant to viruses? Could ripening periods be quickened, or slowed down, depending on the season? If chickens could be developed that were market-ready in as little as two months, could vegetables be produced that would germinate and produce something edible within a fraction of the time of normal seeds? And what about increasing the gallons of milk dairy cows produce? Could these nuisances become issues of the past for farmers?

The answer to those questions appeared to be a resounding yes. Throughout the 1980s, food engineers worked with new technology to create additives like vitamins, flavors, and food colors. Eventually, gene-splicing experiments were conducted to create the first genetically engineered crops. In February 1989 a California-based company by the name of Calgene, Inc., courted the FDA to remove any restrictions preventing it from further developing, and ultimately selling, the genetically altered Flavr Savr tomato. The appeal of the new fruit was that it had a consistent taste as well as an extended shelf life regardless of the time of year it was grown or harvested. Flavr Savr tomatoes came with a pamphlet that was really a form of preemptive damage control: What the company hoped to convey with this disclosure was that consumers would see that there was nothing alien or foreign, nothing to fear, hidden in their genetically altered tomato. "We made a copy of a gene which causes softening of tomatoes," Calgene's brochure read. "Then we put this copy into the plant [technically the plant's DNA structure] backwards to slow down the softening gene." The casual nature and plain talk of the explanation were so understated that Calgene seemed to assume that the restructuring of strands of DNA was the stuff of the average person's everyday conversations, alongside "How was your day?" and "What time is dinner?" Calgene's verbiage was also wisely devoid of any technical jargon that might raise suspicions. In an effort to show there was nothing covert about their experiments, Calgene went one step further and requested that the FDA make all the proceedings regarding their tomato's path to approval public. Interestingly enough, if anyone had any major objections about the FDA's consideration of green-lighting the Flavr Savr, they certainly didn't voice them loudly enough to block the administration from granting approval. More than five years later, in May 1994, the FDA approved the selling of the Flavr Savr, making it the first whole food created by bioengineering to go on the market.

Along the road to granting Calgene approval for the Flavr Savr's production, the FDA also gave the go-ahead to the cattle industry to use bovine somatotropin in 1993. BST, as it became known, was a synthetic hormone created by splicing cow DNA and reconfiguring it with the DNA of a common form of bacteria. The idea of both items—the gene-splicing responsible for the spoil-proof tomato and the bioengineering that resulted in the simulation of the secretion of a cow's pituitary gland—was to generate more sales for farmers and dairy producers by increasing their output and reducing the risk of spoilage.

But genetically altered foods had a PR problem right from the start: While consumers and farmers didn't witness any aspect of the cloning or splicing process that produced the tomatoes, the nature of the BST was more intrusive. The man-made beef hormone required that someone physically insert a syringe into a cow and inject the fluid on a bimonthly basis in order to stimulate more milk production. And since BST received FDA approval first, other bioengineered foods and food products that followed were cast in the same eerie light as the test-tube hormone.

Accusations that food scientists were playing God by creating new forms of life, and monsters at that, had been flung ever since GMOs (genetically modified organisms) first crawled out of the labs and into the headlines in 1987. By the early nineties, the cultural climate wasn't much more receptive toward ideas that sounded as Frankenstein-ish as bioengineering. Even though computer technology was on the cusp of an explosion, the early nineties were a relatively low-tech time. A healthy global living space was more important than cyberspace. The observance of the twentieth anniversary of Earth Day coincided with the beginning of the decade, and a new era of environmental activism was born. The sound track for the movement was grunge, the flannel-clad stepchild of punk rock. Vegetarianism became prominent with the new counterculture of the 1990s. Two of the music scene's most visible and respected artists, singer Eddie Vedder of the band Pearl Jam and Nirvana's singer/songwriter Kurt Cobain, professed to abstain from eating meat. Organizations like People for the Ethical Treatment of Animals (PETA) and Greenpeace were increasingly visible, and volunteerism became an important way to give back to one's community.

The nineties were shaping up to be the antithesis of the flashy, high-tech eighties, and in this kind of climate, Frankenfoods were a tough sell. Organic grocery outlets like Whole Foods and independent farmers' markets were more prevalent than ever, as Americans wanted healthier choices than the selection offered by other supermarkets. To reassure costumers, organic markets wrapped packages of ground beef with labels that read "hormone-free."

The threat to the environment was another aspect of the bioengineering trend that alarmed those who opposed the genetic modification of crops. Insect-resistant strains of corn, potatoes, tomatoes, and squash that housed potential dangers within their new, man-made genetic code were being developed. Inside these new plant varieties was genetic material taken from a bacteria known as *Bacillus thuringiensis*. This bacterium is found naturally in soil and has been used by organic farmers as a way to combat certain types of pests. By introducing the DNA from the *Bacillus thuringiensis* into the genetic structure of corn, for instance, scientists created a brand-new strain of corn with the same natural pest-resistant properties as the bacteria. In the case of the insect-protected corn developed by the Monsanto Company in 1996, the variety of corn produced was genetically engineered and fine-tuned with a type of *Bacillus thuringiensis* that attacks gypsy moths, as well as other types of moths and butterflies. While at first this might seem beneficial, the fact that the corn becomes toxic to species other than the pest the gene from the bacterium is meant to target creates the potential for the type of ecological disruption Rachel Carson feared and warned against in her writings.

This type of genetically spliced resistance isn't limited to natural pests. AgrEvo Incorporated created a variety of corn that was able to withstand any toxic side effects that might result from glufosinate, a common herbicide. When used in fields, glufosinate chokes out weeds and other unwanted vegetation. Corn that has been genetically modified with gene material from glufosinate would be protected from the poison if it were to be used in the same field. According to the Environmental Protection Agency's studies on glufosinate as an agent in genetic engineering, the official conclusion was that "there is a reasonable certainty that no harm will occur to infants and children from aggregate exposure to residues of glufosinate-ammonium." Unfortunately, the wildlife, water supplies, and other vegetation that come in direct contact with the herbicide aren't so lucky. Worries over long-term effects of the herbicide continue to be cause for concern among those opposed to the practice of genetically infusing crops with toxic substances.

The uncertainty of the new creation stems from the lack of experience lab scientists, farmers, and consumers have with the new organism. The genetically engineered plants of the nineties weren't the first new variety of vegetation to be created with the help of humans; grafting and cross-pollination have been used for centuries. Indeed, the pages of *Burpee's Seed Catalog* carry examples of these sorts of hybridized plants, and the produce aisles in grocery stores across the country contain fruits that are the offspring of grafting, such as lemons "grown on orange trees," as John McPhee writes in his book *Oranges*. The difference between these foods and those that are bio-engineered is that nature still has the final say in the grafting and development of the hybrids' fruit. As Dr. Michael Ambrose explains, "Grafting is a form of asexual propagation. Basically it allows one species to grow *through* the body of another, like potato plants that grow tomatoes. The grafting of the tomato top to the potato bottom allows the use of the more sturdy potato trunk with the tomato fruit."

Grafting, Ambrose says, "saves time and money. In fruit trees, a farmer can get more than one variety from a single tree." Similarly, McPhee writes, "A single citrus tree can be turned into a carnival, with lemons, limes, grapefruit, tangerines, kumquats, and oranges all ripening on its branches at the same time." The critical difference is that "there is *no* exchange of genetic material between the grafted plants, and that's the key." Ambrose says. "Grafting has to be done each time to get the same results."

The creation of new plants by cross-pollinating one variety of tomato with another also allows nature to take its course, since "seeds contain the genetic information of their parents, to a point," Ambrose explains.

In other words, natural selection takes place in cross-pollination; in the case of the bioengineered plants, however, the selection has been made *for* the new plant by the scientists who spliced its genes with those of another organism.

Unlike grafting, "genetically modified organisms *do* exchange genetic material through the recombinant DNA," Ambrose says. "The wild type of genome of the corn, strawberry, or tomato is modified by adding *foreign* genes to the genomic material. This material is then passed to each successive generation."

There is also a finality to bioengineering; the type of genetic splicing that produces a new plant such as insect-protected corn "is permanent," Dr. Ambrose says, adding, "until us humans play God again and change it."

Fortunately, not all the things technology helped bring into America's kitchens in the 1990s were as controversial as genetically altered or radiation-blasted foods. (The latter resulted from the deployment of radiation waves to nuke potential theats from harmful bacteria.) The cyber explosion of the decade wired the kitchen to the rest of the world as personal computers, kitchen computer stations, and the Internet made everything from recipes to bags of groceries obtainable with just a simple point and click on the home computer. The proliferation of cooking and food-related Web sites made the contents of countless cookbooks readily available. Recipe-swapping among friends—and even strangers—was made quicker by e-mail, lending an added warmth to the exchange, the resulting dish, and the kitchen itself. Ingredients that were still difficult to find could be ordered from retailers on the other side of the world. But even better, especially for busy families, orders could be placed with local supermarkets as the weekly or monthly grocery shopping was done via the computer.

Peapod, a company originating in Evanston, Illinois, began helping Americans shop online for groceries as early as 1989, when brothers Thomas and Andrew Parkinson envisioned a high-tech version of at-home grocery shopping. The Parkinson brothers gave customers computer software that allowed them to connect directly to the Peapod grocery-shopping service. By placing their orders via their computers—eggs, gallon of milk, salad greens—shoppers eliminated time-consuming trips to their local produce stores. In most cases their deliveries were waiting for them when they got home from work, safely packed in special thermal containers to avoid spoilage. As computer technology became more advanced, and as the growing global market and information facility known as the Internet, or World Wide Web, became more accessible to more home computers, the Parkinson brothers teamed up with larger grocery chains like Giant Food. By the end of the nineties, Peapod's online grocery-shopping experience was available in select areas of the Northeast and Mid-Atlantic regions of the country in addition to Chicago.

The idea of "order now, unpack later" became quite appealing as Americans realized they could restock their kitchens without ever leaving their homes. Companies similar to Peapod began to pop up on the Internet, like the gone-before-its-time Kozmo.com. An eventual victim of the dot-com bust (in which investment futures had ballooned the market by stretching it to unsustainable degrees), in its heyday Kozmo.com gave shoppers access to online warehouses and allowed them to shop for anything from milk to laundry detergent to the latest issue of the *New York Times* to frozen pizzas to a jar of mayonnaise. Items were delivered at a time of the customer's choosing.

While online grocery shopping made the procurement of foodstuffs for the American Kitchen more effortless than ever, critics charged that it widened the chasm between the haves and have-nots in the United States. (Lower-income families still had to spend money on gas, or public transportation, to go to the store to do their shopping, as well as try to find time in their schedules to make the trip.)

* * *

The arrival of countertop computers and on-line shopping were examples of how the growing affluence of the nineties continued to change the landscape of the American Kitchen. The room already had professional-grade appliances, like the Viking and Sub-Zero six-burner, dual-oven stoves; now it also had professionally trained culinary experts handling the family's dinner duties. The United States Personal Chef Assocation was formed in 1991 when busy breadwinners began hiring personal chefs to come into their homes to do their families' cooking.

While at first glance it seemed to run contrary to the zeitgeist, the idea of having a personal chef fell perfectly in line with the 1990s view of the American Kitchen as the new family room. Hectic work and extracurricular-activity schedules limited family time in the nineties. With the chefs' previously prepared meals requiring nothing more than a few minutes of defrosting and reheating time in the microwave, more table time was available for those occasions when every family member was present to enjoy a meal as a unit. Professional chefs also eliminated cleanup time since the meals were prepared during the day while the family was at work and school.

Meanwhile, for those Americans who did choose to dine out, there were countless options. "Never in the history of this country have there been as many great restaurants as there are today," wrote then editor in chief Gail Zweigenthal in *Gourmet* magazine in 1996. The bible of American gourmands had devoted its October issue that year to "Celebrating the Restaurant" in the United States; for as much as Americans loved cooking in their own kitchens during the nineties, they also loved sampling the wares of the top-notch eateries that had turned certain restaurants into culinary travel destinations and the proprietors of those establishments into bona fide stars. The country's celebrity chefs had become the decade's new rock stars, and a meal prepared by their hands was akin to taking in a great concert performance.

The chef as superstar was an inevitable apex, a position reached after years of cultivation by food editors, restaurant critics, and magazine covers. While the excitement caused by Julia Child in the sixties set the stage for chefs to eventually receive star billing, as well as magazine features and covers, the trend really gained momentum in the 1970s. The media machine was being driven by pop culture more than ever, and Hollywood's glamour, coupled with the "California sound" of bands like Fleetwood Mac and the Eagles, made that state the nation's cultural focal point. Before long the dietary trends coming out of California's fields and kitchens made Alice Waters's

Berkeley restaurant, Chez Panisse, a hot spot and turned its chef into a celebrity. By the 1980s, Wolfgang Puck's Oscar-night party at his L.A. restaurant, Spago, was the ticket that separated the A-listers from the rest of the crowd. As *Bon Appétit* wrote in its "American Century in Food" issue in September 1999, the restaurant scene in the eighties was characterized by the way "the struggle for status came down to who could snag a dinner reservation at the likes of Montrachet in New York, Spago in L.A. or Stars in San Francisco." Though the economic downturn that marked the transition from the 1980s to the 1990s created a few empty seats in restaurants across the country, it wasn't long before tables were again booked on a nightly basis. By the end of the decade, the restaurant industry in America was a force to be contended with: In 1999, the National Restaurant Association was named the country's tenth "most powerful lobbying organization" by *Fortune* magazine. That same year was branded "the Year of the Restaurant" by the U.S. Department of Commerce, in honor of the contribution by the restaurant industry to the nation's economy. According to the National Restaurant Association in Washington, D.C., Americans were spending nearly half their household food budgets *outside* the home at the turn of the new century.

So what did the dining-out habits of the country have to do with the workings inside America's home kitchens? Plenty. New culinary trends made their way from professional kitchens to the family dinner table. Editor Zweigenthal noted in *Gourmet*'s "Restaurant Issue" that "bring[ing readers] a taste of the restaurants themselves," via the recipes of the country's top restaurants, was intended to spark "curiosity and [the readers'] appetite." Americans had been rising to new culinary challenges for almost half a century at this point. Trying to match professional chefs spice for spice, whisk for whisk, was part of what distinguished true food enthusiasts from mere culinary tourists.

The superstar status of the creators of the country's hottest restaurant fare was given an extra kick with the 1993 launching of the Food Network. Cooking shows like *The French Chef* or *The Galloping Gourmet* were no longer relegated to Sunday afternoons on public broadcasting stations once the Food Network became available as part of the programming packages offered by cable and satellite TV providers. The new channel was all food, all day, all night, 24-7, and there was a hungry audience waiting to wolf down what the network was offering. According to *Bon Appétit*'s century-spanning roundup issue, as of 1999 the Food Network was "the second-fastest-growing cable channel in the country, reaching 37 million homes." Americans could now cook along with the likes of Mary Sue Milliken and Susan Feniger, the "Two Hot Tamales" from Santa Monica's City Café and Border Grill, or Mario Batali, whose Babbo had food critics grasping for superlatives.

The Food Network's success did nothing to diminish the impact and popularity of the PBS series of Julia Child, who likewise turned her attention to the country's new hot cooking phenoms. In both the books and television series *Cooking with Master Chefs* and *In Julia's Kitchen with Master Chefs*, the culinary queen of America shared the TV spotlight, along with her kitchen, with Milliken and Feniger, Citronelle's Michel Richard, and Emeril Lagasse, as well as veterans like Jeremiah Tower and Alice Waters. Child even stepped out of her familiar home base as her cameras went on-location to the home kitchens of her guest stars. This sort of home-turf approach gave viewers an intimate look at the cooking skills and habits of their idols, demystifying them by allowing a look behind the proverbial wizard's curtain. The "everyday people" appeal of seeing the workings of a pro's kitchen was immediate. It was reassuring to see, for example, that the kitchen in Jeremiah Tower's Bay Area home was, at least as the camera presented it, of a normal scale. Michel Richard's home-cooking laboratory wasn't staffed by sous-chefs but was always on the verge of being overrun by his three children. And, as readers who followed along with the *Master Chefs* television series by way of Julia's companion cookbooks would also learn, it was refreshing to discover that Alice Waters really did rely on the freshest ingredients, yanking garlic bulbs out of the ground from her own backyard stash and knocking the dirt off the roots before getting down to business.

The cachet attached to even the idea of chef-as-icon in the nineties ventured into the art-imitating-life arena on NBC's sitcom *Frasier*. The Crane brothers, Frasier and Niles, were constantly in a tizzy when it came to dining out at the latest haute spots in their hometown of Seattle, often engaging in a game of one-upmanship that went beyond sibling rivalry in their attempts to be the first to secure a table at a new restaurant. In his own kitchen, Frasier Crane was more likely to be seen uncorking a bottle of the white-hot wine of the moment than reducing a pot of veal stock to demi-glace, but he was the most prominent "foodie" to be featured on network TV during the nineties. In addition to *Frasier*, other NBC sitcoms were dotted with many references that showed how much the American Kitchen had influenced America's television-viewing audiences by the century's end. *Seinfeld*'s characters ordered mulligatawny from the Soup Nazi, and while they questioned the popularity of pesto they embraced Snapple as a welcome addition to the culture. Monica Geller, as played by Courteney Cox on *Friends*, was a chef-in-training when the show began and eventually presided over a restaurant kitchen of her own. And domestic doyenne Martha Stewart saved Thanksgiving dinner on an episode of ABC's sitcom *Ellen* when Ellen DeGeneres burned the traditional holiday bird. (Stewart's solution? Order a pizza.)

Elsewhere on TV, for better or for worse, the cause of the American Kitchen and the fascination with its gadgetry was taken up in the 1990s by an oft-maligned messenger: the infomercial. As persistent as a determined housefly, these televised sales pitches became increasingly difficult to avoid while channel surfing. Ranging in length from sixty seconds to sixty minutes, infomercials had been taking over cable channels ever since round-the-clock broadcasting created dead airspace and a need for programming to fill it.

The relationship between the infomercial and America's Kitchen stretched back several decades. Prior to the nineties, manufacturers like Ronco were selling television viewers Ginzu steak knives and multitasking vegetable choppers in commercials featuring rapid-fire editing and breathless voiceovers; volumes of information were delivered in one jam-packed minute. The 1970s saw more than their share of products that not only sliced, diced, and julienned, but which quickly became relegated to "that drawer" in the kitchen—the storage space/graveyard for everything from rubber bands to single-armed scissors to carryout menus from the neighborhood Chinese restaurant to reusable bottle caps—after four easy payments. (In an attempt to help consumers avoid wasting their money, *Good Housekeeping* eventually began critiquing the juicers, smokers, slicers, and peelers and other machines, tools, and utensils being sold on television. A longtime advocate of the harried homemaker, the magazine put the products offered in infomercials to the test and rated them according to their usefulness as well as the accuracy of the TV ad's claims.)

In the 1980s the infomercial format became more sophisticated, expanding beyond its original flash-and-trash format. Not only did the commercials increase in length, they began to mimic talk shows, cooking and craft classes, and training seminars.

Exercise in all its forms—mental, spiritual, and physical—was a favorite topic of infomercial pitches, but controlling one's diet was one of the most popular. And among a certain segment of the American population, few problems were more insurmountable in the 1990s than the battle against obesity. Get-fit-quick programs and machines guaranteed to tighten abdominal muscles or melt away cellulite, as well as diet pills, drinks, and energy bars that offered overweight Americans a way to lose unwanted pounds "without moving a muscle," were favorites of these hour-long "paid programming" ventures. It became almost impossible to distinguish one pitch from another, until one woman's voice, and her message, became instantly recognizable.

As her bio tells the story, Susan Powter was a single mother of two who gained more than 130 pounds before she decided to "stop the insanity" and take control of her weight problem. With a best-selling diet-and-exercise book of the same name, "stop the insanity" became Powter's battle cry as she rallied overweight and unfit Americans into action. The spiky-haired mom from Seattle became the weight-loss spokesperson of the early nineties. Like Richard Simmons, and even Weight Watchers' Jean Nidetch, Powter knew her target audience well, since she had faced the same challenges. But unlike her predecessors, Powter came on like a drill sergeant; though she was sympathetic, she made no bones about the destructive effects of overeating and her opinion of the insanity of indulging in that practice. In paid programming, which she referred to as "specials," Powter relied on jarring visuals like mounds of animal fat to illustrate her point. It was her way of saying, "You are what you eat." She emphasized the importance of having a well-balanced life in addition to maintaining a well-balanced diet. Whether barking out credos like "You gotta eat you gotta breath you gotta move. Every day," or shouting out her trademark line, "Stop the insanity," Powter was hard to ignore. Her popularity wasn't without controversy, however, as her credentials as a weight-loss expert were called into question, right down to doubts about whether the large woman in the "Before" photo was actually her. Whether or not Susan Powter was qualified as an educated professional in a position to advise people on their eating and exercise habits isn't the real issue, anyway: The fact that so many Americans had eaten themselves into such a dangerous state of obesity that their desperation could turn an unknown woman who shared their struggle into an overnight media sensation, let alone a diet and fitness expert, was the real commentary about the mindset in the American Kitchen of the 1990s.

Bearing that in mind, it's no wonder that Susan Powter's *Stop the Insanity* became a best seller in the last decade of the century. Americans wanted to lose weight, but they didn't always have the best role models when it came to healthy diets. The first American president to usher in the decade, George H. W. Bush, had a well-publicized aversion to broccoli, and President Bill Clinton, who led the country from 1992 into the next millennium, was often ribbed for having a fondness for Big Macs. While there was nothing particularly gourmet about either president's menu choices, their tastes were somewhat consistent with those of regular Americans, who were once again welcoming beef and butter into the American Kitchen. Just as iconic cookbooks like *The Silver Palate* were being rereleased and updated with light and low-fat alternatives to recipes that were once much richer, chefs like Emeril Lagasse and Michel Richard were inadvertently launching PR campaigns for foods that had long been eschewed by health-conscious Americans. As Julia Child wrote about Richard in *Cooking with Master Chefs*, "He uses the very best [ingredients] he can find. No butter substitutes, ersatz cream and fake chocolate for him."

This revisiting of some of the kitchen's old favorites wasn't coming from a wanton or reckless desire among Americans to suddenly endanger their health, but was grounded more in the nostalgia and comfort-food trends that began early in the 1990s. On top of that, while some might argue otherwise, when it came to casting a vote for flavor, as light and substitute and nonfat items squared off against the real thing—like butter and cream—there was no contest. In a decade that saw fat substitutes like Olestra and Olean appearing in their favorite snack foods, like potato chips, Americans were definitely making well-informed choices when they opted to chew the fat and worry about burning off the calories later. (Though Olestra didn't have an identifiable taste, critics claimed it changed the "mouth feel" of the foods. Furthermore, the warnings of its side effects—in particular, anal leakage—were enough to make some consumers steer clear.)

For one dietician, the reuniting of Americans with butter, and even bacon, made his weight-loss approach all the more appealing. Dr. Robert C. Atkins had a best seller with his release in the late 1970s of *Dr. Atkins' Diet Revolution*, but the popularity was nothing compared to the way his *New Diet Revolution* was received at the end of the 1990s.

When Atkins's book hit stores in the nineties, it reached a readership who'd been hearing, for most of the 1980s, that fat and cholesterol were the body's enemies. His dismissal of what had been conventional wisdom by encouraging dieters to eat foods high in fat, "liberally" and "luxuriously," was shocking to some. Twenty years earlier Americans weren't as educated about the ill effects of an adverse diet as they were near the century's end; Atkins's high-protein, low-carb diet had its detractors when it was first published, but arguments and debates over the diet's wisdom were for the most part limited to the medical field. But the Atkins revolution of the 1990s, calling for Americans to eat less bread, grains, and pasta, and even cut back on some fruits and vegetables, while at the same time upping their intake of meat, whole milk, butter, and bacon, caused a sharp divide: It sounded like heresy to some and freedom to others. The Atkins diet bucked the medical reports of the last twenty-plus years, not to mention the new Food Pyramid guidelines issued by the U.S. Department of Agriculture, but for Americans who had tried every other diet without lasting success, anything was worth a try. Americans had been trying to keep their fat intake in check, but pulling all the new fat-free items off of grocery store shelves was no longer doing the trick. As Washington, D.C., licensed and registered dietician Caitlyn E. Lorenze explains it, the Atkins program was merely the next logical choice for serial dieters in the 1990s, especially when fat-free foods failed them: "The fat-free foods which flooded the market—the fat-free candy, fat-free cookies, fat-free cakes, and fat-free muffins—were fat-free, but full of calories. Soon dieters saw the pounds start coming back on." Lorenze, who runs a nutritional consulting service called Wholesome Body, says that *The New Diet Revolution* appealed to the fat-free dieters who continued to gain weight even though they thought they were adhering to a weight-loss program. Atkins gave them another target at which to point the finger of blame. "After years of frustration, dieters concluded, 'If it's not the fat that's making us fat, then maybe it's the sugar!' and as a result, Dr. Atkins's book was dusted off and rereleased. The low-carbohydrate diet provided new hope."

In addition to being radically different from what dieters had been hearing for the past two decades, the Atkins approach to losing weight allowed people to continue to eat some of the foods they loved. Cheese? Butter? Real ice cream? Atkins invited them all back into the kitchen. Atkins seemed to offer an unconventional solution to heart disease and other ailments, while at the same time providing a quick fix to correct years of unhealthy eating habits that had changed dieters' bodies, inside and out.

Americans were just as body-conscious as ever in the nineties. The supermodel craze had women longing to look like Cindy Crawford, Christy Turlington, Naomi Campbell, and Linda Evangelista (and straight men hoping their dates would resemble these beauties). In a culture obsessed with beauty, youth, and low body fat, the supermodel was perfection personified— an ideal mere mortals couldn't dream of realizing, certainly not without divine or surgical intervention or superhuman mind control. The stereotype of the fashion model was that of someone who was blessed with good genes and a wickedly fast metabolism; cursed by an eating disorder; outfitted with taste buds that actually favored low-cal, low-fat foods; or else capable of masochistic denial. The conventional wisdom was that the eternally and enviably thin somehow had a leg up on the rest of the world, theirs being an existence that was certainly fueled by air or preternatural willpower. And while *The New Diet Revolution* wasn't going to land everyone who followed it a *Sports Illustrated* swimsuit issue spread or a contract with Calvin Klein, the fact that practitioners of the Atkins program could actually eat real food and still lose weight changed the perception of a diet as something equivalent to denial and misery. That was revolutionary. But for people who simply longed to be able to fit comfortably in a movie theater seat, the Atkins diet offered new hope in their search for what Lorenze calls the "cure-all weight-loss program."

As the return of foods that were once banished from the diet demonstrated, the 1990s were about looking forward just as much as they were about looking back. The new century was on the horizon, and the advancements of computer technology were creating a brave new world, albeit a jittery one as paranoia over problems that were certain to be caused by the so-called Millennium Bug had some Americans stockpiling their kitchens, pantries, basements, and garages with cases of bottled water, shelf-stable preserved foods, generators, batteries, and camping stoves. The American Kitchen had come a long way from the days of root cellars, potted meats, and pickled fruits and vegetables, yet there was something comedic to the doomsday mind-set that caused people to panic at the thought of deprivation. Technology, especially in the areas of food production, packaging, and preservation, had made *access* and *abundance* the operative words in describing the American food experience. The majority of Americans lived a convenient distance from their local food source, the grocery store, which was as it had been for most of the twentieth century. The majority of Americans had a sustainable income, which allowed them to freely shop for enough food to feed themselves and their families. And they lived in homes where there was ample clean and dry storage space where they could stock their provisions. Nearly all of these homes were equipped with appliances that required nothing more than the turn of a knob or the pressing of a button to cook the family's meals. In the case of preserving food until it came time to eat it, there was no expenditure of physical exertion required by the homemaker; refrigerators and freezers quietly did the jobs they were designed to do without any maintenance beyond an occasional cleaning. Even the once-laborious and much-avoided job of defrosting freezers had become a thing of the past.

While the scenario created by the shutting down of the nation's computerized infrastructure as the Millennium Bug stopped computer operations worldwide would have been chaotic, the time elapsed from the onset of the problem to its eventual correction would have been limited. Still, some Americans prepared for the possible arrival of Armageddon at the stroke of midnight on January 1, 2000, the same way that the country's earliest immigrants had readied their ships to cross the Atlantic, or as the westward-bound pioneers had loaded their wagons. This gigantic leap into the unknown, and the anxiety it fostered, may have been one of the reasons for the air of nostalgia that characterized most of the 1990s. People were trying to re-create the look and feel—and even the taste—of happier times from the past, even as the middle of the decade saw a booming economy and rising national optimism. The approach of the new century gave rise to numerous looks back in furniture and design, and retrospectives were featured in magazines and exhibited in museums.

The American Kitchen once again flirted briefly with the mix-and-match look that defined its earliest days. Freestanding sideboards, hutches, and Hoosiers became popular again, as did glass-fronted cabinets and open shelves. Midcentury modernism soon came back into vogue. Americans combed through thrift shops and antique stores, searching for kitchenware designed by Russel and Mary Wright and Eva Zeisel. The works of new designers, who drew inspiration from the movements of the midcentury era and beyond, started popping up on kitchen counters and tables in the late nineties. At the end of the century the ceramic tableware created by Jonathan Adler turned the New York City–based potter into a new American design icon as well as a media magnet. Adler's additions to the American Kitchen took a page from the manifesto of midcentury furniture mainstays Knoll Industries by not only making good design, but making sure that design was exciting and affordable.

Adler's designs were the kind regularly featured in the hip British lifestyle bible of the decade, *Wallpaper**. *Wallpaper** devoted its pages to giving its readers the best of what surrounded them, even if they had to fly thousands of miles to obtain what they wanted. Travel was an important part of the American experience of the 1990s, especially with the economy flourishing, as airfare was relatively inexpensive. This type of accessibility to foreign countries continued to be an important influence on the American Kitchen.

As Julia Child said of the changes in American cooking since her first book came out in 1961, "Although World War II brought some enlightenment, I think the great revolution came through the airplane." This statement, taken from the introduction to her 1995 cookbook, *In Julia's Kitchen with Master Chefs*, was followed by her further observation that beginning in the sixties, globe-trotting Americans had begun "to take a discriminating interest in what they ate," sampling and experimenting "with fine foods" and hoping "for the same quality when they came home." By the 1990s, thirty-plus years after Julia Child first convinced audiences that the American Kitchen was as good a place as any to tackle French cooking, cuisines from around the world could now be sampled in restaurants, carryout shops, supermarket aisles, and even on family dinner tables across America. Jars of Mexican salsa sat on home refrigerator shelves next to Thai fish sauce. Chinese pot-stickers and Italian-style stuffed manicotti shells both became available in the frozen-food section. Television viewers could learn how to prepare authentic curry on PBS or catch an episode of a show devoted to Southern cooking on the Food Network.

Two of the resources that helped the American Kitchen achieve its level of sophistication and worldliness celebrated the century's culinary history with commemorative issues during the 1990s.

Gourmet began the decade by observing its fiftieth anniversary in 1991. In a career-spanning special issue, the magazine of choice for many gourmands selected and published fifty recipes, one for each year the magazine had been in print. A then-and-now assessment of some of the recipes' cultural shelf-lives attested to the timelessness of some foods, like Chili (from 1981) or Tacos de Pollo con Guacamole (surprisingly, from 1961), while other foods seemed, as the editorial content admitted, immediately identifiable with a specific era, like 1956's Chicken Divan ("one of the first recipes that appeared in the 'You Asked for It' column and was requested often during the 1950s") or Grasshopper Pie and Swiss Fondue, both from the sixties (1962 and 1967, respectively).

Gourmet's mission from its inception was a celebration of all aspects of fine living and dining, and the American Kitchen had become more than a means to an end in that regard; as the center of family and communal expression, it had become self-actualized. As Julia Child would write in 1995, "Food is a family affair and every meal (including breakfast) should be a joyous occasion."

Americans loved talking about what they ate and how they cooked in the nineties. Recipe-swapping was popular in magazines like *Cooking Light*, while *Taste of Home* magazine relied exclusively on recipes from home cooks. *Taste of Home*'s recipe contests became so popular among its four million subscribers that an average of fifteen thousand recipes was received each time the magazine called for entries.

Polling readers became a good way to determine what fell into the In and Out columns in American kitchens, and *Bon Appétit* began surveying its audience in 1998 with its first annual "How America Eats" issue. Readers were presented with questions about their likes and dislikes, how often they cooked vegetarian meals, what their favorite comfort foods were, and how often their families had a sit-down meal. The results showed that there were no unanimous trends beyond the obvious—that Americans loved food, and they loved talking about it. A quick glance at the differences between *Gourmet* and *Bon Appétit* as compared to *Taste of Home* supports that shared enthusiasm but also illustrates the disparity between America's home cooks. The two former magazines are popular among those who wish to stay on the cutting edge of culinary movements, and the pages of those magazines are filled with advertisements for professional-grade cookware like All-Clad and restaurant-quality stoves like Wolf; the latter has supported itself entirely on sales of the publication, accepts no advertising, and appeals to a readership that its publisher, Reiman, says favors recipes "that don't call for a lot of exotic ingredients." The differences confirm, however, rather than dispute, Thomas Jefferson's instruction that one should "look into the pots" of a people if one really wants to learn about their culture. The pot on the stove of the American Kitchen of the 1990s was the sum of its parts, and more.

What it meant to cook and eat like an American in the twentieth century could hardly be summarized in one magazine (or even one book), but *Bon Appétit*'s decade-by-decade examination of "The American Century in Food" hit the highlights. Published in September 1999, the special issue honored the restaurants, cookbooks, chefs, and foods that helped define the American Kitchen's experience in the last one hundred years.

As the new century drew nearer, the American Kitchen refined its role as the center of familial operations in the house. Over the course of the twentieth century the workings of the kitchen had received quite a makeover. The greasy, smoky, and smelly by-products of cooking, which had once relegated the room to closed-door quarters in the back of the house, were gone. Cooking for the family was now as quick and lively, or as detail-oriented and time-consuming, as a homemaker desired. *Control* and *convenience* had become the operative words that, along with *access* and *abundance*, characterized the experience in America's kitchens at the end of the 1990s. The breakthroughs of the last one hundred years had contributed to making the room a place that engaged the family, and even guests, as the kitchen's landscape merged with every aspect of the rest of the house.

Epilogue: 2000 and Beyond

The dawn of the twenty-first century came and went without the dreaded Millennium Bug infesting even one home. But soon new fears and anxieties darkened everyday life. Faced with such uncertainty, Americans sought the comfort of the familiar. The American Kitchen offered a refuge, a place to find solace among family and friends. After hundreds of years of history, it remains the warmest room in the house.

What will the next century hold for the American Kitchen? Some familiar patterns are already on the table: a continued focus on healthier food choices, a stronger shift toward organic farming, and further technological breakthroughs that will emphasize the ease of the kitchen's, and the cook's, operation.

Ultimately, it is a history that is written by every cook, with every recipe and every meal. Trends will continue to influence the kitchen, but it will be the desire to share these experiences, and especially these foods, with others that will turn those trends into traditions.

In a survey titled "How America Eats," conducted by *Bon Appétit* in 2001, 61 percent of readers who responded said they made a concerted effort to eat dinner together, as a family unit, more than twice a week. Ann Kaiser, spokesperson for the publication *Taste of Home*, said that their magazine's readership also "feels that sitting down for a family meal is a significant part of their lives." The monthly columns that help homemakers struggling to make mealtime a family affair—like *Cooking Light*'s "Superfast" section or *Bon Appétit*'s "Too Busy to Cook?"—have become magazine mainstays, while the need for kitchen expediency has made a star out of the Food Network's Rachael Ray. Her cooking show, *30-Minute Meals*, and its spin-off cookbooks *30-Minute Meals I* and *II*, turned Ray into a household name.

Like these recipes, technology in the twenty-first century no longer looks to take the cook out of the American Kitchen so much as it focuses on making the most of the time spent there. The "effortless ballet" of the homemaker, as predicted nearly fifty years ago by the Miracle Kitchen unveiled by RCA/Whirlpool in 1964, now moves with a fluidity and speed even its originators didn't imagine. The engineers behind the space-and time-saving oven/fridge combo were astute in their vision of the future—as the Polara combo oven clearly shows—but few forward thinkers could have envisioned a need for refrigerators with videoconferencing capabilities for telecommuters, like LG Electronics' "Internet-enabled cyberfridge," or the ultimate in smart appliances, as featured in *Metropolis* magazine's April 2004 issue: DON'T KNOW HOW TO COOK? the headline asked. "The Kitchen of the Future," as seen in the magazine's pages, "will teach you." Moving beyond the push-of-a-button scenario, the cyberkitchen of tomorrow will display recipes on countertops complete with built-in measuring-cup sensors that can also weigh out portions.

With every recipe made, and with every forkful eaten, food and cooking impart a sense of ancestral as well as communal belonging. In the past few decades Americans have been trying to learn as much about the many chapters of their kitchens' history as possible. The divergent cultures and cooking trends that have influenced American cuisine have all contributed to making an experience that is unique.

Health food and haute cuisine and fast food and ethnic cuisine are all part of the "amazing array of traditions," says Kathleen Iudice, public relations manager at COPIA, the American Center for Wine, Food, and the Arts, "that have made the American kitchen simultaneously a center for diversity and unity."

"As a new country, we have just started to explore the vitality of America's distinct culture and heritage," says Iudice. "These influences, taken as a whole, add up to something distinctively American."

COPIA, which opened in the summer of 2001 in Napa, California, celebrates that uniqueness. The center helps Americans respond to their yearning to know more about the foods that have defined their past. In exhibitions like *Forks in the Road*, which chronicles the change in American eating and cooking habits over the centuries, to installations like *Salad Dressings*, which shows how food trends have influenced fashion, COPIA has created a learning environment that addresses the growing interest in food and cooking among Americans today.

With that interest, a sense of responsibility has also grown. More Americans are opting to eat, and shop, organically in the twenty-first century. The organic-food industry is growing at the rate of 20 percent per year, as of 2004. But it's no longer just the independent purveyor offering organic fare. Companies like General Mills and Coca-Cola are getting in on the action by acquiring smaller businesses that produce organic products. General Mills added Small Planet Foods and began producing a brand of organic breakfast cereals, and Coca-Cola became the parent company of the Odwalla and Fresh Samantha juice companies. Even Heinz has started producing organic spaghetti (in a can) and added organic ketchup to its list of products.

Consumers have been given extra incentive to make healthier choices for their bodies as awareness of the effects of harmful chemicals on the planet has increased. As Rachel Carson warned, the pollutants that go into the atmosphere and into the earth ultimately end up in the human body.

"The [average] American eats five pounds of pesticides a year," says Nora Pouillon, chef and owner of Washington, D.C.'s Restaurant Nora, recognized as the first certified organic restaurant in the United States in 1999.

Pouillon says a shift is occurring toward buying organic foods among consumers, but she admits that dedicating oneself to exclusively organic eating "requires a long vision." And she should know: When Restaurant Nora first opened in 1979, only a handful of farms and dairies were organic. Now she can rely on a network of over thirty providers.

Making healthy food choices in the American Kitchen of the twenty-first century also means avoiding foods that are high in fat—especially trans fats, which are in many processed foods and can raise the LDL, or bad, cholesterol in the bloodstream. The success of the Center for Science in the Public Interest in getting fast-food giants like McDonald's to pledge to switch to a lighter frying oil is a victory for all Americans in the fight against obesity. Since fast foods and processed, prepackaged foods are so readily available, education about their negative effects has to begin early to ensure that America's kitchens in the future are healthier places to cook and eat.

"It's a challenge to teach students why it is important to eat healthy foods: The breakfast of choice for so many of them is a bag of potato chips and a can of Coca-Cola," offers Anna-Frances Slade, a home economics teacher in the Santa Rosa County School District in northwest Florida. Slade notes that the first time her students make spaghetti sauce from scratch, the taste of fresh ingredients is a revelation to many of them. "They are accustomed to eating what they like, and what is convenient, and not necessarily what is good for them," she says.

Barbara Haber, whose cookbook and food-diary studies have made her an expert in the ways Americans have chosen to eat through the centuries, sees a pattern here that must be broken in order to achieve continued success. "There will always be large numbers of people who eat poorly," she says. "And all we can do as a society is continue to try to educate them."

Home economics classes might be the best place to start.

Ultimately what we eat in the American Kitchen of the future, and how that food is prepared, will be most influenced by our past, our own kitchen's history.

As part-owner of a catering service specializing in Italian recipes that have been handed down in his family, Sam Zannino of Baltimore, Maryland, sees the kitchen as the cornerstone of cultural survival: "It's about continuing our heritage, keeping the memory of our grandparents and their homeland alive, and passing on what we have learned to the next generation."

And that is the role the American Kitchen has always played: In its recipes we find our past; in the daily preparations of its meals we celebrate the present; and in our desire to share these recipes, meals, and moments with family and friends again, we look hopefully toward a warm and comforting future.

ACKNOWLEDGMENTS

Other writers have said it before me, so I will continue their tradition: This book could not have been written had it not been for other books, other writers, and other people kind enough to share their knowledge and time.

This has been a long process, and I have so many people to thank. Please forgive any omissions, as they were certainly not intentional. Thanks to: David Dunton, Colin Dickerman, Kathy Belden, Michael O'Connor, JoAnna Kremer, Iris Bass, Philip Rhodes, Kurt B. Reighley, Sarah Bober, Dr. Shirley Wajda, Dr. Terrence Uber, Elizabeth A. Anderson, Adam Johnson, Pat Arcaro, Donna Corbin, Holly Frisbee, Kathy Jesperson, Daniel Stack, Susan Stein, Susan Hofer, Susan Strasser, Barbara Haber, Anthony Bourdain, Cecilia Saad, Dr. Michael F. Jacobson, Anna-Frances Slade, Darin Slade, Nora Pouillon, Camilla Rothchild, Dr. Michael Ambrose, Rodica Stoicoiu, Dr. Christopher Smith, Kathleen Iudice, Betty Teller, Peggy Loar, Faith Echtermeyer, David Bobanick, Shirley Fong-Torres, Joan Nathan, Renee Schettler, Frank Clark, Walter Gagliano, Joan Kohn, John T. Edge, Caitlyn Lorenze, Joyce Fassl, Rolando Rivas-Camp, Helvio Faria, Larry and Rachel Hirsch, Bloomsbury USA, the San Francisco Public Library, the British Library, the Library of Congress, COPIA, the American Center for Food, Wine, and the Arts, *Time* magazine, *Consumer Reports*, Hormel Foods, Campbell Soup Company, Stouffer's, General Mills, the Paley Center for Media (formerly the Museum of Television and Radio), the Johnstown *Tribune-Democrat*, Jim and Cammiel Hussey, Sam Zannino, Margo DeMark, Amy Chapman and family, Seth Chapman and family, Kelly Potchak, Terri Potchak and family, Mark Gdula and family, Judi McIntyre and family, Helen Gdula, Peter Gdula, and Lon Chapman.

ANNOTATED BIBLIOGRAPHY

Books

Ahlstrom, Sydney E. *A Religious History of the American People*. New Haven and London: Yale University Press, 1972. Ahlstrom's book is the go-to guide of America's religious histories. It is an excellent source for understanding the belief system that informed the foodways and farming of groups like the Shakers, Schwenkenfelders, Seventh-Day Adventists, and Puritans.

Albrecht, Donald, Robert Schonfeld, and Lindsay Stamm Shapiro. *Russel Wright: Creating American Lifestyle*. New York: Harry N. Abrams/Smithsonian, 2001. The companion book for the excellent Cooper-Hewitt exhibit that shows why Russel and Mary Wright were the original lifestyle gurus of the twentieth century.

Ambrose, Stephen E. *Undaunted Courage: Meriwether Lewis, Thomas Jefferson, and the Opening of the American West*. New York: Simon & Schuster, 1996. Ambrose's book shows why Jefferson's natural curiosity made him the first "foodie" president. Untapped food resources were one of the reasons Jefferson made the Louisiana Purchase, and he pored over the reports Lewis and Clark sent back about the plants and animals they encountered.

Barnhart, David K., and Allan Metcalf. *America in So Many Words: Words That Have Shaped America*. Boston: Houghton Mifflin, 1997. An amusing and educational look at how words like *cranberry*, *barbecue*, and *chowder* became part of the kitchen as well as part of the vernacular.

Beecher, Catharine E. *A Treatise on Domestic Economy*. Boston: T. H. Webb, 1842. Her emphasis on utility and ease of function made Beecher a nineteenth-century Martha Stewart. Here she tried to bring dignity and order to the labor-intensive housework of the time.

Booth, Sally Smith. *Hung, Strung, & Potted*. New York: Potter, 1971. Booth keeps her focus on eating habits in Colonial America, as her subtitle suggests, with recipes, diary entries, and historical references. A glossary helps readers who can't distinguish their salmagundi from their salamanders.

Bourdain, Anthony. *Typhoid Mary*. New York and London: Bloomsbury, 2001. Using the story of the infamous cook who infected patrons with the typhoid virus as a backdrop, Bourdain presents a case for how the knowledge of disease and germs changed the way the American Kitchen looked, and how that awareness changed the way Americans cooked.

Brooks, Paul. *Rachel Carson: The Writer at Work*. San Francisco: Sierra Club Books, 1989. A look at the impact environmentalist Rachel Carson had on society, and what has and hasn't changed as a result of her efforts to educate the public on the dangers of chemicals.

Brown, Ellen, ed. *Southwest Tastes*. Tucson, Ariz.: HPBooks, 1987. Think of it as *haute tamales*. This cookbook dovetailed with the rethinking of Mexican and Southwestern American foods as a means for chic culinary expression.

Carson, Rachel L. *Silent Spring*. New York: Houghton Mifflin, 1962. Writer, activist, and environmentalist Rachel Carson puts together a scenario in which man's unabated abuse of chemicals would have irreversible effects on life on this planet for generations to come.

Child, Julia. *Cooking with Master Chefs*. New York: Borzoi/Alfred A. Knopf, 1993. Never one to stop learning, in the early nineties Julia Child showcased the chefs and recipes that she admired.

———. *In Julia's Kitchen with Master Chefs*. New York: Alfred A. Knopf, 1995. The follow-up to *Cooking with Master Chefs*, *In Julia's Kitchen* allowed a who's who of the culinary elite to hold court behind her famed kitchen counter.

Critser, Greg. *Fat Land: How Americans Became the Fattest People in the World*. New York: Mariner Books/Houghton Mifflin, 2004. Critser looks at the factors, including various government policies, that have contributed to a glut of fatty and unhealthy foods in the American diet.

Diamond, Jared. *Guns, Germs, and Steel: The Fates of Human Societies*. New York and London: W.W. Norton & Company, 1999. Diamond looks at how the world's haves and have-nots have been determined by such factors as indigenous plants, domesticated animals, and the presence of germs.

Egerton, Ann Bleidt, John Egerton, and Al Clayton. *Southern Foods: At Home, on the Road, in History*. Chapel Hill: North Carolina Press (reprint), 1993. The title says it all. The Egertons aptly handle the huge topic of what defines Southern cuisine.

Fisher, M. F. K. *As They Were*. New York: Vintage, 1983. Meals and memories are shared by one of the great food writers of the twentieth century. Fisher's essays convey the history that remains on the table long after the dishes have been cleared.

Fitch, Noël Riley. *Appetite for Life: The Biography of Julia Child*. New York: Anchor Books, 1999. As the biographer of America's most famous, perhaps best-loved, chef, Fitch treats her subject with reverence yet maintains the human quality that endeared Child to so many. The trials of publishing her first book and her determination that Americans would indeed be willing to cook at a time when kitchens were stocked with prefab food receive particular attention here, and rightfully so.

Franklin, Benjamin. *Poor Richard's Almanack*. New York: Peter Pauper's Press, 1980. Reprint. Words of wisdom from an American classic.

Grey, Johnny. *The Art of Kitchen Design*. London: Cassell Paperbacks, 1995. In addition to providing great visual cues and instruction, Grey provides background info on how the modern kitchen came to look and function the way it does. How many people knew, for example, that the Dutch of the seventeenth century used their kitchens much like Americans use theirs today?

Grun, Bernard, and Eva Simpson. *The Timetables of History: A Horizontal Linkage of People and Events*. Third Revised Edition. English Language Edition. New York: Simon & Schuster, 1991. This gigantic reference book is like having all the cards from every Trivial Pursuit game turned answer-side-up, and then some.

Haber, Barbara. *From Hardtack to Home Fries: An Uncommon History of American Cooks and Meals*. New York: Free Press, 2002. From the curator of Harvard's Schlesinger Library's cookbook and culinary papers collection, a highly readable history of American foodways as necessity and tradition shaped them.

Harrison, Harry. *Make Room! Make Room!* New York: Spectra (reprint), 1994. Harrison's chilling kitchen, and vision, of the future featured edible protein derived from petroleum and restrictions on resources, not conveyor-belt countertops and fabulous appliances.

Hawthorne, Nathaniel. *Mosses from an Old Manse*. New York: A. L. Burt Company, 1846. Hawthorne rails against what he sees as the chilling changes industrialization is bringing, in particular the switch from the down-hearth fireplace to the freestanding cookstove (which he calls a "prison" for fire).

Jacobson, Michael F., Ph.D. *Nutrition Scoreboard: Your Guide to Better Eating*. New York: Avon Books, 1975. Jacobson made phrases like *junk food* and *empty calories* household expressions with his exposé on American eating habits and the nutritional quality of American foods.

Josephy, Alvin M., Jr. *500 Nations: An Illustrated History of North American Indians*. New York: Gramercy Books, 1994. Josephy's book is a poignant look at the life and times of the original inhabitants of North America, who didn't have much of either once settlers from across the oceans began arriving here.

Kittler, Pamela Goyan, and Kathryn P. Sucher. *Cultural Foods: Traditions and Trends*. Belmont, Calif.: Wadsworth/Thomas Learning, 2000. A must for academics and even the casual food enthusiast; a fascinating look into the cultural significance of foods and foodways. The sections covering religion and food practices are of particular value.

Kotz, Nick. *Let Them Eat Promises: The Politics of Hunger in America*. New York: Prentice-Hall, 1969. Kotz won a Pulitzer Prize for his look into the ugly truth that a percentage of the American population was starving, in part because of local government's refusal to help.

Kurlansky, Mark. *Cod: A Biography of the Fish That Changed the World*. New York: Penguin, 1998. Kurlansky tells the surprisingly dramatic story of the importance of cod as an agent of change in the economies and politics of Spain, England, and colonial America.

————. *Salt: A World History*. New York: Penguin Putnam, 2002. Kurlansky's book is filled with the types of facts and anecdotes every *Jeopardy* contestant wishes he could memorize—all in the story of how salt saved, and sometimes ruined, civilizations.

Lawrence, Mary Wells. *A Big Life in Advertising*. New York: Alfred A. Knopf, 2002. Lawrence's retelling of her "ad age" captures the glamour of America's advertising industry and provides insight into the creation of some of the best commercials in TV history—some of which just happened to be food-related.

Loewen, James W. *Lies My Teacher Told Me: Everything Your History Textbook Got Wrong*. New York: Touchstone/Simon & Shuster, 1996. Loewen sullies the whitewashed versions of tales from American history—like the Pilgrims' arrival—by pointing out the messy truth that academic books often omit.

Lovegren, Sylvia. *Fashionable Food: Seven Decades of Food Fads*. New York: Macmillan General Reference, 1995. Recipes, anecdotes, advertisements, and history inform this engaging look at the cooking and eating trends popular in America from 1920 through the 1990s. After being out of print for a few years, it's now—thankfully—available again.

McPhee, John. *The Founding Fish*. New York: Farrar, Straus and Giroux, 2002. McPhee goes fishing for the truth behind the legend of the humble shad as the savior of Washington's troops during the Revolution. What he and his readers discover is a food source that, while essential to the American Kitchen, was often stigmatized, as were the people who ate it.

————. *Oranges*. New York: Farrar, Straus and Giroux, 1967. McPhee examines the orange juice industry and presents a fascinating botanical/horticultural lesson about the role citrus has played in American society (and in other cultures as well).

Mingo, Jack, and Robert Armstrong. *The Official Couch Potato Handbook*. San Francisco: Last Gasp San Francisco, 1982, 1983, and 1988. A soft but effective lampooning of a culture where foods can be sprayed from a can while one lies in repose.

Nichols, Nell B., ed. *Freezing & Canning Cookbook: Prized Recipes from the Farms of America by the Food Editors of* Farm Journal. Garden City, New York: Doubleday & Company, Inc, 1973. This collection continues in the tradition, suggested by Jefferson in *Scheme for a System of Agricultural Societies,* and continued by others, like the farmers' collective started in the mid-nineteenth century that became known as The Grange, that recipes, preservation techniques, and harvest tips be shared among farmers and homemakers for the benefit of all.

Paddock, Paul, and William Paddock. *Famine, 1975!* New York: Little, Brown, 1967. The Paddocks looked at global hunger and projected that a devastating world famine loomed in the near future: The United States' appetite for all things would consume so many resources that it would cause citizens in third-world nations like India to starve to death.

Pearson, Jeanne, ed. *Portal to Good Cooking: Women's American ORT Favorite Recipes.* Lake Region/North Region/Lake County Region: Women's American ORT, 1959. The Women's American ORT was the Organization for Rehabilitation Through Training. This is a collection of recipes aimed primarily at Jewish American women to help them keep traditions alive in their new kitchens.

Pollan, Michael. *The Botany of Desire: A Plant's-Eye View of the World.* New York: Random House, 2001. Pollan looks at how apples and tomatoes (to name two of the book's subjects) developed an "I Want You to Want Me" survival tactic to make sure they stayed on America's kitchen tables.

Randall, Willard Sterne. *George Washington: A Life.* New York: Henry Holt, 1997. A hefty biography of the first president with a fair amount of foodways history included.

Rebora, Giovanni, ed. *Culture of the Fork: A Brief History of Food in Europe.* English translation. New York: Columbia University Press, 2001. A spirited history of how the kitchen utensil was initially a cause of shame and ridicule, as well as a chronicle of how the eating habits of European countries were surprisingly isolated despite their close proximity.

Rountree, Helen C. *The Powhatan Indians of Virginia: Their Traditional Culture.* Norman: University of Oklahoma Press, 1989. Rountree presents detailed information about the farming, hunting, and gathering practices of the Native Americans who all but assured British survival in seventeenth-century Virginia. Through her examination of the Powhatan foodways, Rountree sets the stage for the evolution of the American diet.

Schlink, Frederick, and Arthur Kallet. *100,000,000 Guinea Pigs.* New York: Vanguard Books, 1932. Schlink and Kallet took consumer activism to a new level with this brutal examination of what the American public was being sold, literally and figuratively, in the products they allowed into their kitchens.

Schlosser, Eric. *Fast Food Nation: The Dark Side of the All-American Meal.* New York: Perennial, 2002. Equal parts exposé, gonzo journalism, and academic research make Schlosser's take on the proliferation of the burger-and-fries combo one of the most important food-history books available.

Shapiro, Laura. *Perfection Salad: Women and Cooking at the Turn of the Century.* New York: Farrar, Straus and Giroux, 1986. If you want to know how America's kitchens became a place where foods went from the freezer into the microwave, Shapiro's book takes you back to where it all started, with the evolution of the domestic-science and home-economics movements, from the late nineteenth century into the early twentieth century. One of the best books on American food history there is.

Shephard, Sue. *Pickled, Potted, and Canned: How the Art and Science of Food Preserving Changed the World.* New York: Simon & Schuster, 2000. Shephard knows the subject matter of her title well and her book aptly explains the link between preserved foods and migration, settlements, war, and even space exploration.

Sinclair, Upton. *The Jungle.* New York: Doubleday, Page & Company, 1906. Probably one of the first books of the modern age to convert carnivores to vegetarianism, Sinclair's portrayal of slaughterhouses was grisly, stomach-turning, and essential.

Smith, Jeff. *The Frugal Gourmet on Our Immigrant Ancestors.* New York: Avon Books, 1990. As the book's jacket says, these are recipes your grandmother should have taught you. Each recipe comes with a brief background bio that helps place it in the greater scheme of things in the American Kitchen.

Stark, Steven D. *Glued to the Set: The 60 Television Shows and Events That Made Us Who We Are Today.* New York: Free Press, 1997. Stark could have called his book "We Are What We Watch." A wise and often wry look at how social and economic trends have been presented on the small screen.

Strasser, Susan. *Never Done: A History of American Housework.* New York: Henry Holt (reprint), 2000. A look at the grueling tasks that defined a day in the life of women.

Trager, James. *The Food Chronology: A Food Lover's Compendium of Events and Anecdotes, from Prehistory to the Present.* New York: Henry Holt, 1995. The essential research and fact guide for any food enthusiast. Trager begins at the dawn of civilization and ends, in this volume, in 1995. Along the way he covers migratory trends, crop failures, cookbook publications, restaurant openings, contaminated food-plant closings, and everything in between.

Witt, Doris. *Black Hunger: Food and the Politics of U.S. Identity.* New York: Oxford University Press, 1999. Witt explores the place of food in African American history, as well as the fascination with soul food in American culture.

You Mean a Woman Can Open It . . . ? The Woman's Place in the Classic Age of Advertising. Holbrook, Mass.: Adams Media/Prion Books, 2000. A collection of advertisements (in postcard form) that portray women as helpless dunces paradoxically unable to function in what had always been considered "the woman's domain."

Newspaper, Journal, Magazine Source Materials

Barnes, Dora Russell. "By-Products of Citrus Fruits." *House Beautiful,* January 1919.

Better Homes and Gardens. "First Aid to Old Kitchens." August 1927.

Better Homes and Gardens. "For Better Housekeeping." May 1927.

Better Homes and Gardens. "Hoosier Designs." October 1927.

Better Homes and Gardens. Various product advertisements. August 1927.

Bien, Bettina. "The Liberation of Women: Thoughts on Reading Some Old Cookbooks." *The Freeman* 21, no. 2 (1971).

Bon Appétit. How America Eats. April 2001.

Bon Appétit. Miscellaneous articles, series, advertisements. 1990 through 2005.

Bon Appétit, Millennium Special: The American Century in Food, September 1999.

Boodro, Michael. "Food Fit for Athletics." *Gentlemen's Quarterly,* February 1983.

Caporael, Linda R. "Ergotism: The Satan Loosed in Salem?" *Science Journal* 192 (April 2, 1976).

Claiborne, Craig. "Cooking with Soul." *New York Times,* November 3, 1968.

Cooking Light. Miscellaneous articles, series, advertisements. 1998 through 2002.

De Witt, Katharine. "The Humboldt Hoosier." Special to *The Washington Post,* April 24, 2003.

Dietsch, Deborah K. "Formica, Could This Be Farewell?" Special to *The Washington Post,* March 14, 2002.

Downs, Stacy. "Progress Has By-Passed the Look of a Nook." Knight Ridder newspapers, July 24, 2003.

Ferry, John H. "Food for Thought: A View Toward a Richer Interpretation of the House Museum Kitchen." *Cultural Resource Management* 24, no. 4 (2001).

Food Engineering. "75 Years of Manufacturing Innovation." September 2003.

Gilman, Charlotte Perkins. "Home of Today and Tomorrow." *Good Housekeeping*, September 1907.

Good Housekeeping. "The Law and the Lure of Casseroles." March 1917.

Gourmet. Chinese Cooking. October, November, and December 1979.

Gourmet. Miscellaneous articles, series, advertisements. 1984 through 2005.

Groer, Annie. "Jade-ite, the Green, Green Glass of Home." *Washington Post*, February 13, 2003.

Harper, Ross K., Mary G. Harper, and Bruce Clouette. "Foodways in 18th Century Connecticut." *Cultural Resource Management* 24, no. 4 (2001).

Harper's New Monthly. "Kitchen and Dining Room." February 1877.

House Beautiful. "How Are You Using Your Parks." September 1918.

House Beautiful. "Reconstruction! Are We Ready?" June 1919.

House Beautiful. Various product advertisements. May 1906, July 1927, August 1927.

Ipswich News and Chronicle. "Hints for Housewives: Solving Wartime Meal Problems." March 1943.

Johnstown *Tribune-Democrat*. "The 1930s." Supplement. June 16, 2002.

Kretschmar, Ella Morris. "Her Mess of Pottage." *Good Housekeeping*, September 1907.

Life. "Close Up: Julia Child, TV's Master Chef." October 21, 1966.

Life. "Steak." Labor Day Special Issue, September 1955.

Maddocks, Mildred. "With What Measure Ye Mete." *Good Housekeeping*, January 1917.

Marsh, Dorothy B., and Arthur J. Donniez. "You Can Cook in the Cool of the Morning if You Have a Good Refrigerator." *Good Housekeeping*, July 1929.

Masson, Thomas L. "A Masculine Solution." *Good Housekeeping*, September 1907.

Men's Fitness. History of Diets. Monthly serialized, 2003.

New York Times Magazine. "The 2ⁿᵈ Annual Year in Ideas." December 15, 2002.

New York Times Magazine. "The 3ʳᵈ Annual Year in Ideas." December 14, 2003.

Peeler, Caroline G. "The Home Laboratory in Canning and Drying." *House Beautiful*, December 1918.

Pollan, Michael. "Food: But Not As We Know It." *Sunday Independent*, June 15, 2003.

Ridout, Christine. "The House That Technology Built—in 1807." *Boston Globe*, July 1, 2001.

Ringen, Jonathan. "Kitchen Think" and "Kitchen of the Future." *Metropolis*, April 2004.

Rogers, Patricia Dane. "Banquette on It." *Washington Post*, June 26, 2003.

Schrambling, Regina. "America's Foodie Bible." *New York Times*, March 20, 2002.

Strong, Effa Lyons. "A Convenient Kitchen." *House Beautiful*, April 1905.

Time. "Eating Like Soul Brothers." *Time Magazine*, June 24, 1969.

Time. Letters, The Nation, "Modern Living: Food: Everyone's in the Kitchen," and various advertisements. November 25, 1966.

Time, "Living: Love in the Kitchen." December 19, 1977.

Tingle, Lilian. "Clean Markets." *Good Housekeeping*, September 1907.

Weed, Helen. "Soldiers All!" *House Beautiful*, December 1918.

White, Frank G. "A Cure for Smoking Houses and Scolding Wives." *Old Sturbridge Visitor*, Winter 1980.

Academic Presentations, Educational Materials, Exhibitions, Government Reports, and Miscellaneous Papers and Studies

General Foods Corporation. Consumer Service Department. *Create a Finer Cake*. New York: General Foods Corporation, 1948.

Jefferson, Thomas. "Scheme for a System of Agricultural Societies." *The Writings of Thomas Jefferson*, March, 1811.

Kerr Glass Manufacturing Corporation. *Short Cuts to Good Eating*. An Edition of the Modern Homemaker. Kerr Glass Manufacturing Corporation, 1947–1950.

Kerr Glass Manufacturing Corporation Research and Educational Department. *10 Short Lessons in Home Canning*. Kerr Glass Manufacturing Corporation, 1949.

Koop, C. Everett, M.D. *Surgeon General's Report on Nutrition and Health*. U.S. Department of Health and Human Services, Public Health Service, 1988. DHHS (PHS) 88-50215.

Lee, Royal, and Jerome S. Stolzoff. *The Specific Nutritional Qualities of Natural Foods*. Lee Foundation for Nutritional Research, July 1942.

Linton, Fred B. "Federal Food and Drug Laws: Leaders Who Achieved Their Enactment and Enforcement, Parts I and II." *Food Drug Cosm. L. Quarterly*, 1949, 1950 respectively.

Pillsbury Mills, Inc. Foods Education Department. *Cookin' Up Kitchen Dates*. Minneapolis: Pillsbury Mills, Inc. 1945.

Proctor & Gamble. *Praise for the Cook*. Proctor & Gamble, 1959.

United States Senate Select Committee on Nutrition and Human Needs. *Dietary Goals for the United States*, 2nd edition. U.S. Government Printing, 1977. Revised 1980, 1983–84, 1985.

USDA Economic Research Service Report, Poultry, 1925 through 1965.

Wajda, Shirley Teresa. *Designing Domesticity: Decorating the American Home Since 1876, Part I*. As presented to The Courtauld History of Dress Association Annual Conference July 26–27, 2002.

INDEX

Note: page numbers in *italics* refer to illustrations

corn, genetically modified, 188, 191

Corning Glass Works Company, 29

corn syrup, 170–71

"couch potatoes," 162

countertops, Formica, 14, 143

Cox, Courteney, 197

C-rations, 76–77

cream of mushroom soup, 56, 105

credit, 43

Creole food, 159, 167

Crisco, 121

Critser, Greg, 136–37, 171

Crocker, Betty (fict.), 32, 61

Crock-Pots, xii, 140–41, 142

Cronin, Betty, 85

Crop Loan Act, 46

Crosby, Bing, 76

cross-pollination, 192

CSPI (Center for Science in the Public Interest), 133, 145–46, 208

Cuisinart, 140, 176

cyberkitchens, 207

cyclamates, 119

Daigneau, Kenneth, 57

"dainty" foods, 35–36

Davis, Daisy Adelle, 103–4

DDT, 32, 112–13, 114–15, 147

Dean, James, 101

deep fryers, 141–42

DeGeneres, Ellen, 197

dehydration, 77, 79–80. *See also* freeze-drying

DeLorean, John, 163

Demarest, Michael, 157

DES (diethylstilbestrol), 113

design of kitchens

in 1950s, 89–90

in 1960s, 131–32

in 1970s, 142–43

in 1980s, 178–79

cleanliness and, 15

Desperately Seeking Susan (film), 161, 177

Dexedrine, 101–2

Dietary Goals for the United States, 160, 161

Diet for a Small Planet (Lappé), 150

diethylstilbestrol (DES), 113

dieting and weight

in 1920s, 35–36

in 1950s, 100–4

in 1960s, 111–12, 125–29

in 1970s, 151–52

in 1980s, 160–64, 182

in 1990s, 198–201

Atkins diet, 151, 199–201

drugs for, 101–2

Eskimo diet, 102

low-carbohydrate diets, 102–3, 127, 199–200

obesity, 162, 171, 198

Pennington diet, 102–3

Pritikin diet, 152

Scarsdale diet, 152

Diet Pepsi, 128

Diet Rite cola, 119

digestibility, 35

dinner (1950s), 85–86, 105

diseases from malnourishment, 71

diseases in poultry, 164–65

dishware

1990s nostalgia for midcentury style, 202

Fiestaware, 59

plastic, 143–44

Wright and Wright, 90–91, 92

Zeisel, 92–93

disinfectants, 13

disposals, 55

DNA, 188, 189–90, 192

Doctor's Quick Weight Loss Book, The, 126

domestic help, 11, 20

domestic-science movement, 3–8, 20, 30. *See also* science and technology

Donner party, 25

Dove Bars, 170

Dr. Atkins' Diet Revolution (Atkins), 151, 199

dried foods, 23, 77, 79–80

drifters, 43

Du Pont, 77–78, 88

A NOTE ON THE AUTHOR

Steven Gdula's writing has appeared in *Details*, the *Washington Post*, the *Advocate*, and *Cooking Light* magazine. He lives in Washington, D.C.